TEACHER'S GUIDE TO BEHAVIORAL INTERVENTIONS:

Intervention Strategies for Behavior Problems in the Educational Environment

Kathy Cummins Wunderlich

Copyright © 1988 by Hawthorne Educational Services, Inc

Printed in the
United States of America.
12/00

All rights reserved.

No part of this publication may be reproduced or
transmitted in any form or by any means, electronic or
mechanical, including photocopy, recording, or any
information storage and retrieval systems, without permission in
writing from the publisher.

H A W T H O R N E
Educational Services, Inc.
**800 Gray Oak Drive
Columbia, MO 65201
Telephone: (573) 874-1710
FAX: (800) 442-9509**

Table of Contents

I. Introduction 8

II. Using the *Teacher's Guide to Behavioral Interventions* in Conjunction with the *Behavior Disorders Identification Scale* 10

III. Goals and Objectives 11

    A. Learning 11
    B. Interpersonal Relationships 16
    C. Inappropriate Behavior or Feelings Under Normal Circumstances 22
    D. Unhappiness or Depression 32
    E. Physical Symptoms or Fears 36
    F. Classroom Rules and Expectations 39
    G. Peer Interactions 42
    H. Response to School Environment 43
    I. Response to School and Personal Problems 45
    J. Group Behavior 46
    K. Class Behavior 47
    L. Academic Performance 48

IV. Interventions 50

    A. An Inability to Learn Which Cannot Be Explained by Intellectual, Sensory, or Health Factors

    Behavior Number

    1. Does not perform or complete classroom assignments during class time (e.g., will not perform the assignment or does not use the time provided, will go on to another assignment before completing the first, etc.) 50

    2. Does not turn in homework assignments (e.g., does not do the assignment, loses the assignment after completing it, does not bring the assignment to class to turn in, etc.) 53

    3. Is disorganized to the point of not having necessary materials, losing materials, being unable to find completed assignments, being unable to follow the steps of the assignment in order, etc. 55

    4. Performs assignments so carelessly as to be illegible (e.g., does not care to do well, rushes through tasks, etc.) 58

    5. Is unable to perform assignments independently (e.g., continually asks for assistance or reassurance; will not begin, work on, or complete assignments without assistance; etc.) 60

    6. Performs classroom tests or quizzes at a failing level 62

    7. Is not motivated by rewards at school (e.g., cannot find a reinforcer he/she enjoys) 64

    8. Does not prepare for assigned activities (e.g., does not study for tests or quizzes, does not read assigned material, etc.) 65

    9. Does not remain on-task (e.g., is easily distracted by other students or the teacher, is more interested in other activities, sits and does nothing, etc.) 67

    10. Does not perform academically at his/her ability level (i.e., performs below ability level or at a failing level) 69

    11. Does not follow written directions 72

12. Does not follow verbal directions 75
13. Is reluctant to attempt new assignments or tasks 78
14. Has difficulty with short-term and long-term memory (e.g., cannot remember directions, cannot memorize a poem, cannot recall information previously learned, etc.) 81
15. Has difficulty understanding abstract concepts 84
16. Does not comprehend what he/she reads 86
17. Requires repeated drill and practice to learn what other students master easily 88

B. An Inability to Build or Maintain Satisfactory Interpersonal Relationships with Peers and Teachers

Behavior
Number
18. Fights with other students (e.g., scratches, hits, pulls hair, etc.) 89
19. Becomes physically aggressive with teachers (e.g., pushes, pulls away, grabs, etc.) 91
20. Makes inappropriate comments to teachers (e.g., argues, threatens, calls names, curses, makes rude comments, uses obscenities, etc.) 93
21. Does not respond appropriately to praise or recognition (e.g., gets angry, gets embarrassed, purposely does something inappropriate in response, etc.) 95
22. Is easily angered, annoyed, or upset (e.g., hits, argues, yells, throws things, cries, withdraws, etc.) 96
23. Agitates and provokes peers to a level of verbal or physical assault (e.g., makes derogatory comments or gestures, touches, etc.) 99
24. Has little or no interaction with teachers (e.g., does not talk, make eye contact, ask questions, seek assistance, etc.) 101
25. Has little or no interaction with peers (e.g., does not talk, share in activities, make friends, etc.) 104
26. Makes inappropriate comments to other students (e.g., argues, calls names, curses, uses obscenities, makes rude comments, etc.) 106
27. Responds inappropriately to typical physical exchanges with other students (e.g., being bumped, touched, brushed against, etc.) 108
28. Responds inappropriately to friendly teasing (e.g., jokes, sarcastic remarks, name calling, etc.) 110
29. Is not accepted by other students (e.g., ignored, teased, ridiculed, etc.) 111
30. Bothers other students who are trying to work, listen, etc. 113
31. Responds inappropriately to others' attempts to be friendly, complimentary, sympathetic, etc. 115
32. Does not share possessions or materials 116
33. Does not allow others to take their turns, participate in activities or games, etc. 118

C. Inappropriate Types of Behavior or Feelings Under Normal Circumstances

Behavior
Number
34. Makes inappropriate comments or unnecessary noises in the classroom (e.g., talks to other students without permission, calls out answers, interrupts, makes fun of others, hums, taps, burps, etc.) 120
35. Has unexcused absences (e.g., absent from school, skips classes, etc.) 122
36. Has unexcused tardiness (e.g., late to school, late to class, late to activities, etc.) 124
37. Makes unnecessary physical contact with others (e.g., touches, hugs, etc.) 126
38. Blames other persons or materials to avoid taking responsibility for his/her mistakes (e.g., teachers, other students, books, pencils, pens, etc.) 128

39. Steals or forcibly takes things from other students, teachers, the school building, etc. ... 130
40. Behaves inappropriately when others do well or receive praise or attention (e.g., cannot stand to lose in a game, gets angry, says it is not fair to him/her, etc.) ... 132
41. Engages in inappropriate behaviors while seated (e.g., tips chair or desk, puts feet on desk, touches others as they walk by, taps and makes noises, etc.) ... 134
42. Behaves in a manner inappropriate for the situation (e.g., laughs in a situation where other students would be alarmed or upset, shows no emotion during activities where other students would be laughing and enjoying themselves, etc.) ... 136
43. Tries to avoid situations, assignments, responsibilities (e.g., indicates he/she is sick, injured, does not feel well; requests to leave the classroom to get materials from locker, use the restroom, go to the nurse's office or counselor's office, etc.) ... 138
44. Behaves impulsively, without self-control (e.g., reacts immediately to situations without thinking, is impatient, is unable to wait for a turn or for assistance from an instructor, etc.) ... 140
45. Exhibits extreme mood changes (e.g., from calm to angry, happy to sad, etc.) ... 142
46. Is unpredictable in behavior (e.g., does not respond consistently to situations in the environment) ... 144
47. Does not follow directives from teachers or other school personnel (e.g., refuses to do what he/she is told, goes on doing what he/she was doing, does the opposite of what he/she is told, etc.) ... 146
48. Ignores consequences of his/her behavior (e.g., knows that his/her behavior will result in a negative consequence but engages in the behavior anyway) ... 148
49. Makes sexually-related comments or engages in behavior with sexual overtones (e.g., uses sexual references when talking, makes suggestive sexual comments, makes sexually-related gestures, touches self or others, exposes self, etc.) ... 150
50. Becomes overexcited (e.g., loses control in group activities, forgets rules, becomes loud, etc.) ... 152
51. Lies, denies, exaggerates, distorts the truth ... 154
52. Brings inappropriate or illegal materials to school (e.g., magazines, weapons, drugs, alcohol, etc.) ... 155
53. Destroys school or other students' property (e.g., defaces, damages, vandalizes, etc.) ... 157
54. Cheats (e.g., copies from other students, uses notes during tests or quizzes, copies other students' classwork or homework, etc.) ... 160
55. Demonstrates inappropriate behavior when moving with a group (e.g., fails to stay in line, runs, pushes, etc.) ... 162
56. Responds inappropriately to redirection in academic and social situations (e.g., gets angry when told he/she has made errors on assignments, refuses to return to seat when told to do so, etc.) ... 163
57. Does not accept changes in established routine (e.g., is upset by changes in a schedule, changes in the way assignments are to be performed; behaves inappropriately when a student teacher or substitute teacher is in the classroom; etc.) ... 165
58. Does not follow school rules (e.g., runs in hallways, throws food in cafeteria, is disruptive in library, etc.) ... 168
59. Indicates that he/she does not care or is not concerned about performance, grades, report cards, graduating, consequences of behavior, etc. ... 170
60. Needs immediate rewards/reinforcement in order to demonstrate appropriate behavior ... 172
61. Does not care for personal appearance (e.g., grooming, clothing, etc.) ... 174
62. Engages in inappropriate behaviors related to bodily functions (e.g., talks about bodily functions, masturbates, urinates on restroom floor, smears feces in restroom, etc.) ... 176
63. Does not change behavior from one situation to another (e.g., gets excited at recess and cannot calm down when he/she enters the building, cannot stop one activity and begin another, etc.) ... 178

D. A General Pervasive Mood of Unhappiness or Depression

Behavior Number

64. Does not participate in classroom activities or special events that are interesting to other students (e.g., does not want to participate in group activities, parties, class plays, field trips, assemblies, etc.) 180
65. Blames self for situations beyond his/her control (e.g., classroom situations, accidents, death, divorce, etc.) 183
66. Becomes upset when a suggestion or constructive criticism is given 184
67. Threatens to hurt self or commit suicide (e.g., verbally as well as through pictures and written representations of hurting self or committing suicide) 186
68. Indicates that no one likes him/her, no one cares about him/her, etc. 188
69. Does not smile, laugh, or demonstrate happiness 190
70. Is tired, listless, apathetic, unmotivated, not interested in school 192
71. Is overly critical of self in school-related performance, abilities, personal appearance, etc. (e.g., says he/she cannot perform activities, is dumb, stupid, ugly, etc.) 194
72. Frowns, scowls, looks unhappy during typical classroom situations 196
73. Is pessimistic (e.g., thinks nothing will turn out right) 197

E. A Tendency to Develop Physical Symptoms or Fears Associated with Personal or School Problems

Behavior Number

74. Indicates concern regarding problems or situations in the home or is unable to deal with classroom requirements because of out-of-school situations (e.g., may not be able to concentrate because of family problems, peer relations, personal relationships, etc.) 199
75. Demonstrates self-destructive behavior (e.g., hits, scratches self; destroys clothing or personal property, etc.) 201
76. Moves about unnecessarily (e.g., leaves seat, walks around the classroom, rocks, shakes head, etc.) 203
77. Speaks in an unnatural voice (e.g., falsetto voice, mechanical voice, etc.) 205
78. Speaks incoherently (e.g., statements are disconnected, unrelated, bizarre and unintelligible, etc.) 206
79. Engages in nervous habits (e.g., bites fingernails, twirls hair, chews inside of cheek, chews pencils or pens, spins or twirls objects, etc.) 208
80. Throws temper tantrums 210
81. Reacts physically in response to excitement, disappointment, surprise, happiness, fear, etc. (e.g., flaps hands, shudders, stutters, stammers, trembles, etc.) 212
82. Becomes pale, may throw up, or passes out when anxious or frightened 214
83. Demonstrates phobic-type reactions (e.g., fear of school, speaking in front of a group, uncomfortable changing clothes for physical education, etc.) 215

F. Failure to Follow Classroom Rules and Expectations

Behavior Number

84. Does not follow the rules of the classroom (e.g., talks without permission, leaves seat without permission, etc.) 217
85. Does not wait appropriately for an instructor to arrive (e.g., leaves seat, talks, yells, fights, etc.) 219
86. Does not wait appropriately for assistance or attention from an instructor (e.g., gets out of seat, throws objects, calls out to teacher, talks, etc.) 220

87. Demonstrates inappropriate behavior in the presence of a substitute teacher 221
88. Does not demonstrate appropriate use of school-related materials (e.g., pencil, ruler, industrial arts equipment, etc.) 224
89. Does not demonstrate appropriate care and handling of others' property (e.g., peer and school property) 227
90. Does not raise hand when appropriate (e.g., does not raise hand for assistance, to speak; raises hand to answer questions when he/she does not know the answer; etc.) 230
91. Does not take notes during class when necessary 232

G. Inappropriate Peer Interactions

Behavior Number

92. Does not resolve conflict situations appropriately (e.g., gets angry, cries, fights, runs out of classroom, runs away, etc.) 234
93. Does not make appropriate use of free time (e.g., talks, fails to share materials, fights, etc.) 236
94. Fails to work appropriately with peers in a tutoring situation 238
95. Does not share school materials 240

H. Inappropriate Response to School Environment

Behavior Number

96. Writes and passes notes 242
97. Tattles 243
98. Fails to find necessary locations in the building (e.g., classes, cafeteria, restroom, etc.) 244
99. Does not respond appropriately to environmental cues (e.g., bells, signs, etc.) 246
100. Does not stay in an assigned area for the specified time period (e.g., classroom, building, school grounds, etc.) 248

I. Inappropriate Response to School and Personal Problems

Behavior Number

101. Runs away to avoid problems 250
102. Is under the influence of drugs or alcohol 252
103. Whines or cries 254

J. Inappropriate Group Behavior

Behavior Number

104. Demonstrates inappropriate behavior in a small academic group setting (e.g., reading group, math group, etc.) 256
105. Behaves more appropriately alone or in small groups than with the whole class or in large group activities 259
106. Demonstrates inappropriate behavior in a large academic group setting (e.g., an entire class math activity) 262

K. Inappropriate Out-of-Class Behavior

Behavior
Number
107. Demonstrates inappropriate behavior on the school grounds before and after school (e.g., fights, curses, throws objects, etc.) 265
108. Demonstrates inappropriate behavior going to and from school (e.g., throws objects out of bus window, fights with peers, etc.) 267

L. Concerns Related to Academic Performance

Behavior
Number
109. Does not finish assignments because of reading difficulties (e.g., reads too slowly to finish on time) 269
110. Needs oral questions and directions frequently repeated (e.g., student says, "I don't understand;" needs constant reminders; etc.) 271

V. **Appendix** 273

VI. **Index** 290

I. Introduction

The *Teacher's Guide to Behavioral Interventions* is based on the most commonly encountered behavior problems in the educational environment. The list of behavior problems was compiled as a result of survey activities designed to identify the most common behavior problems encountered by classroom teachers. Input was gathered from 156 classroom teachers and numerous special education personnel from elementary, intermediate, and secondary school settings.

The intent of the *Teacher's Guide to Behavioral Interventions* is to provide educators with a selection of proven interventions for the most common behavior problems encountered in the educational environment. The concept of identifying the most common behavior problems and intervention strategies grew out of years of staffings and in-service presentations where teachers earnestly asked the question over and over again, "What do you do with a student who . . . ?" It is obvious that our educators genuinely want to provide an appropriate behavioral support program for those students in need, and the *Teacher's Guide to Behavioral Interventions* is designed to provide the necessary intervention strategies.

The goals and objectives identified in this manual will serve as samples which may be used in writing IEP's for identified special needs students. Criteria for measuring the success of the student's attainment of the goals and objectives must be determined by those professional educators and parents who are aware of the student's current abilities and program recommendations.

The interventions listed under each behavior problem should serve as a guide for program development or change for any student in need of behavior improvement. Interventions may be chosen by a team of professionals, a special educator in a self-contained class or functioning in a resource or consultant capacity, or by a regular education teacher. Professional judgment should dictate the choice of interventions for any particular student. The student's age, sex, grade level, local community standards, and handicap, if one exists, are all to be considered in selecting appropriate intervention procedures. The interventions have been found appropriate for special education as well as regular education classroom environments.

The assumption is made, in any professionally responsible educational setting, that all related variables will be considered in choosing appropriate interventions designed to facilitate student success. Thorough consideration should identify all related variables influencing student behavior problems in order to appropriately respond to individual situations. Vision, hearing, general health, nutrition, and family case history should be considered in order not to overlook any historical or contemporary determinants of behavior.

The expectation is that the appropriate interventions will be selected, agreed upon, and consistently used by all instructional personnel working with the student. Use of the same interventions by all teachers in all settings greatly enhances the likelihood of student success in the educational environment. These interventions, appropriate for all educational environments, lend themselves particularly well to creating continuity across all the classes and educational settings in which the student functions.

In order to respond to the broad spectrum of implications related to behavior problems, the interventions contained in this manual are designed to represent solutions which are both preventive and reactive. Preventive interventions are environmental modifications used to reduce stimulation, teach the student problem-solving skills, etc. Reactive interventions are more immediately related to the situation, such as removal from the group, increased supervision, natural consequences, etc.

Some interventions in this manual apply to most students and should be considered first in order to provide a more general approach to problem reduction. Other interventions are more specific and should be individually selected for students based on the appropriateness of the intervention to the situation.

For any behavior problem exhibited by students, it will be of value to assess the extent to which institutional variables influence the behavior and possibly contribute to the problem. Limited supervision in play areas, hallways, and during extracurricular activities, as well as arbitrary groupings and seating arrangements are often examples of factors which are inherent in the institutional structure and often contribute to problem behavior. As a first step in improving a situation, these institutional variables should be evaluated and acted upon to reduce the influence of variables which result in unsuccessful behavior.

This manual is designed to respond to the most typical behavior problems exhibited by students in educational settings. The interventions identified herein are appropriate for any student engaging in the behaviors described. The students need not be identified as behaviorally disordered/emotionally disturbed or handicapped in any way. The appropriateness of the interventions relates directly to the behavior problem and not to classification labels. All interventions included have been found to be most successful by administrators, teachers, aides, counselors, parents, and other persons intent on helping students.

Every attempt was made to provide interventions which are likely to contribute to the most positive classroom atmosphere. Additionally, the selection of interventions took into account those interventions which reflect positive teacher behavior expected of educators in our schools. All interventions included in the *Teacher's Guide to Behavioral Interventions* have been proven to contribute to student success in the educational environment.

In addition to providing intervention strategies for the most commonly encountered behavior problems in the educational environment, the *Teacher's Guide to Behavioral Interventions* provides the goals, objectives, and intervention strategies for the behaviors identified by the *Behavior Disorders Identification Scale*. The 83 behaviors included on the *Behavior Disorders Identification Scale: School Version* are included in the *Teacher's Guide to Behavioral Interventions* as well as 27 additional behavior problems which are common in educational environments but were not included on the Behavior Disorders Identification Scale.

Dr. Roy Moeller is to be given special recognition for his assistance in the research involved in this project to identify common behavior problems encountered by teachers. And to all the teachers who face the insurmountable task of helping our students succeed, "God bless you."

K.C.W.

II. Using the *Teacher's Guide to Behavioral Interventions* in Conjunction with the *Behavior Disorders Identification Scale*

*NOTE: If the *Teacher's Guide to Behavioral Interventions* is not being used in conjunction with the *Behavior Disorders Identification Scale*, the following procedural steps need not be followed.

Step 1: The student is rated with the *School Version* of the *Behavior Disorders Identification Scale*.

Step 2: Conversions of raw scores on the are made, subscale scores and percentile scores are determined, and the *Behavior Disorders Identification Scale* results of rating section is completed.

Step 3: Determine on which of the five characteristics (subscales) the student scores one or more standard deviations below the mean (subscale score below 7).

Step 4: Under each of those characteristics (subscales) on which the student scored one standard deviation or more below the mean, determine which behaviors constitute primary concern in the educational environment (the behaviors with the highest raw scores).

Step 5: Find goals and objectives from the *Teacher's Guide to Behavioral Interventions* (section titled: III. Goals and Objectives) which represent each behavior indicated as a primary concern on the *Behavior Disorders Identification Scale*.

Step 6: Determine those interventions from the *Teacher's Guide to Behavioral Interventions* (section IV) which are most appropriate in facilitating the student's success and meeting the goals and objectives chosen in Step 5.

Step 7: If there are any behaviors which are of concern on subscales other than those with scores more than one standard deviation below the mean, goals, objectives, and interventions should be selected and written for those behaviors as well.

Step 8: Share those goals, objectives, and interventions strategies selected for the student with all personnel involved in the student's educational program.

III. Goals and Objectives

BEHAVIOR 1: Does not perform or complete classroom assignments during class time

Goal:
1. The student will complete classroom assignments during class time.

Objectives:
1. The student will complete a task before going on to the next task on ___ out of ___ trials.
2. The student will complete ___ out of ___ assigned tasks per day.
3. The student will attempt ___ out of ___ assigned tasks per day.
4. The student will remain on-task for ___ out of ___ minutes per class period.
5. The student will use the time provided on assigned tasks in order to complete ___ tasks per day.

BEHAVIOR 2: Does not turn in homework assignments

Goal:
1. The student will turn in homework assignments.

Objectives:
1. The student will complete ___ out of ___ homework assignments each day.
2. The student will complete ___ out of ___ homework assignments each week.
3. The student will bring ___ out of ___ of his/her completed homework assignments to school and turn them in each day.
4. The student will bring ___ out of ___ of his/her completed homework assignments to school and turn them in each week.
5. The student will carry his/her homework assignments to and from school in a book bag/backpack in order to prevent loss on ___ out of ___ trials.
6. The student will perform ___ out of ___ homework assignments at home and return them to school each day.
7. The student will perform ___ out of ___ homework assignments at home and return them to school each week.

BEHAVIOR 3: Is disorganized to the point of not having necessary materials, losing materials, being unable to find completed assignments, being unable to follow the steps of the assignment in order, etc.

Goal:
1. The student will improve his/her organizational skills related to assignments.

Objectives:
1. The student will have the necessary materials for assigned activities on ___ out of ___ trials.
2. The student will carry his/her materials and assignments to and from activities in a book bag/backpack in order to prevent loss on ___ out of ___ trials.
3. The student will return materials to their specified locations on ___ out of ___ trials.
4. The student will place his/her completed work in a specified location (folder, "mailbox," etc.) on ___ out of ___ trials.
5. The student will be organized and prepared to work within ___ minutes of the beginning of class.
6. The student will complete one step of the task before going on to the next step on ___ out of ___ trials.
7. The student will complete the steps of the assigned task in sequential order on ___ out of ___ trials.
8. The student will prioritize and complete assignments with the help of the teacher on ___ out of ___ opportunities.
9. The student will independently prioritize and complete assignments on ___ out of ___ opportunities.

10. The student will organize his/her materials at the beginning and end of each assigned task on ___ out of ___ trials.

BEHAVIOR 4: Performs assignments so carelessly as to be illegible

Goal:
1. The student will perform assignments legibly.

Objectives:
1. The student will perform written tasks in a legible manner on ___ out of ___ trials.
2. The student will take his/her time when performing a written task in order to make it legible on ___ out of ___ tasks.
3. The student will turn in written work which is legible on ___ out of ___ trials.
4. The student will turn in written assignments that are clean, free of tears, neat, etc., on ___ out of ___ trials.
5. The student will recopy his/her written assignments before turning them in on ___ out of ___ trials.

BEHAVIOR 5: Is unable to perform assignments independently

Goal:
1. The student will independently perform assignments.

Objectives:
1. The student will attempt to perform a given assignment before asking for teacher assistance on ___ out of ___ trials.
2. The student will read necessary directions, instructions, explanations, etc., before asking for teacher assistance on ___ out of ___ trials.
3. The student will independently complete ___ out of ___ assignments per school day.
4. The student will ask for teacher assistance only when necessary when performing assignments on ___ out of ___ trials.
5. The student will work for ___ minutes without requiring assistance from the teacher on ___ out of ___ trials.

BEHAVIOR 6: Performs classroom tests or quizzes at a failing level

Goals:
1. The student will improve his/her performance on classroom tests.
2. The student will improve his/her performance on classroom quizzes.

Objectives:
1. The student will perform classroom tests with ___% accuracy. (Gradually increase expectations as the student demonstrates success.)
2. The student will perform classroom quizzes with ___% accuracy. (Gradually increase expectations as the student demonstrates success.)
3. The student will meet a ___% level of mastery on classroom tests. (Gradually increase expectations as the student demonstrates success.)
4. The student will meet a ___% level of mastery on classroom quizzes. (Gradually increase expectations as the student demonstrates success.)

BEHAVIOR 7: Is not motivated by rewards at school

Goal:
1. The student will be motivated by rewards at school.

Objectives:
1. The student will identify something he/she enjoys doing when asked by the teacher on ___ out of ___ occasions.

2. The student will identify something he/she would like to earn when asked by the teacher on ___ out of ___ occasions.
3. The student will identify a reinforcer he/she will work toward earning on ___ out of ___ trials.
4. The student will earn ___ identified reinforcer(s) per day.
5. The student will earn ___ identified reinforcer(s) per week.

BEHAVIOR 8: **Does not prepare for assigned activities**

Goal:
1. The student will be prepared for assigned activities.

Objectives:
1. The student will study for ___ out of ___ tests.
2. The student will study for ___ out of ___ quizzes.
3. The student will study and perform classroom tests with ___% accuracy. (Gradually increase expectations as the student demonstrates success.)
4. The student will study and perform classroom quizzes with ___% accuracy. (Gradually increase expectations as the student demonstrates success.)
5. The student will be prepared for assigned activities by reading the assigned material for ___ out of ___ activities.
6. The student will complete his/her assigned tasks, such as book reports, projects, etc., by the due date on ___ out of ___ trials.
7. The student will complete his/her homework prior to coming to the assigned activity on ___ out of ___ trials.
8. The student will correctly answer questions covering the assigned reading material on ___ out of ___ trials.
9. The student will read necessary information prior to coming to the assigned activity on ___ out of ___ trials.

BEHAVIOR 9: **Does not remain on-task**

Goal:
1. The student will remain on-task.

Objectives:
1. The student will demonstrate on-task behavior by sitting quietly at his/her seat, looking at his/her materials, and performing the task for ___ minutes at a time. (Gradually increase expectations as the student demonstrates success.)
2. The student will remain on-task for ___ minutes at a time. (Gradually increase expectations as the student demonstrates success.)
3. The student will remain on-task long enough to complete the task on ___ out of ___ tasks.
4. The student will remain on-task through its completion on ___ out of ___ tasks.
5. The student will maintain eye contact with the teacher for ___ minutes at a time.

BEHAVIOR 10: **Does not perform academically at his/her ability level**

Goal:
1. The student will perform academically at his/her ability level.

Objectives:
1. The student will perform academic tasks with ___% accuracy. (Gradually increase expectations as the student demonstrates success.)
2. The student will meet a ___% level of mastery on academic tasks. (Gradually increase expectations as the student demonstrates success.)
3. The student will perform academic tasks on his/her ability level on ___ out of ___ trials.
4. The student will perform tasks designed to meet his/her level of functioning with ___% accuracy. (Gradually increase expectations as the student demonstrates success.)

BEHAVIOR 11:   Does not follow written directions

Goal:
1. The student will follow written directions.

Objectives:
1. The student will follow written directions in correct sequential order on ___ out of ___ trials.
2. The student will follow ___ out of ___ written directions.
3. The student will demonstrate the ability to follow written directions by reading the directions carefully and completing the task with ___% accuracy.
4. The student will follow written directions with teacher assistance on ___ out of ___ trials.
5. The student will independently follow written directions on ___ out of ___ trials.
6. The student will read directions written on his/her ability level and follow them in correct sequential order on ___ out of ___ trials.
7. The student will complete one step of the written direction before going on to the next step on ___ out of ___ trials.
8. The student will follow one-step written directions on ___ out of ___ trials. (Gradually increase expectations as the student demonstrates success.)

BEHAVIOR 12:   Does not follow verbal directions

Goal:
1. The student will follow verbal directions.

Objectives:
1. The student will follow verbal directions in correct sequential order on ___ out of ___ trials.
2. The student will follow ___ out of ___ verbal directions.
3. The student will demonstrate the ability to follow verbal directions by listening carefully and completing the task with ___% accuracy.
4. The student will follow verbal directions with teacher assistance on ___ out of ___ trials.
5. The student will independently follow verbal directions on ___ out of ___ trials.
6. The student will listen to verbal directions on his/her ability level and follow them in correct sequential order on ___ out of ___ trials.
7. The student will complete one step of the verbal direction before going on to the next step on ___ out of ___ trials.
8. The student will follow one-step verbal directions on ___ out of ___ trials. (Gradually increase expectations as the student demonstrates success.)

BEHAVIOR 13:   Is reluctant to attempt new assignments or tasks

Goals:
1. The student will attempt new assignments.
2. The student will attempt new tasks.

Objectives:
1. The student will attempt new assignments or tasks with teacher assistance on ___ out of ___ trials.
2. The student will independently attempt new assignments or tasks on ___ out of ___ trials.
3. The student will read the directions when attempting a new assignment or task on ___ out of ___ trials.
4. The student will perform a new assignment or task along with a peer on ___ out of ___ trials.
5. The student will attempt ___ out of ___ new assignments or tasks per day.
6. The student will begin a new assignment or task within ___ minutes.
7. The student will listen to directions prior to attempting a new assignment or task on ___ out of ___ trials.
8. The student will attempt to perform a new assignment or task before asking for teacher assistance on ___ out of ___ trials.

9. The student will work for ___ minutes without requiring teacher assistance on ___ out of ___ trials.

BEHAVIOR 14: **Has difficulty with short-term and long-term memory**

Goals:
1. The student will improve his/her short-term memory.
2. The student will improve his/her long-term memory.
3. The student will improve his/her information retrieval skills.

Objectives:
1. The student will independently follow one-step directions on ___ out of ___ trials.
2. The student will independently follow two- or three-step directions on ___ out of ___ trials.
3. The student will memorize a short poem and recite it word-for-word on ___ out of ___ trials.
4. The student will immediately remember information that was presented and removed on ___ out of ___ trials.
5. The student will recall information at short intervals of 10-15 minutes on ___ out of ___ trials.
6. The student will recall information at intervals of several hours or more on ___ out of ___ trials.
7. The student will recall information at intervals of several days or weeks on ___ out of ___ trials.

BEHAVIOR 15: **Has difficulty understanding abstract concepts**

Goals:
1. The student will develop an understanding of abstract concepts.
2. The student will improve his/her abstract reasoning skills.

Objectives:
1. The student will demonstrate an understanding of spatial relationships such as near-far, above-below, over-under, etc., on ___ out of ___ trials.
2. The student will use manipulatives to further develop his/her abstract reasoning skills on ___ out of ___ trials.
3. The student will match pictures of abstract concepts such as dimensionality, size, shape, space, etc., with tangible representations on ___ out of ___ trials.
4. The student will identify abstract concepts such as dimensionality, size, shape, space, etc., with visual and verbal cues on ___ out of ___ trials.
5. The student will independently identify abstract concepts such as dimensionality, size, shape, space, etc., on ___ out of ___ trials.

BEHAVIOR 16: **Does not comprehend what he/she reads**

Goal:
1. The student will improve his/her reading comprehension skills.

Objectives:
1. The student will read and correctly answer ___ out of ___ comprehension questions about sight words on his/her level of functioning.
2. The student will read and correctly answer ___ out of ___ comprehension questions covering individual phrases on his/her level of functioning.
3. The student will read and correctly answer ___ out of ___ comprehension questions covering individual sentences on his/her level of functioning.
4. The student will read and correctly answer ___ out of ___ comprehension questions covering individual paragraphs on his/her level of functioning.
5. After reading a short passage on his/her level of functioning, the student will correctly answer ___ out of ___ comprehension questions covering the material.
6. After reading a short passage on his/her level of functioning to the teacher, the student will be able to correctly answer ___ out of ___ comprehension questions.

7. After independently reading a three-page passage on his/her level of functioning, the student will correctly answer ___ out of ___ comprehension questions.

BEHAVIOR 17: Requires repeated drill and practice to learn what other students master easily

Goal:
1. The student will improve his/her ability to grasp concepts at a faster pace.

Objectives:
1. The student will use visual cues to aid his/her ability to grasp concepts at a faster pace with ___% accuracy.
2. The student will use auditory cues to aid his/her ability to grasp concepts at a faster pace with ___% accuracy.
3. The student will use visual and auditory cues to aid his/her ability to grasp concepts at a faster pace with ___% accuracy.
4. The student will learn ____ new concepts per week. (Gradually increase expectations as the student demonstrates success.)
5. The student will independently review concepts and pass a weekly review with the teacher with ___% accuracy.
6. The student will independently review concepts and pass a monthly review with the teacher with ___% accuracy.

BEHAVIOR 18: Fights with other students

Goal:
1. The student will interact appropriately with other students.

Objectives:
1. The student will refrain from touching other students during ___ out of ___ interactions.
2. The student will be able to settle minor conflicts with peers without becoming physically aggressive during ___ out of ___ interactions.
3. The student will seek teacher assistance when he/she is experiencing difficulty interacting with peers during ___ out of ___ interactions.
4. The student will walk away from peer conflicts during ___ out of ___ interactions.
5. The student will verbally, rather than physically, express his/her feelings toward a peer during ___ out of ___ interactions.

BEHAVIOR 19: Becomes physically aggressive with teachers

Goal:
1. The student will interact appropriately with teachers.

Objectives:
1. The student will refrain from touching the teacher during ___ out of ___ interactions.
2. The student will sit/stand quietly when the teacher discusses the student's behavior with him/her during ___ out of ___ interactions.
3. The student will verbally, rather than physically, express his/her feelings toward the teacher during ___ out of ___ interactions.
4. The student will control his/her anger to the extent of not requiring to be physically restrained by the teacher in ___ out of ___ anger-producing situations.

BEHAVIOR 20: Makes inappropriate comments to teachers

Goal:
1. The student will make appropriate comments to teachers.

Objectives:
1. The student will make appropriate comments to the teacher in ___ out of ___ interactions.
2. The student will refrain from arguing with the teacher when given a direction, new task, etc., on ___ out of ___ trials.
3. The student will converse with the teacher in a calm tone of voice during ___ out of ___ interactions.
4. The student will verbally express his/her feelings in an appropriate manner when interacting with the teacher on ___ out of ___ trials.
5. The student will use socially acceptable language in public settings on ___ out of ___ trials.

BEHAVIOR 21: Does not respond appropriately to praise or recognition

Goals:
1. The student will respond appropriately to praise.
2. The student will respond appropriately to recognition.

Objectives:
1. The student will respond appropriately when given praise by saying "Thank you," smiling, etc., on ___ out of ___ trials.
2. The student will respond appropriately when given recognition by saying "Thank you," smiling, etc., on ___ out of ___ trials.
3. The student will respond appropriately when praised by the teacher by saying "Thank you," smiling, etc., on ___ out of ___ trials.
4. The student will respond appropriately when recognized by the teacher by saying "Thank you," smiling, etc., on ___ out of ___ trials.
5. The student will respond appropriately when praised by a peer by saying "Thank you," smiling, etc., on ___ out of ___ trials.
6. The student will respond appropriately when recognized by a peer by saying "Thank you," smiling, etc., on ___ out of ___ trials.

BEHAVIOR 22: Is easily angered, annoyed, or upset

Goals:
1. The student will demonstrate appropriate behavior when angry.
2. The student will demonstrate appropriate behavior when annoyed with others.
3. The student will demonstrate appropriate behavior when upset.

Objectives:
1. The student will be able to settle minor conflicts with others without arguing, yelling, crying, hitting, etc., during ___ out of ___ interactions.
2. The student will tolerate a peer's inappropriate behavior by demonstrating patience and refraining from being verbally or physically aggressive during ___ out of ___ interactions.
3. The student will walk away from a peer or group situation when he/she becomes angry, annoyed, or upset during ___ out of ___ interactions.
4. The student will demonstrate self-control when angered, annoyed, or upset by a peer on ___ out of ___ trials.
5. The student will refrain from arguing, using a harsh tone of voice, yelling, etc., during ___ out of ___ interactions.
6. The student will continue to demonstrate appropriate behavior and interact with others when angry, annoyed, or upset during ___ out of ___ interactions.

BEHAVIOR 23: Agitates and provokes peers to a level of verbal or physical assault

Goals:
1. The student will demonstrate behaviors that will cause peers to react in a positive manner.
2. The student will refrain from agitating peers.
3. The student will refrain from provoking peers to a level of verbal or physical assault.

4. The student will interact appropriately with peers.

Objectives:
1. The student will interact with others in an appropriate manner during ___ out of ___ interactions.
2. The student will interact with others in a physically appropriate manner during ___ out of ___ interactions.
3. The student will make positive comments when interacting with peers during ___ out of ___ interactions.
4. The student will refrain from touching peers during ___ out of ___ interactions.
5. The student will avoid interacting with peers who are easily agitated and provoked by his/her behavior on ___ out of ___ trials.
6. The student will develop appropriate social interaction skills and use the skills when interacting with others ___% of the time. (Gradually increase expectations as the student demonstrates success.)

BEHAVIOR 24: Has little or no interaction with teachers

Goal:
1. The student will increase his/her interactions with teachers.

Objectives:
1. The student will verbally respond to ___ out of ___ questions asked by the teacher.
2. The student will make eye contact with the teacher when spoken to on ___ out of ___ trials.
3. The student will make eye contact with the teacher when speaking on ___ out of ___ trials.
4. The student will maintain eye contact with the teacher for ___ minutes during a conversation.
5. The student will seek assistance from the teacher when necessary on ___ out of ___ trials.
6. The student will interact with the teacher ___ times per day. (Gradually increase expectations as the student demonstrates success.)
7. The student will initiate ___ interaction(s) with the teacher per day. (Gradually increase expectations as the student demonstrates success.)
8. The student will interact for ___ minutes per day with the teacher. (Gradually increase expectations as the student demonstrates success.)

BEHAVIOR 25: Has little or no interaction with peers

Goal:
1. The student will increase his/her interactions with peers.

Objectives:
1. The student will verbally respond to ___ out of ___ questions asked by a peer.
2. The student will interact with a peer for ___ minutes at a time.
3. The student will engage in parallel play with a peer for ___ minutes at a time.
4. The student will share materials with a peer during ___ out of ___ interactions.
5. The student will demonstrate appropriate peer-interaction skills by sharing materials, waiting his/her turn, and talking in an acceptable manner on ___ out of ___ trials.
6. The student will interact with a peer ___ times per day. (Gradually increase expectations as the student demonstrates success.)
7. The student will initiate ___ interaction(s) with a peer per day. (Gradually increase expectations as the student demonstrates success.)
8. The student will make eye contact with a peer when interacting on ___ out of ___ trials.

BEHAVIOR 26: Makes inappropriate comments to other students

Goal:
1. The student will make appropriate comments to other students.

Objectives:
1. The student will make appropriate comments to a peer during ___ out of ___ interactions.

2. The student will settle minor conflicts with a peer during ___ out of ___ interactions.
3. The student will refrain from arguing with a peer during ___ out of ___ interactions.
4. The student will demonstrate appropriate interaction skills such as sharing, waiting his/her turn, talking in an acceptable manner, and making appropriate gestures during ___ out of ___ interactions with a peer.
5. The student will refrain from calling names during ___ out of ___ interactions with a peer.
6. The student will refrain from cursing during ___ out of ___ interactions with a peer.
7. The student will refrain from using obscenities during ___ out of ___ interactions with a peer.
8. The student will refrain from making rude comments during ___ out of ___ interactions with a peer.
9. The student will demonstrate respect for a peer on ___ out of ___ trials.
10. The student will make comments that are appropriate to the situation on ___ out of ___ trials.
11. The student will make gestures that are appropriate to the situation on ___ out of ___ trials.

BEHAVIOR 27: **Responds inappropriately to typical physical exchanges with other students**

Goals:
1. The student will respond appropriately to typical physical exchanges with other students.
2. The student will not become upset as a result of typical physical exchanges with other students.

Objectives:
1. The student will respond appropriately by saying "Excuse me," moving aside, ignoring, etc., to typical physical exchanges with other students during ___ out of ___ interactions.
2. The student will respond appropriately when accidentally bumped by a peer on ___ out of ___ occasions.
3. The student will respond appropriately when touched by a peer on ___ out of ___ occasions.
4. The student will respond appropriately when brushed against by a peer on ___ out of ___ occasions.
5. The student will move about the room in an appropriate manner on ___ out of ___ trials.
6. The student will move throughout the halls in an appropriate manner on ___ out of ___ trials.
7. The student will continue working, playing, etc., when typical physical exchanges with other students occur on ___ out of ___ trials.

BEHAVIOR 28: **Responds inappropriately to friendly teasing**

Goal:
1. The student will respond appropriately to friendly teasing.

Objectives:
1. The student will respond appropriately to friendly teasing on ___ out of ___ trials.
2. When teased, the student will tease in return on ___ out of ___ trials.
3. The student will laugh in response to friendly teasing on ___ out of ___ trials.
4. The student will joke with peers on ___ out of ___ trials.
5. The student will walk away from a peer when he/she has difficulty accepting friendly teasing on ___ out of ___ trials.
6. The student will avoid those peers who engage in excessive friendly teasing on ___ out of ___ trials.

BEHAVIOR 29: **Is not accepted by other students**

Goal:
1. The student will demonstrate behaviors that will be accepted by other students.

Objectives:
1. The student will develop interaction skills and use them when interacting with a peer(s) during ___ out of ___ interactions.
2. The student will demonstrate acceptable physical contact such as a handshake, pat on the back, "high five," etc., when appropriate on ___ out of ___ trials.
3. The student will gain others' attention in an appropriate manner by standing quietly or raising his/her hand until recognized on ___ out of ___ trials.

4. The student will use a normal tone of voice when talking on ___ out of ___ trials.
5. The student will interact with other students in a physically appropriate manner on ___ out of ___ trials.
6. The student will develop hygiene skills and manners and use them when interacting with other students on ___ out of ___ trials.
7. The student will talk to his/her peers in a socially acceptable manner during ___ out of ___ interactions.
8. The student will show emotion that is appropriate for the situation during ___ out of ___ situations.
9. The student will wait quietly for his/her turn when engaged in activities with peers on ___ out of ___ trials.
10. The student will demonstrate consideration/regard for his/her peers on ___ out of ___ trials.
11. The student will demonstrate peer-interaction skills by sharing materials, waiting his/her turn, and talking in an acceptable manner on ___ out of ___ trials.
12. The student will successfully interact with a peer ___ times per day.
13. The student will successfully interact with a peer ___ times per week.

BEHAVIOR 30: Bothers other students who are trying to work, listen, etc.

Goals:
1. The student will refrain from bothering other students who are trying to work, listen, etc.
2. The student will stay on-task.

Objectives:
1. The student will refrain from bothering other students who are trying to work, listen, etc., on ___ out of ___ trials.
2. The student will stay on-task for ___ minutes at a time. (Gradually increase expectations as the student demonstrates success.)
3. The student will interact with other students when appropriate on ___ out of ___ trials.
4. The student will interact with other students during free time, break time, lunch time, etc., on ___ out of ___ trials.
5. The student will ask the teacher's permission prior to interacting with a peer(s) on ___ out of ___ trials.
6. The student will remain appropriately seated until given teacher permission to do otherwise on ___ out of ___ trials.

BEHAVIOR 31: Responds inappropriately to others' attempts to be friendly, complimentary, sympathetic, etc.

Goals:
1. The student will respond appropriately to others' attempts to be friendly.
2. The student will respond appropriately to others' attempts to be complimentary.
3. The student will respond appropriately to others' attempts to be sympathetic.
4. The student will respond appropriately to others' attempts to interact with him/her.

Objectives:
1. The student will respond appropriately to others' attempts to be friendly during ___ out of ___ interactions.
2. The student will respond appropriately to others' attempts to be complimentary during ___ out of ___ interactions.
3. The student will respond appropriately to others' attempts to be sympathetic during ___ out of ___ interactions.
4. The student will respond appropriately to others' attempts to interact with him/her on ___ out of ___ trials.
5. The student will respond appropriately to others' attempts to interact for ___ minutes at a time. (Gradually increase expectations as the student demonstrates success.)
6. The student will be friendly when interacting with others on ___ out of ___ trials.
7. The student will say "Thank you" when given a compliment on ___ out of ___ trials.

8. The student will appropriately acknowledge others' attempts to be sympathetic on ___ out of ___ trials.
9. The student will appropriately interact with others on ___ out of ___ trials.

BEHAVIOR 32: Does not share possessions or materials

Goals:
1. The student will share possessions.
2. The student will share materials.

Objectives:
1. The student will share possessions on ___ out of ___ trials.
2. The student will share materials on ___ out of ___ trials.
3. The student will share possessions without being asked to do so on ___ out of ___ trials.
4. The student will share materials when directed by the teacher on ___ out of ___ trials.
5. The student will share materials without being asked to do so on ___ out of ___ trials.
6. The student will allow a peer to play with his/her possessions for ___ minutes at a time.
7. The student will allow a peer to use materials for ___ minutes at a time.
8. The student will ask permission to use materials before taking them on ___ out of ___ trials.
9. The student will not bring possessions to school that he/she does not want to share on ___ out of ___ trials.

BEHAVIOR 33: Does not allow others to take their turns, participate in activities or games, etc.

Goals:
1. The student will allow others to take their turns.
2. The student will allow others to participate in activities and games.
3. The student will demonstrate appropriate interaction skills.

Objectives:
1. The student will allow others to take their turns on ___ out of ___ trials.
2. The student will demonstrate the ability to wait his/her turn by allowing others to take their turn on out of ___ trials.
3. The student will take turns with a peer for ___ minutes at a time. (Gradually increase expectations as the student demonstrates success.)
4. The student will take turns with two peers for ___ minutes at a time. (Gradually increase expectations as the student demonstrates success.)
5. The student will take turns with four to six peers for ___ minutes at a time. (Gradually increase expectations as the student demonstrates success.)
6. The student will allow others to participate in activities and games on ___ out of ___ trials.
7. The student will demonstrate the ability to appropriately interact with others by allowing them to participate in activities and games on ___ out of ___ trials.
8. The student will participate with a peer in an activity or game for ___ minutes at a time. (Gradually increase expectations as the student demonstrates success.)
9. The student will participate with two peers in an activity or game for ___ minutes at a time. (Gradually increase expectations as the student demonstrates success.)
10. The student will participate with four to six peers in an activity or game for ___ minutes at a time. (Gradually increase expectations as the student demonstrates success.)
11. The student will demonstrate appropriate interaction skills during ___ out of ___ activities or games.
12. The student will demonstrate appropriate interaction skills when engaged in highly structured/supervised activities or games on ___ out of ___ trials.
13. The student will demonstrate appropriate interaction skills when engaged in structured activities and games with minimal supervision on ___ out of ___ trials.

14. The student will demonstrate appropriate interaction skills when engaged in unstructured activities such as free time, lunch, recess, etc., on ___ out of ___ trials.

BEHAVIOR 34:   Makes inappropriate comments or unnecessary noises in the classroom

Goals:
1. The student will communicate with others in an acceptable manner in the classroom.
2. The student will work quietly in the classroom.

Objectives:
1. The student will gain permission from the teacher, by raising his/her hand, when he/she needs to talk with a peer on ___ out of ___ trials.
2. The student will contribute his/her opinion/answer after being recognized by the teacher on ___ out of ___ trials.
3. The student will wait his/her turn to talk when engaged, or attempting to engage, in interactions with others on ___ out of ___ trials.
4. The student will make comments which are relevant to the situation on ___ out of ___ trials.
5. The student will refrain from making sounds which are inappropriate for the situation on ___ out of ___ trials.
6. The student will make positive comments about others on ___ out of ___ trials.

BEHAVIOR 35:   Has unexcused absences

Goals:
1. The student will improve his/her attendance at school.
2. The student will improve his/her attendance in class.

Objectives:
1. The student will attend ___ out of ___ school days per week. (Gradually increase expectations as the student demonstrates success.)
2. The student will attend ___ out of ___ school days per month. (Gradually increase expectations as the student demonstrates success.)
3. The student will attend ___ out of ___ class periods per week. (Gradually increase expectations as the student demonstrates success.)
4. The student will attend ___ out of ___ class periods per month. (Gradually increase expectations as the student demonstrates success.)

BEHAVIOR 36:   Has unexcused tardiness

Goal:
1. The student will improve his/her punctuality.

Objectives:
1. The student will be on time to school on ___ out of ___ days per week. (Gradually increase expectations as the student demonstrates success.)
2. The student will be on time to school on ___ out of ___ days per month. (Gradually increase expectations as the student demonstrates success.)
3. The student will be on time to class on ___ out of ___ class periods per day. (Gradually increase expectations as the student demonstrates success.)
4. The student will be on time to class on ___ out of ___ class periods per week. (Gradually increase expectations as the student demonstrates success.)
5. The student will be on time to (specified activity) on ___ out of ___ days per week. (Gradually increase expectations as the student demonstrates success.)
6. The student will be on time to (specified activity) on ___ out of ___ days per month. (Gradually increase expectations as the student demonstrates success.)

BEHAVIOR 37:   Makes unnecessary physical contact with others

Goal:
1. The student will make physical contact with others when appropriate.

Objectives:
1. The student will interact with others in a physically appropriate manner on ___ out of ___ trials.
2. The student will refrain from making unnecessary contact such as hugging, touching, etc., when interacting with others on ___ out of ___ trials.
3. The student will touch others in only designated areas such as on the arm, shoulder, or hand on ___ out of ___ trials.
4. The student will gain others' attention in an appropriate manner by standing quietly or raising his/her hand until recognized on ___ out of ___ trials.
5. The student will demonstrate acceptable physical contact such as a handshake, pat on the back, "high five," etc., when appropriate on ___ out of ___ trials.

BEHAVIOR 38:   Blames other persons or materials to avoid taking responsibility for his/her mistakes

Goal:
1. The student will take responsibility for his/her mistakes.

Objectives:
1. The student will take responsibility for his/her mistakes on ___ out of ___ trials.
2. The student will correct his/her mistakes when asked to do so by the teacher on ___ out of ___ trials.
3. The student will immediately correct his/her mistakes when he/she becomes aware of them on ___ out of ___ trials.
4. The student will independently correct his/her mistakes when assignments are returned to him/her for corrections on ___ out of ___ trials.

BEHAVIOR 39:   Steals or forcibly takes things from other students, teachers, the school building, etc.

Goal:
1. The student will not take things that belong to others.

Objectives:
1. The student will refrain from stealing on ___ out of ___ trials.
2. The student will refrain from forcibly taking things from others on ___ out of ___ trials.
3. The student will ask the owner's permission before using materials, possessions, etc., on ___ out of ___ trials.
4. The student will ask the user's permission before using materials, equipment, etc., on ___ out of ___ trials.
5. The student will ask to use materials, share materials, and return materials in the same or better condition on ___ out of ___ trials.
6. The student will ask to borrow materials, equipment, possessions, etc., before taking them on ___ out of ___ trials.

BEHAVIOR 40:   Behaves inappropriately when others do well or receive praise or attention

Goals:
1. The student will behave appropriately when others do well.
2. The student will behave appropriately when others receive praise or attention.

Objectives:
1. The student will congratulate others when they do well on ___ out of ___ trials.
2. The student will congratulate others when they receive praise or attention on ___ out of ___ trials.
3. The student will clap/cheer, when appropriate for the situation, for others when they do well on ___ out of ___ trials.

4. The student will clap/cheer, when appropriate for the situation, for others when they receive praise or attention on ___ out of ___ trials.
5. The student will make a positive comment when others do well on ___ out of ___ trials.
6. The student will make a positive comment when others receive praise or attention on ___ out of ___ trials.
7. The student will continue to participate in the game/activity when others are doing better than he/she on ___ out of ___ trials.
8. The student will encourage others to do well when competing for an award, prize, etc., on ___ out of ___ trials.
9. The student will demonstrate good sportsmanship by helping his/her teammates, playing fairly, cheering for the opposing team, etc., during ___ out of ___ competitive activities.
10. The student will remove himself/herself from an activity when he/she begins to experience difficulty behaving appropriately during ___ out of ___ competitive activities.
11. The student will shake the opponent's hand and make a positive comment such as "Good game," after losing to the opponent on ___ out of ___ trials.

BEHAVIOR 41: Engages in inappropriate behaviors while seated

Goals:
1. The student will engage in appropriate behaviors while seated.
2. The student will sit appropriately in his/her seat.

Objectives:
1. The student will demonstrate appropriate in-seat behavior by sitting quietly with his/her feet on the floor under the desk and keeping all four legs of the chair in contact with the floor for ___ minutes at a time. (Gradually increase expectations as the student demonstrates success.)
2. The student will refrain from tipping his/her chair for ___ minutes at a time. (Gradually increase expectations as the student demonstrates success.)
3. The student will refrain from tipping his/her desk while seated for ___ minutes at a time. (Gradually increase expectations as the student demonstrates success.)
4. The student will keep his/her feet on the floor while seated for ___ minutes at a time. (Gradually increase expectations as the student demonstrates success.)
5. The student will sit quietly while seated for ___ minutes at a time. (Gradually increase expectations as the student demonstrates success.)
6. The student will refrain from touching others as they walk by on ___ out of ___ trials.
7. The student will refrain from tapping objects such as a pencil, paper clip, eraser, ruler, etc., for ___ minutes at a time. (Gradually increase expectations as the student demonstrates success.)

BEHAVIOR 42: Behaves in a manner inappropriate for the situation

Goal:
1. The student will behave in a manner appropriate for the situation.

Objectives:
1. The student will laugh when appropriate during ___ out of ___ situations.
2. The student will appear alarmed or upset when appropriate during ___ out of ___ situations.
3. The student will show emotion that is appropriate for the situation during ___ out of ___ situations.
4. The student will demonstrate emotion like that of his/her peers during ___ out of ___ situations.
5. The student will cry when appropriate during ___ out of ___ situations.
6. The student will demonstrate anger when appropriate during ___ out of ___ situations.

BEHAVIOR 43: Tries to avoid situations, assignments, responsibilities

Goals:
1. The student will respond appropriately to situations, assignments, or responsibilities in the classroom.

2. The student will attempt new situations in the classroom.
3. The student will attempt new assignments in the classroom.
4. The student will accept responsibilities in the classroom.

Objectives:
1. The student will refrain from making somatic complaints on ___ out of ___ trials in order to avoid situations, assignments, or responsibilities.
2. The student will complain of physical discomfort when appropriate in ___ out of ___ situations.
3. The student will attempt new situations in the classroom on ___ out of ___ trials.
4. The student will attempt new assignments on ___ out of ___ trials.
5. The student will accept responsibilities in the classroom on ___ out of ___ trials.
6. The student will not ask to use the restroom, go to his/her locker, go to the office, etc., in order to avoid situations in the classroom on ___ out of ___ trials.
7. The student will not ask to use the restroom, go to his/her locker, go to the office, etc., in order to avoid assignments in the classroom on ___ out of ___ trials.
8. The student will not ask to use the restroom, go to his/her locker, go to the office, etc., in order to avoid accepting responsibilities in the classroom on ___ out of ___ trials.

BEHAVIOR 44: Behaves impulsively, without self-control

Goal:
1. The student will demonstrate self-control.

Objectives:
1. The student will wait quietly for assistance from an instructor on ___ out of ___ trials.
2. The student will wait his/her turn when engaged in activities with peers on ___ out of ___ trials.
3. The student will make decisions appropriate to the situation on ___ out of ___ trials.
4. The student will attempt a task before asking for assistance on ___ out of ___ trials.
5. The student will ask to use materials before taking them on ___ out of ___ trials.
6. The student will use materials appropriately and return them in the same or better condition on ___ out of ___ trials.
7. The student will stay in his/her seat for ___ minutes at a time. (Gradually increase expectations as the student demonstrates success.)
8. The student will raise his/her hand to leave his/her seat on ___ out of ___ trials.
9. The student will raise his/her hand to gain the teacher's attention on ___ out of ___ trials.
10. The student will listen to directions before beginning a task on ___ out of ___ trials.
11. The student will read directions before beginning a task on ___ out of ___ trials.
12. The student will refrain from touching others during ___ out of ___ interactions.
13. The student will demonstrate consideration/regard for others on ___ out of ___ trials.

BEHAVIOR 45: Exhibits extreme mood changes

Goal:
1. The student will demonstrate behavior appropriate to the situation.

Objectives:
1. The student will demonstrate behavior that is appropriate to the situation on ___ out of ___ trials.
2. The student will show emotion that is appropriate to the situation during ___ out of ___ situations.
3. The student will maintain consistency in his/her mood for ___ day(s) at a time.
4. The student will react in a consistent manner in similar situations on ___ out of ___ trials.
5. The student will recognize his/her mood changes on ___ out of ___ occasions.
6. The student will remove himself/herself from the group when he/she experiences difficulty behaving appropriately on ___ out of ___ trials.

BEHAVIOR 46: **Is unpredictable in behavior**

Goals:
1. The student will demonstrate behavior that is predictable.
2. The student will respond to situations in a predictable manner.

Objectives:
1. The student will respond consistently to similar situations in the environment on ___ out of ___ trials.
2. The student will respond consistently to situations in the environment for ___ day(s) at a time.
3. The student will respond consistently to situations in the environment for ___ week(s) at a time.
4. The student will respond consistently to situations in the environment for ___ month(s) at a time.
5. The student will show emotion that is appropriate to the situation on ___ out of ___ trials.
6. The student will react in a manner appropriate to the situation on ___ out of ___ trials.
7. The student will maintain his/her orientation to time and place for ___ day(s) at a time.
8. The student will maintain his/her orientation to time and place for ___ week(s) at a time.
9. The student will maintain his/her orientation to time and place for ___ month(s) at a time.

BEHAVIOR 47: **Does not follow directives from teachers or other school personnel**

Goals:
1. The student will follow directives from teachers.
2. The student will follow directives from school personnel.

Objectives:
1. The student will follow through with teacher directives within ___ minutes. (Gradually increase expectations as the student demonstrates success.)
2. The student will follow through with directions given by school personnel within ___ minutes. (Gradually increase expectations as the student demonstrates success.)
3. The student will follow teacher directives when given ___ cues. (Gradually decrease number of cues as the student demonstrates success.)
4. The student will follow school personnel directives when given ___ cues. (Gradually decrease number of cues as the student demonstrates success.)
5. The student will stop an activity when told to do so by the teacher on ___ out of ___ trials.
6. The student will stop an activity when told to do so by school personnel on ___ out of ___ trials.

BEHAVIOR 48: **Ignores consequences of his/her behavior**

Goals:
1. The student will consider consequences of his/her behavior.
2. The student will demonstrate consideration of consequences of his/her behavior.

Objectives:
1. The student will identify appropriate consequences of his/her behavior with the teacher on ___ out of ___ trials.
2. The student will behave in such a way as to demonstrate that he/she considered consequences of his/her behavior on ___ out of ___ trials.
3. The student will refrain from reacting impulsively on ___ out of ___ trials.
4. The student will demonstrate behaviors that will result in positive consequences on ___ out of ___ trials.

BEHAVIOR 49: **Makes sexually-related comments or engages in behavior with sexual overtones**

Goals:
1. The student will refrain from making sexually-related comments.

2. The student will refrain from engaging in behaviors with sexual overtones.
3. The student will demonstrate appropriate behavior in carrying out his/her social-sexual role at school.

Objectives:
1. The student will make appropriate comments when talking with others during ___ out of ___ interactions.
2. The student will make appropriate gestures on ___ out of ___ trials.
3. The student will refrain from touching others on ___ out of ___ trials.
4. The student will not expose himself/herself to others on ___ out of ___ trials.
5. The student will touch himself/herself in appropriate areas on ___ out of ___ trials.
6. The student will refrain from inappropriately touching himself/herself on ___ out of ___ trials.
7. The student will remain appropriately clothed on ___ out of ___ trials.
8. The student will make appropriate comments on ___ out of ___ trials.

BEHAVIOR 50: Becomes overexcited

Goal:
1. The student will maintain self-control in stimulating activities.

Objectives:
1. The student will temporarily remove himself/herself from an activity when he/she begins to become overexcited on ___ out of ___ trials.
2. The student will ask for teacher assistance when he/she becomes overexcited on ___ out of ___ trials.
3. The student will use a tone of voice appropriate to the situation on ___ out of ___ trials.
4. The student will maintain self-control when involved in ___ out of ___ stimulating activities.
5. The student will walk away from a stimulating situation and return when he/she has gained control of his/her behavior on ___ out of ___ trials.
6. The student will stop an activity when told to do so by the teacher on ___ out of ___ trials.
7. The student will physically interact with others in an appropriate manner on ___ out of ___ trials.
8. The student will refrain from reacting impulsively in ___ out of ___ stimulating activities.
9. The student will remain on-task in the presence of stimuli in the classroom on ___ out of ___ trials.
10. The student will remain quietly seated in the presence of stimuli on ___ out of ___ trials.
11. The student will follow rules in the presence of stimuli on ___ out of ___ trials.

BEHAVIOR 51: Lies, denies, exaggerates, distorts the truth

Goals:
1. The student will relate information in an accurate manner.
2. The student will accept responsibility for his/her behavior.
3. The student will tell the truth.

Objectives:
1. The student will relate information in an accurate manner on ___ out of ___ trials.
2. The student will accept responsibility for his/her behavior when confronted by the teacher on ___ out of ___ trials.
3. The student will tell the truth on ___ out of ___ trials.
4. The student will refrain from denying his/her behavior on ___ out of ___ trials.
5. The student will accurately represent information on ___ out of ___ trials.
6. The student will report details in an accurate manner on ___ out of ___ trials.
7. The student will admit to his/her behavior on ___ out of ___ trials.

BEHAVIOR 52: Brings inappropriate or illegal materials to school

Goals:
1. The student will bring appropriate materials to school.

2. The student will bring legal materials to school.
3. The student will follow the school's code of conduct.

Objectives:
1. The student will bring appropriate materials to school ___ out of ___ days per week.
2. The student will bring appropriate materials to school ___ out of ___ days per month.
3. The student will bring appropriate materials to school ___ out of ___ days per semester.
4. The student will bring legal materials to school ___ out of ___ days per week.
5. The student will bring legal materials to school ___ out of ___ days per month.
6. The student will bring legal materials to school ___ out of ___ days per semester.
7. The student will refrain from bringing magazines to school ___ out of ___ days per week.
8. The student will refrain from bringing magazines to school ___ out of ___ days per month.
9. The student will refrain from bringing magazines to school ___ out of ___ days per semester.
10. The student will refrain from bringing weapons to school ___ out of ___ days per week.
11. The student will refrain from bringing weapons to school ___ out of ___ days per month.
12. The student will refrain from bringing weapons to school ___ out of ___ days per semester.
13. The student will refrain from bringing drugs to school ___ out of ___ days per week.
14. The student will refrain from bringing drugs to school ___ out of ___ days per month.
15. The student will refrain from bringing drugs to school ___ out of ___ days per semester.
16. The student will refrain from bringing alcohol to school ___ out of ___ days per week.
17. The student will refrain from bringing alcohol to school ___ out of ___ days per month.
18. The student will refrain from bringing alcohol to school ___ out of ___ days per semester.
19. The student will arrive at school sober ___ out of ___ days per week.
20. The student will arrive at school sober ___ out of ___ days per month.
21. The student will arrive at school sober ___ out of ___ days per semester.
22. The student will be free from the influence of drugs ___ out of ___ days per week.
23. The student will be free from the influence of drugs ___ out of ___ days per month.
24. The student will be free from the influence of drugs ___ out of ___ days per semester.
25. The student will not consume drugs or alcohol at school ___ out of ___ days per week.
26. The student will not consume drugs or alcohol at school ___ out of ___ days per month.
27. The student will not consume drugs or alcohol at school ___ out of ___ days per semester.
28. The student will not possess drugs or alcohol at school ___ out of ___ days per week.
29. The student will not possess drugs or alcohol at school ___ out of ___ days per month.
30. The student will not possess drugs or alcohol at school ___ out of ___ days per semester.

BEHAVIOR 53: **Destroys school or other students' property**

Goals:
1. The student will take proper care of school property.
2. The student will care for school property in a responsible manner.
3. The student will take proper care of other students' property.
4. The student will care for other students' property in a responsible manner.

Objectives:
1. The student will return school property to a designated location in the same or better condition on ___ out of ___ trials.
2. The student will return other students' property in the same or better condition on ___ out of ___ trials.
3. The student will care for school property in a responsible manner on ___ out of ___ trials.
4. The student will care for other students' property in a responsible manner on ___ out of ___ trials.
5. The student will demonstrate appropriate care and handling of school property on ___ out of ___ trials.
6. The student will demonstrate appropriate care and handling of other students' property on ___ out of ___ trials.
7. The student will refrain from defacing school property on ___ out of ___ trials.

8. The student will refrain from defacing other students' property on ___ out of ___ trials.
9. The student will refrain from damaging school property on ___ out of ___ trials.
10. The student will refrain from damaging other students' property on ___ out of ___ trials.
11. The student will refrain from vandalizing school property on ___ out of ___ trials.
12. The student will refrain from vandalizing other students' property on ___ out of ___ trials.

BEHAVIOR 54: Cheats

Goals:
1. The student will independently perform his/her assignments.
2. The student will not cheat.

Objectives:
1. The student will independently perform his/her assignments on ___ out of ___ trials.
2. The student will refrain from cheating on ___ out of ___ tasks.
3. The student will independently perform ___ out of ___ tasks.
4. The student will refrain from copying other students' work on ___ out of ___ trials.
5. The student will refrain from using notes during ___ out of ___ quizzes.
6. The student will independently perform ___ out of ___ homework assignments.
7. The student will ask for teacher assistance when necessary on ___ out of ___ trials.

BEHAVIOR 55: Demonstrates inappropriate behavior when moving with a group

Goal:
1. The student will demonstrate appropriate behavior when moving with a group.

Objectives:
1. The student will demonstrate appropriate behavior when moving with a group on ___ out of ___ trials.
2. The student will stay in line when moving with a group on ___ out of ___ trials.
3. The student will walk quietly when moving with a group on ___ out of ___ trials.
4. The student will keep his/her hands to his/her sides when moving with a group on ___ out of ___ trials.
5. The student will demonstrate appropriate behavior for ___ minutes at a time when moving with a group.
6. The student will walk quietly by the teacher when moving with a group on ___ out of ___ trials.
7. The student will walk quietly by a peer when moving with a group on ___ out of ___ trials.

BEHAVIOR 56: Responds inappropriately to redirection in academic and social situations

Goals:
1. The student will respond appropriately to redirection in academic situations.
2. The student will respond appropriately to redirection in social situations.

Objectives:
1. The student will follow teacher directives in academic situations on ___ out of ___ trials.
2. The student will follow teacher directives in social situations on ___ out of ___ trials.
3. The student will make the correct response to redirection in academic situations on ___ out of ___ trials.
4. The student will make the correct response to redirection in social situations on ___ out of ___ trials.
5. The student will correct errors when told to do so by the teacher on ___ out of ___ trials.
6. The student will refrain from arguing when told to correct errors on assigned tasks on ___ out of ___ trials.
7. The student will return to his/her seat when told to do so by the teacher on ___ out of ___ trials.
8. The student will follow teacher directives when given ___ cues. (Gradually increase expectations as the student demonstrates success.)

9. The student will immediately respond to redirection on ___ out of ___ trials.
10. The student will maintain self-control when redirected in an academic situation on ___ out of ___ trials.
11. The student will maintain self-control when redirected in a social situation on ___ out of ___ trials.
12. The student will stop an activity when told to do so by the teacher on ___ out of ___ trials.

BEHAVIOR 57: Does not accept changes in established routine

Goals:
1. The student will accept changes in an established routine.
2. The student will demonstrate appropriate behavior when an established routine is temporarily altered.

Objectives:
1. The student will accept changes in an established routine on ___ out of ___ trials.
2. The student will demonstrate appropriate behavior when an established routine is temporarily altered on ___ out of ___ trials.
3. The student will maintain self-control when changes in his/her schedule have been made on ___ out of ___ trials.
4. The student will demonstrate flexibility in performing tasks in a variety of ways on ___ out of ___ trials.
5. The student will demonstrate appropriate behavior in the presence of a student teacher on ___ out of ___ trials.
6. The student will demonstrate appropriate behavior in the presence of a substitute teacher on ___ out of ___ trials.
7. The student will follow established rules and behavioral expectations when changes in an established routine occur on ___ out of ___ trials.
8. The student will follow teacher directives when given ___ cues. (Gradually increase expectations as the student demonstrates success.)
9. The student will immediately respond to redirection on ___ out of ___ trials.
10. The student will maintain self-control when redirected in an academic situation on ___ out of ___ trials.
11. The student will maintain self-control when redirected in a social situation on ___ out of ___ trials.
12. The student will stop an activity when told to do so by the teacher on ___ out of ___ trials.

BEHAVIOR 58: Does not follow school rules

Goal:
1. The student will follow school rules.

Objectives:
1. The student will follow school rules on ___ out of ___ trials.
2. The student will walk in the halls when moving from one location to another on ___ out of ___ trials.
3. The student will refrain from throwing food in the cafeteria on ___ out of ___ trials.
4. The student will keep his/her food on his/her plate on ___ out of ___ trials.
5. The student will work quietly in the library on ___ out of ___ trials.
6. The student will talk quietly with a peer when in the library on ___ out of ___ trials.
7. The student will handle school property with care on ___ out of ___ trials.
8. The student will walk quietly through the halls on ___ out of ___ trials.
9. The student will interact appropriately with his/her peers during lunch, recess, break time, etc., on ___ out of ___ trials.

BEHAVIOR 59: Indicates that he/she does not care or is not concerned about performance, grades, report cards, graduating, consequences of behavior, etc.

Goals:
1. The student will demonstrate concern about his/her classroom performance.

2. The student will demonstrate consideration of consequences of his/her behavior.
3. The student will demonstrate an interest in graduating from high school.

Objectives:
1. The student will demonstrate concern about his/her classroom performance on ___ out of ___ trials.
2. The student will demonstrate consideration of consequences of his/her behavior on ___ out of ___ trials.
3. The student will demonstrate behaviors that will result in positive consequences on ___ out of ___ trials.
4. The student will perform academic tasks designed to meet his/her level of functioning with ___% accuracy. (Gradually increase expectations as the student demonstrates success.)
5. The student will demonstrate an interest in graduating from high school by talking about graduation, making plans for college or future employment, etc., on ___ out of ___ trials.
6. The student will demonstrate pride in his/her classroom performance by making positive comments, displaying his/her work for others to view, asking to take on new responsibilities, etc., on ___ out of ___ trials.
7. The student will attend ___ out of ___ classes per week.
8. The student will attend ___ out of ___ classes per month.
9. The student will attend ___ out of ___ classes per semester.
10. The student will be on time to ___ out of ___ classes per week.
11. The student will be on time to ___ out of ___ classes per month.
12. The student will be on time to ___ out of ___ classes per semester.

BEHAVIOR 60: Needs immediate rewards/reinforcement in order to demonstrate appropriate behavior

Goal:
1. The student will demonstrate the ability to delay rewards/reinforcement.

Objectives:
1. The student will delay rewards/reinforcement for ___ minutes at a time. (Gradually increase expectations as the student demonstrates success.)
2. The student will delay rewards/reinforcement until he/she has successfully completed ___ task(s). (Gradually increase expectations as the student demonstrates success.)
3. The student will delay rewards/reinforcement until the end of the school day on ___ out of ___ trials.
4. The student will delay rewards/reinforcement for ___ week(s). (Gradually increase expectations as the student demonstrates success.)
5. The student will delay rewards/reinforcement for up to ___ month(s). (Gradually increase expectations as the student demonstrates success.)
6. The student will work for ___ minutes without requiring rewards/reinforcement. (Gradually increase expectations as the student demonstrates success.)
7. The student will complete ___ tasks without requiring rewards/reinforcement. (Gradually increase expectations as the student demonstrates success.)

BEHAVIOR 61: Does not care for personal appearance

Goals:
1. The student will care for his/her personal appearance.
2. The student will improve his/her hygiene skills.

Objectives:
1. The student will come to class with his/her hair combed ___ out of ___ classes per week.
2. The student will come to class free of offending odors on ___ out of ___ trials.
3. The student will wear clothing to school that is clean, properly fitted, and free of tears and holes on ___ out of ___ trials.

4. The student will wash his/her hands after using the restroom, eating, playing outside, etc., on ___ out of ___ trials.
5. The student will blow his/her nose in an appropriate manner on ___ out of ___ trials.
6. The student will wear clothing that matches in color and style on ___ out of ___ trials.

BEHAVIOR 62: Engages in inappropriate behaviors related to bodily functions

Goals:
1. The student will engage in appropriate behavior related to bodily functions.
2. The student will use school facilities in an appropriate manner.

Objectives:
1. The student will engage in appropriate behaviors related to bodily functions on ___ out of ___ trials.
2. The student will use school facilities in an appropriate manner on ___ out of ___ trials.
3. The student will use acceptable language when referring to bodily functions on ___ out of ___ trials.
4. The student will only make references to bodily functions when appropriate on ___ out of ___ trials.
5. The student will use the toilet appropriately on ___ out of ___ trials.
6. The student will use the urinal appropriately on ___ out of ___ trials.
7. The student will refrain from masturbating for ___ minutes at a time. (Gradually increase expectations as the student demonstrates success.)
8. The student will interact appropriately with others during ___ out of ___ interactions.
9. The student will appropriately perform necessary bodily functions with supervision on ___ out of ___ trials.
10. The student will independently perform necessary bodily functions in an appropriate manner on ___ out of ___ trials.
11. The student will maintain control of bodily functions ___ out of ___ days per week.
12. The student will ask for assistance related to bodily function when necessary on ___ out of ___ trials.

BEHAVIOR 63: Does not change behavior from one situation to another

Goals:
1. The student will change his/her behavior from one situation to another.
2. The student will demonstrate flexibility in his/her behavior.

Objectives:
1. The student will change his/her behavior from one situation to another on ___ out of ___ trials.
2. The student will demonstrate flexibility in his/her behavior on ___ out of ___ trials.
3. The student will stop an activity when cued by the teacher on ___ out of ___ trials.
4. The student will stop an activity and begin another within ___ minutes. (Gradually increase expectations as the student demonstrates success.)
5. The student will demonstrate behavior appropriate for the situation on ___ out of ___ trials.
6. The student will calm down when he/she enters the building on ___ out of ___ trials.
7. At the end of recess, the student will calm down within ___ minutes and enter the building in a quiet manner.
8. The student will engage in a relaxation activity following a stimulating activity on ___ out of ___ trials.
9. The student will begin a task within ___ minutes. (Gradually increase expectations as the student demonstrates success.)

BEHAVIOR 64: Does not participate in classroom activities or special events that are interesting to other students

Goal:
1. The student will participate in classroom activities or special events.

Objectives:
1. The student will participate in ___ out of ___ classroom activities each week.
2. The student will participate in ___ out of ___ special events per month.
3. The student will demonstrate an interest in classroom activities by asking about the activities, talking about the activities, helping prepare for the activities, etc., in ___ out of ___ activities.
4. The student will demonstrate an interest in special events by asking about the events, talking about the events, helping prepare for the events, etc., in ___ out of ___ special events.
5. The student will passively participate in a classroom activity by sitting quietly, assisting the teacher, taking notes, etc., during ___ out of ___ activities.
6. The student will actively participate in a classroom activity by being the group leader or spokesperson, answering questions, providing his/her opinion, etc., during ___ out of ___ activities.
7. The student will passively participate in a special event by sitting/standing quietly, walking with the group, watching others play games, etc., during ___ out of ___ events.
8. The student will actively participate in a special event by having a role in the play, producing the play, decorating the room, performing in the assembly, etc., during ___ out of ___ events.

BEHAVIOR 65: Blames self for situations beyond his/her control

Goal:
1. The student will demonstrate realistic, objective self-appraisal.

Objectives:
1. The student will make ____ positive statement(s) about himself/herself per day. (Gradually increase expectations as the student demonstrates success.)
2. The student will demonstrate the ability to accept mistakes by refraining from crying, making negative self-statements, etc., on ___ out of ___ trials.
3. The student will demonstrate the ability to refrain from expecting perfection on his/her own part, by working on a specific task for a realistic amount of time on ___ out of ___ trials.
4. Given five situations over which the student has control and five situations over which he/she has no control, the student will correctly identify ___ of which he/she either has control or no control.
5. The student will make an accurate appraisal of his/her performance, at the end of each activity, on ___ out of ___ trials.

BEHAVIOR 66: Becomes upset when a suggestion or constructive criticism is given

Goals:
1. The student will respond appropriately when he/she receives a suggestion.
2. The student will respond appropriately when he/she receives a constructive criticism.

Objectives:
1. The student will correct his/her errors when told to by the teacher on ___ out of ___ trials.
2. The student will change the manner in which he/she performs, talks to others, etc., when given constructive criticism on ___ out of ___ trials.
3. The student will refrain from crying, tantruming, yelling, etc., when he/she receives a suggestion on ___ out of ___ trials.
4. The student will refrain from crying, tantruming, yelling, etc., when he/she receives a constructive criticism on ___ out of ___ trials.
5. The student will respond appropriately to a suggestion by saying "Thank you", talking about alternative ways to perform a task, etc., on ___ out of ___ trials.
6. The student will respond appropriately to constructive criticism by discussing alternative ways to behave, perform the task, etc., on ___ out of ___ trials.

BEHAVIOR 67: Threatens to hurt self or commit suicide

Goals:
1. The student will not threaten to hurt self.

2. The student will not threaten to commit suicide.

Objectives:
1. The student will express his/her feelings in an appropriate manner on ___ out of ___ trials.
2. The student will talk to the teacher when he/she is feeling depressed, anxious, upset, hopeless, etc., on ___ out of ___ occasions.

BEHAVIOR 68: Indicates that no one likes him/her, no one cares about him/her, etc.

Goals:
1. The student will improve his/her self-esteem.
2. The student will develop a friendship.

Objectives:
1. The student will make ___ positive self-statement(s) per day.
2. The student will interact with a peer(s) when asked on ___ out of ___ trials.
3. The student will initiate an interaction with a peer(s) ___ times per day.
4. The student will participate in assigned activities on ___ out of ___ trials.
5. The student will demonstrate emotions that are appropriate to the situation on ___ out of ___ trials.
6. The student will talk about situations in a realistic manner on ___ out of ___ trials.
7. The student will develop ___ friendship(s) in a month period.
8. The student will indicate that he/she is liked by others on ___ out of ___ trials.
9. The student will indicate that others care about him/her on ___ out of ___ trials.

BEHAVIOR 69: Does not smile, laugh, or demonstrate happiness

Goals:
1. The student will smile.
2. The student will laugh.
3. The student will demonstrate happiness.

Objectives:
1. The student will smile when appropriate on ___ out of ___ trials.
2. The student will laugh when appropriate on ___ out of ___ trials.
3. The student will demonstrate happiness when appropriate on ___ out of ___ trials.
4. The student will demonstrate happiness by smiling, laughing, joking with peers, etc., on ___ out of ___ trials.
5. The student will laugh or smile when humorous events or activities take place on ___ out of ___ trials.

BEHAVIOR 70: Is tired, listless, apathetic, unmotivated, not interested in school

Goals:
1. The student will participate in classroom activities.
2. The student will demonstrate interest by participating in classroom activities.

Objectives:
1. The student will participate in ___ out of ___ classroom activities per day.
2. The student will participate in ___ out of ___ classroom activities per week.
3. The student will participate in ___ out of ___ classroom activities per month.
4. The student will demonstrate an interest in classroom activities by asking about the activities, talking about the activities, helping prepare for the activities, etc., in ___ out of ___ activities.
5. The student will passively participate in classroom activity by sitting quietly, assisting the teacher, taking notes, etc., during ___ out of ___ activities.
6. The student will actively participate in a classroom activity by being the group leader or spokesperson, answering questions, providing his/her opinion, etc., during ___ out of ___ activities.
7. The student will interact with a peer for ___ minutes per day. (Gradually increase expectations as the student demonstrates success.)

8. The student will initiate ____ interactions with a peer per day. (Gradually increase expectations as the student demonstrates success.)
9. The student will interact with the teacher for ____ minutes per day. (Gradually increase expectations as the student demonstrates success.)
10. The student will initiate ____ interactions with the teacher per day. (Gradually increase expectations as the student demonstrates success.)
11. The student will perform academic tasks with ____% accuracy. (Gradually increase expectations as the student demonstrates success.)
12. The student will identify something he/she enjoys doing at school when asked by the teacher on ____ out of ____ occasions.
13. The student will identify a reinforcer he/she would like to earn for participating in classroom activities on ____ out of ____ trials.
14. The student will perform ____ out of ____ academic tasks per day. (Gradually increase expectations as the student demonstrates success.)

BEHAVIOR 71: Is overly critical of self in school-related performance, abilities, personal appearance, etc.

Goals:
1. The student will demonstrate realistic, objective self-appraisal.
2. The student will improve his/her perception of self.

Objectives:
1. The student will make an accurate appraisal of his/her performance at the end of each activity on ____ out of ____ trials.
2. The student will discuss his/her abilities in a realistic manner on ____ out of ____ trials.
3. The student will make ____ positive comment(s) about himself/herself per day. (Gradually increase expectations as the student demonstrates success.)
4. The student will refrain from making self-depreciating remarks such as "I'm stupid," "I'm dumb," "I'm ugly," etc., on ____ out of ____ trials.
5. The student will attempt ____ out of ____ assigned tasks per day. (Gradually increase expectations as the student demonstrates success.)
6. The student will ask for teacher assistance only when necessary on ____ out of ____ trials.
7. The student will work for ____ minutes without requiring teacher assistance. (Gradually increase expectations as the student demonstrates success.)

BEHAVIOR 72: Frowns, scowls, looks unhappy during typical classroom situations

Goals:
1. The student will smile during typical classroom situations.
2. The student will demonstrate happiness during typical classroom situations.
3. The student will refrain from frowning, scowling, and looking unhappy during typical classroom situations.
4. The student will behave in a manner appropriate for the situation.

Objectives:
1. The student will smile when appropriate during ____ out of ____ typical classroom situations.
2. The student will demonstrate happiness during ____ out of ____ typical classroom situations.
3. The student will refrain from frowning, scowling, and looking unhappy during ____ out of ____ typical classroom situations.
4. The student will show emotion that is appropriate for the situation during ____ out of ____ occasions.
5. The student will demonstrate happiness by smiling, laughing, joking, etc., when appropriate during ____ out of ____ typical classroom situations.
6. The student will laugh or smile when humorous events or activities take place on ____ out of ____ trials.
7. The student will demonstrate emotion like that of his/her peers during ____ out of ____ typical classroom situations.

BEHAVIOR 73:   Is pessimistic

Goals:
1. The student will become more optimistic.
2. The student will improve his/her perception of school-related activities.

Objectives:
1. The student will make optimistic statements regarding expected outcomes on ___ out of ___ trials.
2. The student will improve his/her perception of school-related activities on ___ out of ___ trials.
3. The student will attempt ___ out of ___ tasks. (Gradually increase expectations as the student demonstrates success.)
4. The student will passively participate in classroom activity by sitting quietly, assisting the teacher, taking notes, etc., during ___ out of ___ activities.
5. The student will actively participate in a classroom activity by being the group leader or spokesperson, answering questions, providing his/her opinion, etc., during ___ out of ___ activities.
6. The student will interact with others for ___ minutes at a time. (Gradually increase expectations as the student demonstrates success.)
7. The student will work on ___ short-term projects per month.
8. The student will work on ___ long-term projects per month.
9. The student will voluntarily participate in competitive activities on ___ out of ___ trials.
10. The student will participate in one or more extracurricular activities per semester.

BEHAVIOR 74:   Indicates concern regarding problems or situations in the home or is unable to deal with classroom requirements because of out-of-school situations

Goal:
1. The student will function successfully at school despite problems or situations in the home or out of school.

Objectives:
1. The student will stay on-task for ___ minutes at a time. (Gradually increase expectations as the student demonstrates success.)
2. The student will complete ___% of his/her assigned tasks each day. (Gradually increase expectations as the student demonstrates success.)
3. The student will attend ___ out of ___ school days per week. (Gradually increase expectations as the student demonstrates success.)
4. The student will attend ___ out of ___ school days per month. (Gradually increase expectations as the student demonstrates success.)
5. The student will be on time to school on ___ out of ___ days per week. (Gradually increase expectations as the student demonstrates success.)
6. The student will be on time to school on ___ out of ___ days per month. (Gradually increase expectations as the student demonstrates success.)
7. The student will be on time to class or activities ___ times per day. (Gradually increase expectations as the student demonstrates success.)
8. The student will perform assigned tasks with ___% accuracy.
9. The student will perform tests or quizzes with ___% accuracy.
10. The student will socially interact in an appropriate manner during ___ out of ___ interactions.

BEHAVIOR 75:   Demonstrates self-destructive behavior

Goals:
1. The student will demonstrate self-regard.
2. The student will not demonstrate self-destructive behaviors.

Objectives:
1. The student will refrain from engaging in self-destructive behaviors when experiencing stress, anger, frustration, etc., during ___ out of ___ situations.

2. The student will care for his/her clothing in an appropriate manner when experiencing stress, anger, unhappiness, etc., during ___ out of ___ situations.
3. The student will care for personal property in an appropriate manner when experiencing stress, anger, anxiety, etc., during ___ out of ___ situations.
4. The student will walk away from stressful, anger-producing situations on ___ out of ___ trials.
5. The student will seek assistance from the teacher when experiencing anger, frustration, hopelessness, etc., during ___ out of ___ trials.
6. The student will refrain from tearing his/her clothing when angry, upset, frustrated, etc., on ___ out of ___ trials.
7. The student will refrain from damaging personal property when angry, upset, anxious, etc., on ___ out of ___ trials.
8. The student will refrain from demonstrating self-destructive behaviors upon receiving constructive criticism from the teacher on ___ out of ___ trials.

BEHAVIOR 76: Moves about unnecessarily

Goals:
1. The student will move about the classroom when necessary.
2. The student will demonstrate body movements appropriate to the situation.

Objectives:
1. The student will leave his/her seat when given permission by the teacher on ___ out of ___ trials.
2. The student will move about the classroom when given permission by the teacher on ___ out of ___ trials.
3. The student will go directly to a specific location and immediately return to his/her seat when given permission by the teacher on ___ out of ___ trials.
4. The student will demonstrate body movements appropriate to the situation on ___ out of ___ trials.
5. The student will refrain from making unnecessary body movements for ___ minutes at a time. (Gradually increase expectations as the student demonstrates success.)
6. The student will stop unnecessary body movements when cued by the teacher on ___ out of ___ trials.
7. The student will ask to have a break from the activity, go to a specific location in the classroom, etc., when he/she begins to feel anxious, upset, frustrated, etc., on ___ out of ___ trials.

BEHAVIOR 77: Speaks in an unnatural voice

Goals:
1. The student will speak in a natural voice.
2. The student will use a natural tone of voice when speaking.

Objectives:
1. The student will speak in a natural voice on ___ out of ___ trials.
2. The student will use a natural tone of voice when speaking on ___ out of ___ trials.

BEHAVIOR 78: Speaks incoherently

Goal:
1. The student will speak coherently.

Objectives:
1. The student will speak coherently on ___ out of ___ trials.
2. The student will make statements that are connected on ___ out of ___ trials.
3. The student will make statements that are related on ___ out of ___ trials.
4. The student will make comments that are intelligible on ___ out of ___ trials.

BEHAVIOR 79: Engages in nervous habits

Goals:
1. The student will maintain self-control in stimulating activities.
2. The student will not engage in nervous habits.

Objectives:
1. The student will discontinue engaging in the nervous habit when cued by the teacher on ___ out of ___ trials.
2. The student will temporarily remove himself/herself from a stimulating activity on ___ out of ___ trials.
3. The student will maintain self-control when engaged in ___ out of ___ stimulating activities.
4. The student will refrain from biting his/her fingernails during ___ out of ___ stimulating activities.
5. The student will refrain from twirling his/her hair during ___ out of ___ stimulating activities.
6. The student will refrain from chewing the inside of his/her cheek during ___ out of ___ stimulating activities.
7. The student will refrain from chewing pencils or pens during ___ out of ___ stimulating activities.
8. The student will refrain from spinning/twirling objects during ___ out of ___ stimulating activities.

BEHAVIOR 80: Throws temper tantrums

Goals:
1. The student will handle anger, frustration, disappointment, anxiety, etc., in an appropriate manner.
2. The student will demonstrate self-control.
3. The student will not throw temper tantrums.

Objectives:
1. The student will handle anger, frustration, disappointment, anxiety, etc., in an appropriate manner on ___ out of ___ trials.
2. The student will demonstrate self-control when angry, frustrated, disappointed, anxious, etc., on ___ out of ___ trials.
3. The student will not throw temper tantrums when angry, frustrated, disappointed, anxious, etc., on ___ out of ___ trials.
4. The student will demonstrate appropriate ways in which to express his/her anger, frustration, disappointment, anxiety, etc., on ___ out of ___ trials.

BEHAVIOR 81: Reacts physically in response to excitement, disappointment, surprise, happiness, fear, etc.

Goals:
1. The student will demonstrate self-control in stimulating situations.
2. The student will control his/her physical response to stimulating situations.

Objectives:
1. The student will demonstrate self-control in ___ out of ___ stimulating situations.
2. The student will control his/her physical response to ___ out of ___ stimulating situations.
3. The student will refrain from flapping his/her hands in ___ out of ___ stimulating situations.
4. The student will refrain from shuddering or trembling in response to ___ out of ___ stimulating situations.
5. The student will refrain from stuttering or stammering in response to ___ out of ___ stimulating situations.
6. The student will temporarily remove himself/herself from a stimulating situation in order to avoid physically responding to the situation on ___ out of ___ trials.
7. The student will refrain from physically responding to stimulating situations when cued by the teacher on ___ out of ___ trials.

BEHAVIOR 82: Becomes pale, may throw up, or passes out when anxious or frightened

Goals:
1. The student will reduce the number of times he/she becomes pale, throws up, or passes out.

2. The student will react in an appropriate manner when anxious or frightened.
3. The student will deal with anxiety or fright in an appropriate manner.

Objectives:
1. The student will reduce the number of times he/she becomes pale, throws up, or passes out by _____% when anxious or frightened. (Gradually increase expectations as the student demonstrates success.)
2. The student will react in an appropriate manner when anxious or frightened on ___ out of ___ trials.
3. The student will deal with anxiety or fright in an appropriate manner on ___ out of ___ trials.
4. The student will temporarily remove himself/herself from anxiety or fright-provoking situations on ___ out of ___ trials.
5. The student will engage in relaxation activities when he/she is anxious or frightened on ___ out of ___ trials.
6. The student will prepare for assignments, tests, or quizzes on ___ out of ___ trials.
7. The student will communicate his/her anxiety or fright to the teacher on ___ out of ___ trials.

BEHAVIOR 83: Demonstrates phobic-type reactions

Goals:
1. The student will demonstrate appropriate behavior in response to typical school experiences.
2. The student will not demonstrate phobic-type reactions.

Objectives:
1. The student will demonstrate appropriate behavior in response to typical school experiences on ___ out of ___ trials.
2. The student will demonstrate appropriate behavior in response to speaking in front of a group on ___ out of ___ trials.
3. The student will demonstrate appropriate behavior in response to changing clothes for physical education on ___ out of ___ trials.
4. The student will attend school ___ out of ___ days per week.
5. The student will attend school ___ out of ___ days per month.
6. The student will attend school ___ out of ___ days per semester.
7. The student will speak in front of a peer for ___ minutes at a time. (Gradually increase expectations as the student demonstrates success.)
8. The student will speak in front of a group for ___ minutes at a time. (Gradually increase expectations as the student demonstrates success.)
9. The student will change clothes for physical education in the presence of a peer on ___ out of ___ trials.
10. The student will change clothes for physical education in the presence of several peers on ___ out of ___ trials.
11. The student will remove himself/herself from a stressful situation on ___ out of ___ trials.
12. The student will attempt ___ out of ___ tasks per day.
13. The student will engage in relaxation activities when he/she begins to demonstrate phobic-type reactions on ___ out of ___ trials.

BEHAVIOR 84: Does not follow the rules of the classroom

Goal:
1. The student will follow the rules of the classroom.

Objectives:
1. The student will follow the rules of the classroom on ___ out of ___ trials.
2. The student will talk only after being given permission on ___ out of ___ trials.
3. The student will ask to leave his/her seat before doing so on ___ out of ___ trials.

4. The student will immediately respond to redirection on ___ out of ___ trials.
5. The student will follow the rules of the classroom with ___ reminders.
6. The student will independently follow the rules of the classroom on ___ out of ___ trials.
7. The student will follow classroom rules when interacting with peers during group activities, free time, etc., on ___ out of ___ trials.
8. The student will handle classroom materials and equipment with care on ___ out of ___ trials.
9. The student will walk quietly in the classroom on ___ out of ___ trials.
10. The student will complete ___ out of ___ assigned tasks per day.

BEHAVIOR 85: Does not wait appropriately for an instructor to arrive

Goal:
1. The student will wait appropriately for an instructor to arrive.

Objectives:
1. The student will wait appropriately for an instructor to arrive on ___ out of ___ trials.
2. The student will stay in his/her seat while waiting for an instructor to arrive on ___ out of ___ trials.
3. The student will wait quietly until an instructor arrives on ___ out of ___ trials.
4. The student will use a quiet tone of voice while waiting for an instructor to arrive on ___ out of ___ trials.
5. The student will interact appropriately with his/her peers by taking turns, sharing materials, talking in an acceptable manner, etc., while waiting for an instructor to arrive on ___ out of ___ trials.
6. The student will go on to the next problem, assignment, etc., while waiting for an instructor to arrive on ___ out of ___ trials.
7. The student will find a structured activity such as reading a library book, studying, etc., while waiting for an instructor to arrive on ___ out of ___ trials.

BEHAVIOR 86: Does not wait appropriately for assistance or attention from an instructor

Goal:
1. The student will wait appropriately for assistance or attention from an instructor.

Objectives:
1. The student will wait appropriately for assistance or attention from an instructor on ___ out of ___ trials.
2. The student will stay in his/her seat while waiting for assistance or attention from an instructor on ___ out of ___ trials.
3. The student will sit quietly while waiting for assistance or attention from an instructor on ___ out of ___ trials.
4. The student will refrain from throwing objects while waiting for assistance or attention from an instructor on ___ out of ___ trials.
5. The student will go on to the next problem, assignment, etc., while waiting for assistance or attention on ___ out of ___ trials.
6. The student will refrain from calling out to the teacher while waiting for assistance or attention on ___ out of ___ trials.
7. The student will refrain from talking while waiting for assistance or attention from an instructor on ___ out of ___ trials.
8. The student will refrain from making noises such as belching, rustling papers, tapping pencil, drumming fingers, etc., while waiting for assistance or attention from an instructor on ___ out of ___ trials.

BEHAVIOR 87: Demonstrates inappropriate behavior in the presence of a substitute teacher

Goal:
1. The student will demonstrate appropriate behavior in the presence of a substitute teacher.

Objectives:
1. The student will demonstrate appropriate behavior in the presence of a substitute teacher on ___ out of ___ trials.
2. The student will follow directions given by a substitute teacher on ___ out of ___ trials.
3. The student will work on assigned tasks in the presence of a substitute teacher on ___ out of ___ trials.
4. The student will interact appropriately with his/her peers by sharing materials, waiting his/her turn, using acceptable language, etc., on ___ out of ___ trials.
5. The student will provide accurate information for the substitute teacher when requested to do so on ___ out of ___ trials.
6. The student will follow the rules of the classroom in the presence of a substitute teacher on ___ out of ___ trials.

BEHAVIOR 88: Does not demonstrate appropriate use of school-related materials

Goals:
1. The student will demonstrate appropriate use of school-related materials.
2. The student will care for school-related materials in a responsible manner.
3. The student will take proper care of school-related materials.

Objectives:
1. The student will return school-related materials to designated locations in the same or better condition on ___ out of ___ trials.
2. The student will demonstrate appropriate use of school-related materials on ___ out of ___ trials.
3. The student will care for school-related materials in a responsible manner on ___ out of ___ trials.
4. The student will take proper care of school-related materials on ___ out of ___ trials.
5. The student will demonstrate appropriate care and handling of school-related materials on ___ out of ___ trials.
6. The student will use school-related materials such as pencils, rulers, industrial arts equipment, etc., for their intended use on ___ out of ___ trials.
7. The student will refrain from damaging school-related materials on ___ out of ___ trials.

BEHAVIOR 89: Does not demonstrate appropriate care and handling of others' property

Goal:
1. The student will demonstrate appropriate care and handling of others' property.

Objectives:
1. The student will demonstrate appropriate care and handling of others' property on ___ out of ___ trials.
2. The student will return others' property in the same or better condition on ___ out of ___ trials.
3. The student will use others' property for its intended use on ___ out of ___ trials.
4. The student will demonstrate appropriate care and handling of peers' property on ___ out of ___ trials.
5. The student will demonstrate appropriate care and handling of school property on ___ out of ___ trials.
6. The student will care for others' property in a responsible manner on ___ out of ___ trials.
7. The student will take proper care of others' property on ___ out of ___ trials.

BEHAVIOR 90:   Does not raise hand when appropriate

Goal:
1. The student will raise his/her hand when appropriate.

Objectives:
1. The student will raise his/her hand when appropriate on ___ out of ___ trials.
2. The student will raise his/her hand to gain the teacher's attention on ___ out of ___ trials.
3. The student will raise his/her hand for assistance on ___ out of ___ trials.
4. The student will raise his/her hand for permission to speak on ___ out of ___ trials.
5. The student will raise his/her hand only when he/she knows the correct answer on ___ out of ___ trials.
6. The student will raise his/her hand to leave his/her seat on ___ out of ___ trials.
7. The student will raise his/her hand to participate on ___ out of ___ trials.
8. The student will raise his/her hand to make a relevant comment during ___ out of ___ discussions.
9. The student will raise his/her hand to ask a question on ___ out of ___ trials.

BEHAVIOR 91:   Does not take notes during class when necessary

Goal:
1. The student will take notes during class when necessary.

Objectives:
1. The student will take notes during class when necessary on ___ out of ___ trials.
2. The student will take notes during class when necessary with the aid of a peer on ___ out of ___ trials.
3. The student will independently take notes during class when necessary on ___ out of ___ trials.
4. The student will write down pertinent information when taking notes on ___ out of ___ trials.

BEHAVIOR 92:   Does not resolve conflict situations appropriately

Goal:
1. The student will improve his/her ability to resolve conflict situations.

Objectives:
1. The student will remain calm during ___ out of ___ conflict situations.
2. The student will refrain from crying during ___ out of ___ conflict situations.
3. The student will refrain from fighting during ___ out of ___ conflict situations.
4. The student will stay in the classroom during ___ out of ___ conflict situations.
5. The student will not run away during ___ out of ___ conflict situations.
6. The student will call upon an arbitrator when involved in a conflicting situation on ___ out of ___ trials.
7. The student will remove himself/herself from a conflicting situation by walking away, returning to his/her seat, finding a different activity, etc., on ___ out of ___ trials.
8. The student will attempt to resolve a conflict with a peer(s) by quietly discussing behavioral options, cooperating, etc., on ___ out of ___ trials.

BEHAVIOR 93:   Does not make appropriate use of free time

Goal:
1. The student will make appropriate use of free time.

Objectives:
1. The student will use free time to find an activity, interact quietly with a peer(s), follow directions, etc., on ___ out of ___ trials.
2. The student will use acceptable language during free time on ___ out of ___ trials.
3. The student will share materials with a peer(s) during free time on ___ out of ___ trials.
4. The student will take turns with a peer(s) during free time on ___ out of ___ trials.
5. The student will interact appropriately with peers during free time by sharing materials, working cooperatively, using acceptable language, etc., on ___ out of ___ trials.
6. The student will find an activity and work cooperatively with peers for ___ minutes during free time.
7. The student will find an activity and work independently for ___ minutes during free time.

BEHAVIOR 94: Fails to work appropriately with peers in a tutoring situation

Goal:
1. The student will be able to work appropriately with a peer(s) in a tutoring situation.

Objectives:
1. The student will work appropriately with a peer(s) in a tutoring situation on ___ out of ___ trials.
2. The student will work appropriately with a peer(s) in a tutoring situation for ___ minutes at a time. (Gradually increase expectations as the student demonstrates success.)
3. The student will share materials with a peer(s) in a tutoring situation on ___ out of ___ trials.
4. The student will work cooperatively with a peer(s) in a tutoring situation on ___ out of ___ trials.
5. The student will settle minor conflicts with a peer(s) in a tutoring situation on ___ out of ___ trials.
6. The student will refrain from fighting with a peer(s) in a tutoring situation on ___ out of ___ trials.
7. The student will stay on-task for ___ minutes when involved in a tutoring situation with a peer(s).
8. The student will complete the task with ___% accuracy when involved in a tutoring situation with a peer(s).
9. The student will follow directions when involved in a tutoring situation with a peer(s) on ___ out of ___ trials.

BEHAVIOR 95: Does not share school materials with other students

Goal:
1. The student will share school materials with other students.

Objectives:
1. The student will share school materials with other students on ___ out of ___ trials.
2. The student will share school materials with other students when directed by the teacher on ___ out of ___ trials.
3. The student will share school materials with other students without being asked to do so on ___ out of ___ trials.
4. The student will allow a peer(s) to use school materials for ___ minutes at a time.
5. The student will ask to use school materials before taking them on ___ out of ___ trials.

BEHAVIOR 96: Writes and passes notes

Goal:
1. The student will not write and pass notes.

Objective:
1. The student will not write and pass notes during ___ out of ___ classes.

BEHAVIOR 97: Tattles

Goals:
1. The student will not tattle.
2. The student will not report the behavior of others.

Objectives:
1. The student will not tattle in ___ out of ___ situations.
2. The student will not report the behavior of others in ___ out of ___ situations.
3. The student will not tattle for ___ minutes at a time.
4. The student will not report the behavior of others for ___ minutes at a time.

BEHAVIOR 98: Fails to find necessary locations in the building

Goal:
1. The student will be able to find necessary locations in the building.

Objectives:
1. The student will be able to find necessary locations in the building such as his/her classes, cafeteria, restroom, etc., on ___ out of ___ trials.
2. The student will be able to find his/her classes on ___ out of ___ trials.
3. The student will be able to go from one class to another within ___ minutes. (Gradually increase expectations as the student demonstrates success.)
4. The student will be able to find the cafeteria on ___ out of ___ trials.
5. The student will be able to find the restroom on ___ out of ___ trials.
6. The student will be able to find the restroom and return to class within ___ minutes. (Gradually increase expectations as the student demonstrates success.)
7. The student will be able to find his/her locker on ___ out of ___ trials.
8. The student will be able to find the office on ___ out of ___ trials.
9. The student will be able to find necessary locations in the building with assistance from a peer on ___ out of ___ trials.
10. The student will independently find necessary locations in the building on ___ out of ___ trials.

BEHAVIOR 99: Does not respond appropriately to environmental cues

Goals:
1. The student will respond appropriately to environmental cues.
2. The student will use environmental cues to help him/her function successfully in the educational environment.

Objectives:
1. The student will respond appropriately to environmental cues such as bells, signs, etc., on ___ out of ___ trials.
2. The student will follow environmental cues such as bells, signs, etc., on ___ out of ___ trials.
3. The student will use environmental cues such as bells, signs, etc., to help him/her function successfully in the educational environment on ___ out of ___ trials.
4. The student will use environmental cues such as bells to remember when to change from one activity to another on ___ out of ___ trials.
5. The student will use environmental cues such as signs to remember how to get from one location to another on ___ out of ___ trials.
6. The student will use environmental cues such as behavioral checklists, posted rules, etc., to remind him/her to demonstrate appropriate behavior on ___ out of ___ trials.
7. The student will use environmental cues such as signs and symbols to help him/her find unfamiliar locations on ___ out of ___ trials.

BEHAVIOR 100: Does not stay in an assigned area for the specified time period

Goal:
1. The student will stay in an assigned area for the specified time period.

Objectives:
1. The student will stay in an assigned area for the specified time period on ___ out of ___ trials.
2. The student will stay in an assigned area for ___ minutes. (Gradually increase expectations as the student demonstrates success.)
3. The student will stay in an assigned area with the aid of physical barriers such as a row of chairs, rope, partition, desk, etc., for the specified time period on ___ out of ___ trials.
4. The student will independently stay in an assigned area for the specified time period on ___ out of ___ trials.
5. The student will stay in the classroom for ___ minutes at a time. (Gradually increase expectations as the student demonstrates success.)
6. The student will stay in the building for ___ minutes at a time. (Gradually increase expectations as the student demonstrates success.)
7. The student will stay on the school grounds for ___ minutes at a time. (Gradually increase expectations as the student demonstrates success.)
8. The student will stay on the playground for ___ minutes at a time. (Gradually increase expectations as the student demonstrates success.)
9. The student will stay in his/her seat for ___ minutes at a time. (Gradually increase expectations as the student demonstrates success.)
10. The student will stay in assigned areas such as the cafeteria, library, gym, etc., for the specified time period on ___ out of ___ trials.

BEHAVIOR 101: Runs away to avoid problems

Goals:
1. The student will accept responsibility for his/her problems.
2. The student will attempt to resolve his/her problems.

Objectives:
1. The student will accept responsibility for his/her problems on ___ out of ___ trials.
2. The student will attempt to resolve his/her problems by talking, cooperating, etc., on ___ out of ___ trials.
3. The student will attempt new tasks on ___ out of ___ trials.
4. The student will ask for teacher assistance when necessary in order to help resolve his/her problems on ___ out of ___ trials.

BEHAVIOR 102: Is under the influence of drugs or alcohol while at school

Goals:
1. The student will not take drugs at school.
2. The student will not drink alcohol at school.
3. The student will follow the school's code of conduct.

Objectives:
1. The student will not take drugs at school for ___ out of ___ days per week.
2. The student will not take drugs at school for ___ out of ___ days per month.
3. The student will not take drugs at school for ___ out of ___ days per semester.
4. The student will not drink alcohol at school for ___ out of ___ days per week.
5. The student will not drink alcohol at school for ___ out of ___ days per month.
6. The student will not drink alcohol at school for ___ out of ___ days per semester.
7. The student will be sober at school for ___ out of ___ days per week.
8. The student will be sober at school for ___ out of ___ days per month.

9. The student will be sober at school for ___ out of ___ days per semester.
10. The student will be free from the influence of drugs for ___ out of ___ days per week.
11. The student will be free from the influence of drugs for ___ out of ___ days per month.
12. The student will be free from the influence of drugs for ___ out of ___ days per semester.

BEHAVIOR 103:   Whines or cries in response to personal or school experiences

Goals:
1. The student will respond appropriately to personal experiences.
2. The student will respond appropriately to school experiences.

Objectives:
1. The student will respond appropriately to personal experiences on ___ out of ___ trials.
2. The student will respond appropriately to school experiences on ___ out of ___ trials.
3. The student will refrain from whining or crying in response to personal experiences on ___ out of ___ trials.
4. The student will refrain from whining or crying in response to school experiences on ___ out of ___ trials.
5. The student will talk with the teacher when he/she has difficulty handling a personal experience on ___ out of ___ trials.
6. The student will talk with the teacher when he/she has difficulty handling a school experience on ___ out of ___ trials.
7. The student will continue to engage in an activity when he/she experiences difficulty on ___ out of ___ trials.
8. The student will be actively involved in assigned activities for ___ minutes at a time.

BEHAVIOR 104:   Demonstrates inappropriate behavior in a small academic group setting

Goal:
1. The student will demonstrate appropriate behavior in a small academic group setting.

Objectives:
1. The student will demonstrate appropriate behavior in ___ out of ___ small academic group settings.
2. The student will share materials during ___ out of ___ small academic group settings.
3. The student will wait his/her turn during ___ out of ___ small academic group settings.
4. The student will talk in an acceptable manner during ___ out of ___ small academic group settings.
5. The student will stay in his/her seat during ___ out of ___ small academic group settings.
6. The student will raise his/her hand to talk during ___ out of ___ small academic group settings.
7. The student will passively participate in small academic group settings by listening quietly, taking notes, reading to self, etc., on ___ out of ___ trials.
8. The student will actively participate in small academic group settings by being the group leader or spokesperson, answering questions, sharing his/her opinion, etc., on ___ out of ___ trials.

BEHAVIOR 105:   Behaves more appropriately alone or in small groups than with the whole class or in large group activities

Goals:
1. The student will behave appropriately when involved in class activities.
2. The student will behave appropriately in large group activities.

Objectives:
1. The student will behave appropriately when involved in class activities on ___ out of ___ trials.
2. The student will behave appropriately in large group activities on ___ out of ___ trials.

3. The student will behave appropriately in class activities by following rules, sharing materials, waiting his/her turn, actively participating, following teacher directives, etc., on ___ out of ___ trials.
4. The student will behave appropriately in large group activities by following rules, sharing materials, waiting his/her turn, actively participating, following teacher directives, etc., on ___ out of ___ trials.

BEHAVIOR 106: Demonstrates inappropriate behavior in a large academic group setting

Goal:
1. The student will demonstrate appropriate behavior in a large academic group setting.

Objectives:
1. The student will demonstrate appropriate behavior in ___ out of ___ large academic group settings.
2. The student will share materials during ___ out of ___ large academic group settings.
3. The student will wait his/her turn during ___ out of ___ large academic group settings.
4. The student will talk in an acceptable manner during ___ out of ___ large academic group settings.
5. The student will stay in his/her seat during ___ out of ___ large academic group settings.
6. The student will raise his/her hand to talk during ___ out of ___ large academic group settings.
7. The student will passively participate in large academic group settings by listening quietly, taking notes, reading to self, etc., on ___ out of ___ trials.
8. The student will actively participate in large academic group settings by being the group leader or spokesperson, answering questions, sharing his/her opinion, etc., on ___ out of ___ trials.

BEHAVIOR 107: Demonstrates inappropriate behavior on the school grounds before and after school

Goals:
1. The student will demonstrate appropriate behavior on the school grounds before school.
2. The student will demonstrate appropriate behavior on the school grounds after school.

Objectives:
1. The student will demonstrate appropriate behavior on the school grounds before school on ___ out of ___ trials.
2. The student will demonstrate appropriate behavior on the school grounds after school on ___ out of ___ trials.
3. The student will refrain from fighting with peers on the school grounds before school on ___ out of ___ trials.
4. The student will refrain from fighting with peers on the school grounds after school on ___ out of ___ trials.
5. The student will refrain from cursing on the school grounds before school on ___ out of ___ trials.
6. The student will refrain from cursing on the school grounds after school on ___ out of ___ trials.
7. The student will refrain from throwing objects such as rocks, sticks, bottles, cans, etc., on the school grounds before school on ___ out of ___ trials.
8. The student will refrain from throwing objects such as rocks, sticks, bottles, cans, etc., on the school grounds after school on ___ out of ___ trials.
9. The student will demonstrate appropriate behavior by interacting appropriately with peers and refraining from damaging, vandalizing, etc., school property before school on ___ out of ___ trials.
10. The student will demonstrate appropriate behavior by interacting appropriately with peers and refraining from damaging, vandalizing, etc., school property after school on ___ out of ___ trials.

BEHAVIOR 108: Demonstrates inappropriate behavior going to and from school

Goals:
1. The student will demonstrate appropriate behavior going to and from school.
2. The student will demonstrate appropriate behavior on the school bus.

3. The student will demonstrate appropriate behavior walking to and from school.

Objectives:
1. The student will demonstrate appropriate behavior going to and from school on ___ out of ___ trials.
2. The student will demonstrate appropriate behavior on the school bus on ___ out of ___ trials.
3. The student will demonstrate appropriate behavior walking to and from school on ___ out of ___ trials.
4. The student will sit quietly on the school bus on ___ out of ___ trials.
5. The student will talk quietly to peers on the school bus on ___ out of ___ trials.
6. The student will refrain from throwing objects out of bus windows on ___ out of ___ trials.
7. The student will interact appropriately with peers on the school bus by sitting quietly, talking in an acceptable manner, respecting personal space, etc., on ___ out of ___ trials.
8. The student will remain quietly seated from the time he/she boards the bus until the time he/she gets off on ___ out of ___ trials.
9. The student will refrain from touching, talking to, distracting, etc., the bus driver on ___ out of ___ trials.
10. The student will keep his/her hands, arms, head, etc., inside the bus on ___ out of ___ trials.
11. The student will walk directly to school and home on ___ out of ___ trials.
12. The student will refrain from fighting, arguing, name calling, etc., with peers when walking to and from school on ___ out of ___ trials.
13. The student will refrain from throwing objects such as rocks, sticks, bottles, cans, etc., when walking to and from school on ___ out of ___ trials.
14. The student will interact appropriately with peers by walking quietly, talking in an acceptable manner, respecting personal space, etc., when walking to and from school on ___ out of ___ trials.

BEHAVIOR 109: Does not finish assignments because of reading difficulties

Goals:
1. The student will improve his/her reading skills.
2. The student will increase his/her reading rate.

Objectives:
1. The student will increase his/her rate of reading to ___ sentences per ___ minute time period.
2. The student will increase his/her rate of reading to ___ paragraphs per ___ minute time period.
3. The student will finish a reading assignment within a ___ minute time period.
4. The student will complete ___ out of ___ activities that require reading per day.
5. The student will use the time provided to read, in order to complete ___ out of ___ assigned activities per day,

BEHAVIOR 110: Needs oral questions and directions frequently repeated

Goals:
1. The student will improve his/her listening comprehension skills.
2. The student will auditorially attend to the source of information.

Objectives:
1. The student will maintain eye contact with the teacher when information is being communicated on ___ out of ___ trials.
2. The student will listen quietly when verbal directions are given on ___ out of ___ trials.
3. The student will successfully reiterate (paraphrase) the information he/she has previously received on ___ out of ___ trials.
4. The student will correctly respond to auditory information with ___ reminders.

5. The student will immediately respond to information he/she receives auditorially on ___ out of ___ trials.
6. The student will follow one-step verbal directions on ___ out of ___ trials.
7. The student will follow two-step verbal directions on ___ out of ___ trials.
8. The student will follow multi-step verbal directions on ___ out of ___ trials.
9. The student will write down pertinent information when it is auditorially presented to him/her on ___ out of ___ trials.

IV. Interventions

1. Does not perform or complete classroom assignments during class time

1. Reinforce the student for attempting and completing class assignments: (a) give the student a tangible reward (e.g., classroom privileges, line leading, passing out materials, five minutes free time, etc.) or (b) give the student an intangible reward (e.g., praise, handshake, smile, etc.).

2. Speak with the student to explain: (a) what he/she is doing wrong (e.g., not completing assignments) and (b) what he/she should be doing (e.g., completing assignments during class).

3. Establish classroom rules (e.g., work on-task, work quietly, remain in your seat, finish task, meet task requirements). Reiterate rules often and reinforce students for following rules.

4. Reinforce those students in the classroom who attempt and complete assignments during class time.

5. Reinforce the student for attempting and completing assignments based on the amount of work that he/she can successfully complete. Gradually increase the amount of work required for reinforcement as the student demonstrates success.

6. Write a contract with the student specifying what behavior is expected (e.g., attempting and completing class assignments) and what reinforcement will be made available when the terms of the contract have been met.

7. Have the student keep a chart or graph representing the number of class assignments completed.

8. Evaluate the appropriateness of the task to determine if: (a) the task is too easy, (b) the task is too difficult, and (c) the length of time scheduled for the task is appropriate.

9. Assign a peer to help the student with class assignments.

10. Assess the degree of task difficulty in comparison with the student's ability to perform the task.

11. Assign the student shorter tasks (e.g., modify a 20-problem math activity to 4 activities of 5 problems each to be done at various times during the day). Gradually increase the number of problems over time.

12. Present tasks in the most attractive and interesting manner possible.

13. Reduce distracting stimuli (e.g., place the student in the front row, provide a carrel or quiet place away from distractions). This is used as a means of reducing stimuli and not as a form of punishment.

14. Interact frequently with the student in order to maintain involvement with class assignments (e.g., ask the student questions, ask the student's opinions, stand close to the student, seat the student near the teacher's desk, etc.).

15. Allow the student additional time to complete class assignments.

16. Supervise the student during class assignments in order to maintain on-task behavior.

17. Deliver directions orally in order to increase the probability of the student's understanding of class assignments.

18. Repeat directions in order to increase the probability of understanding.

19. Encourage the student to ask for clarification of directions for classroom assignments.

20. Follow a less desirable task with a highly desirable task, making the completion of the first necessary to perform the second.

21. Give directions in a variety of ways to increase the probability of understanding (e.g., if the student fails to understand verbal directions, present them in written form).

22. Provide the student with step-by-step written directions for doing class assignments.

23. Make certain the student understands the natural consequences of failing to complete assignments (e.g., students who do not finish their work do not get to do more desirable activities).

24. Allow the student to perform alternative assignments. Gradually introduce more components of the regular assignments until those assignments are routinely performed.

25. Explain to the student that work not done during work time will have to be done during other times (e.g., break time, recreational time, after school, etc.).

26. Take steps to deal with student refusal to perform an assignment in order that the rest of the group will not be exposed to contagion (e.g., refrain from arguing with the student, place the student at a carrel or other quiet place to work, remove the student from the group or classroom, etc.).

27. Maintain consistency of expectations while keeping expectations within the ability level of the student.

28. Allow the student the option of performing the assignment at another time (e.g., earlier in the day, later, another day, or take the assignment home).

29. Provide the student with a selection of assignments and require him/her to choose a minimum number from the total amount (e.g., present the student with 10 academic tasks from which he/she must finish 6 that day).

30. Maintain consistency in daily routine.

31. Work a few problems with the student on an assignment in order to serve as a model and help the student begin a task.

32. Reinforce the student for beginning, staying on, and completing assignments.

33. Communicate with parents (e.g., notes home, phone calls, etc.) in order to share information concerning the student's progress and so that they may reinforce the student at home for completing assignments at school.

34. Identify a peer to act as a model for the student to imitate appropriate completion of assignments.

35. Have the student question any directions, explanations, instructions he/she does not understand.

36. Assess the quality and clarity of directions, explanations, and instructions given to the student.

37. Structure the environment in such a way as to provide the student with increased opportunity for help or assistance.

38. Communicate clearly to the student the length of time he/she has to complete the assignment.

39. Communicate clearly to the student when the assignment should be completed.

40. Have the student time his/her assignments in order to monitor his/her own behavior and accept time limits.

41. Structure time units in order that the student knows exactly how long he/she has to work and when he/she must be finished.

42. Provide the student with more than enough time to finish an activity and decrease the amount of time as the student demonstrates success.

43. Have the student repeat the directions orally to the teacher.

44. Rewrite directions at a lower reading level.

45. Provide the student with a schedule of daily events in order that he/she knows exactly what and how much there is to do in a day. (See Appendix for Schedule of Daily Events.)

46. Prevent the student from becoming over stimulated by an activity (e.g., frustrated, angry, etc.).

47. Specify exactly what is to be done for the completion of the task (e.g., indicate definite starting and stopping points, indicate a minimum requirement, etc.).

48. Require the student to begin each assignment within a specified period of time (e.g., three minutes, five minutes, etc.).

49. Provide the student with shorter tasks given more frequently.

50. Provide clearly stated directions in written or verbal form (i.e., make the directions as simple and concrete as possible).

51. Interact frequently with the student in order to help him/her follow directions for the assignments.

52. Provide alternatives for the traditional format of directions (e.g., tape record, summarize directions, directions given by peers, etc.).

53. Practice direction-following skills on nonacademic tasks.

54. Reduce directions to steps (e.g., give the student each additional step after completion of the previous step).

55. Make certain the student achieves success when following directions.

56. Reduce the emphasis on early completion. Hurrying to complete assignments may cause the student to fail to follow directions.

57. Establish assignment rules (e.g., listen to directions, wait until all directions have been given, ask questions about anything you do not understand, begin assignment only when you are certain about what you are supposed to do, make certain you have all necessary materials, etc.).

58. Allow the student access to pencils, pens, etc., only after directions have been given.

59. Make certain that the student is attending to the teacher when directions are given (e.g., eye contact, hands free of writing materials, looking at assignment, etc.).

60. Maintain visibility to and from the student in order to make certain the student is attending. The teacher should be able to see the student and the student should be able to see the teacher, making eye contact possible at all times.

61. Along with the student, chart those assignments that have been completed in a given period of time.

62. Present one assignment at a time. As each assignment is completed, deliver reinforcement along with the presentation of the next assignment.

63. Have the student use a timer in order to complete tasks within a given period of time.

64. Reduce emphasis on academic and social competition. Fear of failure may cause the student to not want to complete the required number of assignments in a given period of time.

65. Have the student complete his/her assignments in a private place (e.g., carrel, "office," quiet study area, etc.) in order to reduce the anxiety of public failure.

66. Provide the student with the opportunity to perform assignments/activities in a variety of ways (e.g., on tape, with a calculator, orally, etc.).

67. Have the student explain to the teacher what he/she should do in order to perform the assignments.

2 Does not turn in homework assignments

1. Reinforce the student for turning in homework assignments: (a) give the student a tangible reward (e.g., classroom privileges, line leading, passing out materials, five minutes free time, etc.) or (b) give the student an intangible reward (e.g., praise, handshake, smile, etc.).

2. Speak to the student to explain: (a) what he/she is doing wrong (e.g., not turning in homework assignments) and (b) what he/she should be doing (e.g., completing homework assignments and returning them to school).

3. Establish homework assignment rules (e.g., work on-task, finish task, meet task expectations, turn in task). Reiterate rules often and reinforce students for following rules.

4. Reinforce those students in the classroom who turn in their homework assignments.

5. Reinforce the student for turning in his/her homework. Gradually increase the number of time required for reinforcement as the student demonstrates success.

6. Write a contract with the student specifying what behavior is expected (e.g., turning in homework) and what reinforcement will be made available when the terms of the contract have been met.

7. Communicate with parents (e.g., notes home, phone calls, etc.) in order to share information concerning the student's progress and so that they may reinforce the student at home for turning in homework at school.

8. Evaluate the appropriateness of the homework assignment to determine: (a) if the task is too easy, (b) if the task is too difficult, and (c) if the length of time scheduled to complete the task is appropriate.

9. Identify a peer to act as a model for the student to imitate turning in homework assignments.

10. Have the student keep a chart or graph the number of homework assignments he/she turns in to the teacher.

11. Have the student question any directions, explanations, instructions he/she does not understand.

12. Assess the appropriateness of assigning the student homework if his/her ability or circumstances at home make it impossible to complete and return the assignments.

13. Meet with parents to instruct them in appropriate ways to help the student with homework.

14. Assign a peer to help the student with homework.

15. Present the tasks in the most attractive and interesting manner possible.

16. Allow the student additional time to turn in homework assignments.

17. Deliver directions orally in order to increase the probability of the student's understanding of homework assignments.

18. Chart homework assignments completed.

19. Repeat directions in order to increase the student's probability of understanding.

20. Allow the student to perform a highly desirable task when his/her homework has been turned in to the teacher.

21. Give directions in a variety of ways in order to increase the probability of understanding (e.g., if the student fails to understand verbal directions, present them in written form).

22. Provide the student with written directions for doing homework assignments.

23. Allow natural consequences to occur for failure to turn in homework assignments (e.g., students who do not finish their homework do not get to engage in more desirable activities).

24. Encourage the parents to provide the student with a quiet, comfortable place, and adequate time to do homework.

25. Introduce the student to other resource persons who may be of help in doing homework (e.g., other teachers, librarian, etc.).

26. Allow the student to perform alternative homework assignments. Gradually introduce more components of the regular homework assignments until the assignments are routinely performed and returned to school.

27. Take proactive steps to deal with student refusal to perform a homework assignment in order that the rest of the group will not be exposed to contagion (e.g., refrain from arguing with the student, place the student at a carrel or other quiet place to work, remove the student from the group or classroom, etc.).

28. Maintain consistency of expectations and keep the expectations within the ability level of the student.

29. Work a few problems with the student on homework assignments in order to serve as a model and start the student on a task.

30. Make certain that homework is designed to provide drill activities rather than introduce new information.

31. Develop a contract with the student and his/her parents requiring that homework be done before more desirable activities take place at home (e.g., playing, watching television, going out for the evening, etc.).

32. Should the student fail to take necessary materials home, provide a set of these materials to be kept at home and send directions for homework with the student.

33. Assign small amounts of homework initially, gradually increase the amount as the student demonstrates success (e.g., one or two problems to perform may be sufficient to begin the homework process).

34. Find a tutor (e.g., peer, volunteer, etc.) to work with the student at home.

35. Maintain consistency in assigning homework (i.e., assign the same amount or length of homework each day).

36. Provide time at school for homework completion when the student cannot be successful in performing assignments at home.

37. Provide the student with a book bag, back pack, etc., to take homework assignments and materials to and from home.

38. Send homework assignments and materials directly to the home with someone other than the student (e.g., brother or sister, neighbor, bus driver, etc.).

39. Schedule the student's time at school in order that homework will not be absolutely necessary if he/she takes advantage of the time provided to complete assignments at school.

40. Reinforce those students who complete their assignments at school during the time provided.

41. Create a learning center at school, open the last hour of each school day, where professional educators are available to help with homework assignments.

42. Do not use homework as a punishment (i.e., homework should not be assigned as a consequence for inappropriate behavior at school).

3. Is disorganized to the point of not having necessary materials, losing materials, being unable to find completed assignments, being unable to follow the steps of the assignment in order, etc.

1. Reinforce the student for being organized/prepared for specified activities: (a) give the student a tangible reward (e.g., classroom privileges, line leading, passing out materials, five minutes free time, etc.) or (b) give the student an intangible reward (e.g., praise, handshake, smile, etc.).

2. Speak to the student to explain: (a) what he/she is doing wrong (e.g., failing to bring necessary materials for specified activities) and (b) what he/she should be doing (e.g., having necessary materials for specified activities).

3. Establish classroom rules (e.g., have necessary materials, work on-task, work quietly, remain in your seat, finish task, and meet task expectations). Reiterate rules often and reinforce students for following rules.

4. Reinforce those students in the classroom who are organized/prepared for specified activities.

5. Reinforce the student for being organized/prepared for specified activities based on the number of times he/she can be successful. Gradually increase the number of times required for reinforcement as the student demonstrates success.

6. Write a contract with the student specifying what behavior is expected (e.g., having necessary materials for specified activities) and what reinforcement will be made available when the terms of the contract have been met.

7. Communicate with parents (e.g., notes home, phone calls, etc.) in order to share information concerning the student's progress and so that they may reinforce the student at home for being organized/prepared for specified activities at school.

8. Evaluate the appropriateness of the task to determine: (a) if the task is too easy, (b) if the task is too difficult, and (c) if the length of time scheduled to complete the task is appropriate.

9. Identify a peer to act as a model for the student to imitate being organized/prepared for specified activities.

10. Have the student question any directions, explanations, instructions he/she does not understand.

11. Assign a peer to accompany the student to specified activities in order to make certain the student has the necessary materials.

12. Provide the student with a list of necessary materials for each activity of the day.

13. Provide the student with verbal reminders of necessary materials required for each activity.

14. Provide time at the beginning of each day for the student to organize his/her materials.

15. Provide time at various points throughout the day for the student to organize his/her materials (e.g., before school, recess, lunch, end of the day, etc.).

16. Provide storage space for materials the student is not using at any particular time.

17. Act as a model for being organized/prepared for specified activities.

18. Make certain that work not completed because necessary materials were not brought to the specified activity must be completed during recreational or break time.

19. Have the student chart the number of times he/she is organized/prepared for specified activities.

20. Remind the student at the end of the day when materials are required for specified activities for the next day (e.g., note sent home, verbal reminder, etc.).

21. Have the student establish a routine to follow before coming to class (e.g., check which activity is next, determine what materials are necessary, collect materials, etc.).

22. Have the student leave necessary materials at specified activity areas.

23. Provide the student with a container in which to carry necessary materials for specified activities (e.g., back pack, book bag, briefcase, etc.).

24. Provide adequate transition time between activities for the student to organize his/her materials.

25. Establish a routine to be followed for organization and appropriate use of work materials. Provide the routine for the student in written form or verbally reiterate often.

26. Provide adequate time for the completion of activities.

27. Assess the quality and clarity of directions, explanations, and instructions given to the student.

28. Provide the student with structure for all academic activities (e.g., specific directions, routine format for tasks, time units, etc.).

29. Minimize materials needed for specified activities.

30. Provide an organizer for materials inside the student's desk.

31. Provide the student with an organizational checklist (e.g., routine activities, materials needed, and steps to follow).

32. Make certain that all personal property is labeled with the student's name.

33. Teach the student how to conserve rather than waste materials (e.g., amount of glue, paper, tape, etc., to use; putting lids, caps, tops on such materials as markers, pens, bottles, jars, cans, etc.).

34. Teach the student to maintain care of personal property and school materials (e.g., keep property with him/her, know where property is at all times, secure property in lockers, leave valuable property at home, etc.).

35. Provide the student with an appropriate place to store/secure personal property (e.g., desk, locker, closet, etc.) and require that the student store all property when not in use.

36. Limit the student's freedom to take property from school if he/she is unable to remember to return such items.

37. Make certain that failure to have necessary materials results in loss of opportunity to participate in activities or a failing grade for that day's activity.

38. Reduce the number of materials for which the student is responsible. Increase the number as the student demonstrates appropriate use of property.

39. Require that lost or damaged property be replaced by the student. If the student cannot replace the property, restitution can be made by working at school.

40. Make certain that the student is not inadvertently reinforced for losing materials. Provide the student with used materials, copies of the materials, etc., rather than new materials if he/she fails to care for the materials in an appropriate manner.

41. Provide the student with more work space (e.g., a larger desk or table at which to work).

42. Reduce distracting stimuli (e.g., place the student on the front row, provide a carrel or quiet place away from distractions, etc.). This is used as a means of reducing distracting stimuli and not as a form of punishment.

43. Interact frequently with the student in order to prompt organizational skills and appropriate use of materials.

44. Assign the student organizational responsibilities in the classroom (e.g., equipment, software materials, etc.).

45. Limit the student's use of materials (i.e., provide the student only those materials necessary at any given time).

46. Act as a model for organization and appropriate use of work materials (e.g., putting materials away before getting others out, having a place for all materials, maintaining an organized desk area, following a schedule for the day, etc.).

47. Have the student maintain an assignment notebook which indicates those materials needed for each activity.

48. Provide the student with a schedule of daily events in order that he/she knows exactly what and how much there is to do in a day. (See Appendix for Schedule of Daily Events.)

49. Supervise the student while he/she is performing school work in order to monitor quality.

50. Allow natural consequences to occur as the result of the student's inability to organize or use materials appropriately (e.g., work not done during work time must be made up during recreational time, materials not maintained will be lost or not serviceable, etc.).

51. Assist the student in beginning each task in order to reduce impulsive behavior.

52. Provide the student with structure for all academic activities (e.g., specific directions, routine format for tasks, time units, etc.).

53. Provide a color-coded organizational system (e.g., notebook, folders, etc.).

54. Teach the student to prioritize assignments (e.g., according to importance, length, etc.).

55. Provide adequate time for completion of activities.

56. Develop monthly calendars to keep track of important events, due dates, assignments, etc.

4 Performs assignments so carelessly as to be illegible

1. Reinforce conscientiousness in improving handwriting (e.g., double checking spelling, proper positioning of letters, spacing, etc.): (a) give the student a tangible reward (e.g., classroom privileges, line leading, passing out materials, five minutes free time, etc.) or (b) give the student an intangible reward (e.g., praise, handshake, smile, etc.).

2. Speak with the student to explain: (a) what he/she is doing wrong (e.g., turning in work which has spelling errors, spacing errors, work that is illegible, etc.) and (b) what he/she should be doing (e.g., taking time to check for spelling, spacing errors, etc.).

3. Establish classroom rules (e.g. work on-task, work quietly, remain in your seat, finish task, meet task expectations). Reiterate rules often and reinforce students for following rules.

4. Reinforce those students in the classroom who turn in assignments which are legible.

5. Reinforce the student for improving the quality of his/her handwriting based on his/her ability. Gradually increase the amount of improvement expected for reinforcement as the student demonstrates success.

6. Write a contract with the student specifying what behavior is expected (e.g., improving the quality of his/her handwriting) and what reinforcement will be made available when the terms of the contract have been met.

7. Communicate with parents (e.g., notes home, phone calls, etc.) in order to share information concerning the student's progress and so that they may reinforce the student at home for improving the quality of his/her handwriting at school.

8. Evaluate the appropriateness of the task to determine: (a) if the task is too easy, (b) if the task is too difficult, and (c) if the length of time scheduled to complete the task is appropriate.

9. Assign a peer to work with the student in order to provide an acceptable model for the student to imitate.

10. Allow the student to perform school work in a quiet place (e.g., study carrel, library, resource room, etc.) in order to reduce distractions.

11. Assign the student shorter tasks while increasing quality expectations.

12. Supervise the student while he/she is performing school work in order to monitor handwriting quality.

13. Provide the student with clearly stated criteria for acceptable work.

14. Have the student read/go over school work with the teacher in order that the student can become more aware of the quality of his/her work.

15. Provide the student with samples of work which may serve as models for acceptable quality (e.g., the student is to match the quality of the sample before turning in the assignment).

16. Provide the student additional time to perform school work in order to achieve quality.

17. Teach the student procedures for doing quality work (e.g., listen to directions, make certain directions are understood, work at an acceptable pace, check for errors, correct for neatness, copy the work over, etc.).

18. Recognize quality (e.g., display student's work, congratulate the student, etc.).

19. Conduct a preliminary evaluation of the work, requiring the student to make necessary corrections before final grading.

20. Establish levels of expectations for quality of handwriting performance and require the student to correct or repeat assignments until the expectations are met.

21. Provide the student with quality materials to perform the assignment (e.g., pencil with eraser, paper, dictionary, handwriting sample, etc.).

22. Provide the student with ample opportunity to master handwriting skills (e.g., instruction in letter positioning, direction, spacing, etc.).

23. Provide the student with an appropriate model of handwriting (e.g., other students' work, teacher samples, commercial samples, etc.) to use at his/her desk.

24. Model appropriate handwriting at all times.

25. Provide a multitude of handwriting opportunities for the student to practice handwriting skills (e.g., writing letters to sports and entertainment figures, relatives, friends; writing for free information on a topic in which the student is interested, etc.).

26. Have the student trace handwriting models and fade the model as the student develops the skill.

27. Gradually reduce the space between lines as the student's handwriting improves.

28. Use primary paper to assist the student in sizing upper-case and lower-case letters. Use standard lined paper when the student's skills improve.

29. Use paper that is also vertically lined (e.g., | | | | |) to teach the student appropriate spacing skills (e.g., K|a|t|h|y|).

30. Use adhesive material (e.g., tape, Dycem material, etc.) to keep paper positioned appropriately for handwriting.

31. Use a pencil grip (e.g., three-sided, foam rubber, etc.) in order to provide the student assistance in appropriate positioning of the pencil or pen.

32. Use handwriting models with arrows that indicate the direction in which the student should correctly form the letters.

33. Provide older students with functional handwriting opportunities (e.g., job application forms, reinforcer surveys, order forms, check writing, etc.).

34. Make certain that all educators who work with the student maintain consistent expectations of handwriting quality.

5. Fails to perform assignments independently

1. Reinforce the student for communicating his/her needs to others only when necessary: (a) give the student a tangible reward (e.g., classroom privileges, line leading, passing out materials, five minutes free time, etc.) or (b) give the student an intangible reward (e.g., praise, handshake, smile, etc.).

2. Reinforce the student for performing assignments independently.

3. Speak to the student to explain: (a) what he/she is doing wrong (e.g., asking for teacher assistance when not necessary) and (b) what he/she should be doing (e.g., asking for teacher assistance when necessary).

4. Establish classroom rules (e.g., work on-task, work quietly, request assistance when needed, remain in your seat, finish task, meet task expectations). Reiterate rules often and reinforce students for following rules.

5. Reinforce those students in the classroom who communicate their needs to others when necessary.

6. Reinforce the student for communicating his/her needs to others based on the number of times he/she can be successful. Gradually increase the number of times required for reinforcement as the student demonstrates success.

7. Write a contract with the student specifying what behavior is expected (e.g., asking for teacher assistance when necessary) and what reinforcement will be made available when the terms of the contract have been met.

8. Communicate with parents (e.g., notes home, phone calls, etc.) in order to share information concerning the student's progress and so that they may reinforce the student at home for communicating his/her needs to others when necessary at school.

9. Identify a peer to act as a model for the student to imitate communication of needs to others.

10. Encourage the student to question any directions, explanations, instructions he/she does not understand.

11. Evaluate the appropriateness of expecting the student to communicate his/her needs to others when necessary.

12. Maintain mobility throughout the classroom in order to determine the student's needs.

13. Offer the student assistance frequently throughout the day.

14. Make certain that directions, explanations, and instructions are delivered on the student's ability level.

15. Structure the environment in order that the student is not required to communicate all needs to others (i.e., make certain the student's tasks are on his/her ability level, instructions are clear, and maintain frequent interactions with the student in order to ensure his/her success).

16. In order to detect the student's needs, communicate with the student as often as opportunities permit.

17. Demonstrate accepting behavior (e.g., willingness to help others, making criticisms constructive and positive, demonstrating confidentiality in personal matters, etc.).

18. Communicate to the student an interest in his/her needs.

19. Communicate to the student that he/she is a worthwhile individual.

20. Call on the student often in order to encourage communication.

21. Teach the student communication skills (e.g., hand raising, expressing needs in written and/or verbal forms, etc.).

22. Encourage communication skills in the classroom.

23. Communicate your own personal needs and feelings to the student.

24. Encourage the student to communicate his/her needs to other personnel in the educational environment (e.g., school counselor, school psychologist, principal, etc.).

25. Communicate with parents, agencies, or appropriate parties in order to inform them of the problem, determine the cause of the problem, and solutions to the problem.

26. Teach the student to communicate his/her needs in an appropriate manner (e.g., raise hand, use a normal tone of voice when speaking, verbally express problems, etc.).

27. Recognize the student's attempts to communicate his/her needs (e.g., facial expressions, gestures, inactivity, self-depreciating comments, etc.).

28. Have the student interact with a peer in order to encourage him/her to communicate his/her needs to others. Gradually increase the number of peers the student interacts with as he/she demonstrates success in communicating his/her needs to others.

29. Pair the student with a non-threatening peer, a peer with similar interests and ability level, etc.

30. Give the student responsibilities in the classroom in order to increase the probability of communication (e.g., passing out materials, collecting lunch money, collecting school work, etc.).

31. Give the student responsibilities in the classroom that require communication (e.g., peer tutor, group leader, teacher assistant, etc.).

32. Have the student keep a chart or graph representing the number of assignments he/she completes independently.

33. Assess the degree of task difficulty in comparison with the student's ability to perform the task.

34. Assign the student shorter tasks (e.g., modify a 20-problem math activity to 4 activities of 5 problems each to be done at various times during the day). Gradually increase the number of problems as the student demonstrates success.

35. Present the task in the most interesting manner possible.

36. Reduce distracting stimuli (e.g., place the student in the front row, provide a carrel or quiet place away from distractions, etc.). This is to be used as a means of reducing distracting stimuli and not as a form of punishment.

37. Allow the student additional time to complete assignments when working independently.

38. Encourage the student to ask for clarification of directions for assignments.

39. Provide the student with step-by-step written directions for performing assignments.

40. Allow the student to perform alternative assignments. Gradually introduce more components of the regular assignments until those assignments are routinely performed.

41. Explain to the student that work not done during work time will have to be done during other times (e.g., break time, recreational time, after school, etc.).

42. Maintain consistency of expectations while keeping expectations within the ability level of the student.

43. Maintain consistency in daily routine.

44. Work a few problems with the student on an assignment in order to serve as a model and help the student begin a task.

45. Reinforce the student for beginning, working on, and completing assignments.

6 Performs classroom tests or quizzes at a failing level

1. Reinforce improved test or quiz scores: (a) give the student a tangible reward (e.g., classroom privileges, line leading, passing out materials, five minutes free time, etc.) or (b) give the student an intangible reward (e.g., praise, handshake, smile, etc.).

2. Speak with the student to explain: (a) what he/she is doing wrong (e.g., not attending in class, not using study time, etc.) and (b) what he/she should be doing (e.g., attending during class, asking questions, using study time, etc.).

3. Establish classroom rules (e.g., work on-task, work quietly, remain in your seat, finish task, meet task expectations). Reiterate rules often and reinforce students for following rules.

4. Reinforce those students who demonstrate improved test or quiz scores. (It may be best to reinforce privately rather than publicly.)

5. Write a contract with the student specifying what behavior is expected (e.g., improved test or quiz scores) and what reinforcement will be made available when the terms of the contract have been met.

6. Communicate with the parents (e.g., notes home, phone calls, etc.) in order to share information concerning the student's progress and so that they may reinforce the student at home for improved test or quiz scores.

7. Evaluate the appropriateness of the task to determine if: (a) the task is too easy, (b) the task is too difficult, and (c) the length of time scheduled for the task is appropriate.

8. Have the student question anything he/she does not understand while taking tests or quizzes.

9. Make certain that the tests or quizzes measure knowledge of content and not related skills, such as reading or writing.

10. Teach the student test-taking strategies (e.g., answer questions you are sure of first, learn to summarize, recheck each answer, etc.).

11. Give shorter tests or quizzes but more frequently. Increase the length of tests or quizzes over time as the student demonstrates success.

12. Have tests or quizzes read to the student.

13. Have the student answer tests or quizzes orally.

14. Have the tests or quizzes tape recorded and allow the student to listen to questions as often as necessary.

15. Allow the student to take tests or quizzes in a quiet place in order to reduce distractions (e.g., study carrel, library, resource room, etc.).

16. Have the student take tests or quizzes in the resource room where the resource teacher can clarify questions, offer explanations, etc.

17. Provide the student with opportunities for review before taking tests or quizzes.

18. Teach and encourage the student to practice basic study skills (e.g., reading for the main point, note taking, summarizing, highlighting, studying in an appropriate environment, using time wisely, etc.) before taking tests or quizzes.

19. Assess student performance in a variety of ways (e.g., have the student give verbal explanations, simulations, physical demonstrations of a skill, etc.).

20. Have the student maintain a performance record for each subject in which he/she is experiencing difficulty.

21. Arrange a time for the student to study with a peer tutor before taking tests or quizzes.

22. Provide a variety of opportunities for the student to learn the information covered by tests or quizzes (e.g., films, visitors, community resources, etc.).

23. Allow the student to respond to alternative test or quiz questions (e.g., more generalized questions which represent global understanding).

24. Provide the opportunity for the student to study daily assignments with a peer.

25. Have the student take a sample test or quiz before the actual test.

26. Remove the threat of public knowledge of failure (e.g., test or quiz results are not read aloud or posted, test ranges are not made public, etc.).

27. Reduce the emphasis on formal testing by grading the student on his/her daily performance.

28. Provide parents with information on test and quiz content (e.g., what material will be covered by the test or quiz, format, types of questions, etc.).

29. Modify instruction to include more concrete examples in order to enhance student learning.

30. Monitor student performance in order to detect errors and determine where learning problems exist.

31. Reduce the emphasis on competition. Students who compete academically and fail may cease to try to succeed and do far less than they are capable of achieving.

32. Only give tests and quizzes when the student is certain to succeed (e.g., after he/she has learned the information).

7 Is not motivated by rewards at school

1. Conduct a reinforcer survey with the student in order to determine his/her reinforcer preferences. (See Appendix for Reinforcer Survey)

2. Communicate with parents in order to determine what the student finds reinforcing at home.

3. Make an agreement with the parents in order that enjoyable activities at home (e.g., watching television, riding bike, visiting with friends, etc.) are contingent upon appropriate behavior at school.

4. Write a contract with the student in order that he/she can earn reinforcement at home for appropriate behavior at school.

5. Make certain that the student can be successful at school in order to earn reinforcement.

6. Provide a wide variety of reinforcers for the student at school (e.g., eating lunch with the teacher, one-to-one time with the teacher, principal's assistant, assistant to the custodian, extra time in a favorite class, etc.).

7. Present tasks in the most attractive and interesting manner possible.

8. Communicate with parents, agencies, or appropriate parties in order to inform them of the problem, determine the cause of the problem, and solutions to the problem.

9. Provide reinforcers that are social in nature (e.g., extracurricular activities, clubs, community organizations such as 4-H, scouting, YMCA, YWCA, etc.).

10. Help the student develop an interest in a hobby which can be used as a reinforcer at school (e.g., stamp collecting, rock collecting, model building, photography, art, reading, sewing, cooking, etc.).

8. Does not prepare for assigned activities

1. Reinforce the student for being prepared for assigned activities: (a) give the student a tangible reward (e.g., classroom privileges, line leading, passing out materials, five minutes free time, etc.) or (b) give the student an intangible reward (e.g., praise, handshake, smile, etc.).

2. Speak to the student to explain: (a) what he/she is doing wrong (e.g., failing to study, complete assignments, bring materials to class, etc.) and (b) what he/she should be doing (e.g., studying, completing assignments, bringing materials to class, etc.).

3. Establish classroom rules (e.g., work on-task, work quietly, remain in your seat, finish task, meet task expectations). Reiterate rules often and reinforce students for following rules.

4. Reinforce those students in the classroom who are prepared for assigned activities.

5. Reinforce the student for being prepared for assigned activities based on the number of times he/she can be successful. Gradually increase the number of times required for reinforcement as the student demonstrates success.

6. Write a contract with the student specifying what behavior is expected (e.g., study for tests or quizzes) and what reinforcement will be made available when the terms of the contract have been met.

7. Communicate with parents (e.g., notes home, phone calls, etc.) in order to share information concerning the student's progress and so that they may reinforce the student at home for being prepared for assigned activities at school.

8. Evaluate the appropriateness of the task to determine: (a) if the task is too easy, (b) if the task is too difficult, and (c) if the length of time scheduled to complete the task is appropriate.

9. Identify a peer to act as a model for the student to imitate being prepared for assigned activities.

10. Have the student question any directions, explanations, instructions he/she does not understand.

11. Assign a peer to accompany the student to specified activities in order to make certain the student has the necessary materials.

12. Provide the student with a list of necessary materials for each activity of the day.

13. Provide the student with verbal reminders of materials required for each activity.

14. Provide time at the beginning of each day for the student to organize his/her materials (e.g., before school, recess, lunch, end of the day, etc.).

15. Act as model for being prepared for assigned activities.

16. At the end of the day, remind the student when materials are required for specified activities for the next day (e.g., send a note home, verbal reminder, etc.).

17. Have the student establish a routine to follow before coming to class (e.g., check which activity is next, determine what materials are necessary, collect materials, etc.).

18. Have the student leave necessary materials at specified activity areas.

19. Provide the student with a container in which to carry necessary materials for specified activities (e.g., backpack, book bag, briefcase, etc.).

20. Assess the quality and clarity of directions, explanations, and instructions given to the student.

21. Provide the student with structure for all academic activities (e.g., specific directions, routine format for tasks, time units, etc.).

22. Minimize materials needed.

23. Make certain that failure to be prepared for assigned activities results in loss of the opportunity to participate in activities or a failing grade for that day's activity.

24. Provide the student with adequate time at school to prepare for assigned activities (e.g., supervised study time).

25. Assign a peer tutor to work with the student in order to prepare him/her for assigned activities.

26. Reduce the number/length of assignments. Gradually increase the number/length of assignments as the student demonstrates success.

27. Specify exactly what is to be done for the completion of assignments (e.g., make definite starting and topping points, determine a minimum requirement, etc.).

28. Allow natural consequences to occur when the student is unprepared for assigned activities (e.g., the student will fail a test or quiz, work not done during work time must be completed during recreational time, etc.).

29. Ask the student why he/she is unprepared for assigned activities. The student may have the most accurate perception.

30. Communicate with parents or guardians in order to inform them of the student's homework assignments and what they can do to help him/her prepare for assigned activities.

31. Provide the student with written directions to follow in preparing for all assigned activities.

32. Provide the student with a written list of assignments to be performed each day and have him/her check each assignment as it is completed.

33. Provide individual assistance to the student in order to help him/her prepare for assigned activities (e.g., time set aside during the day, study hall, after school, etc.).

34. Identify other personnel in the school who may assist the student in preparing for assigned activities (e.g., aide, librarian, other teachers, etc.).

9 Does not remain on-task

1. Reinforce the student for staying on-task in the classroom: (a) give the student a tangible reward (e.g., classroom privileges, line leading, passing out materials, five minutes free time, etc.) or (b) give the student an intangible reward (e.g., praise, handshake, smile, etc.).

2. Speak to the student to explain: (a) what he/she is doing wrong (e.g., failing to attend to tasks) and (b) what he/she should be doing (e.g., attending to tasks).

3. Establish classroom rules (e.g., work on-task, work quietly, remain in your seat, finish task, meet task expectations). Reiterate rules often and reinforce students for following rules.

4. Reinforce those students in the classroom who demonstrate on-task behavior.

5. Reinforce the student for attending to task based on the length of time he/she can be successful. Gradually increase the length of time required for reinforcement as the student demonstrates success.

6. Write a contract with the student specifying what behavior is expected (establish a reasonable length of time to stay on-task) and what reinforcement will be made available when the terms of the contract have been met.

7. Communicate with parents (e.g., notes home, phone calls, etc.) in order to share information concerning the student's progress and so that they may reinforce the student at home for staying on-task in the classroom.

8. Identify a peer to act as a model for the student to imitate on-task behavior.

9. Have the student question any directions, explanations, instructions he/she does not understand.

10. Evaluate the auditory and visual stimuli in the classroom in order to determine what level of stimuli the student can respond to in an appropriate manner.

11. Reduce auditory and visual stimuli to a level at which the student can successfully function. Gradually allow auditory and visual stimuli to increase as the student demonstrates that he/she can successfully tolerate the increased levels.

12. Seat the student so that he/she experiences the least amount of auditory and visual stimuli possible.

13. Provide the student with a quiet place in which to work where auditory and visual stimuli is reduced. This is used to reduce distracting stimuli and not as a form of punishment.

14. Seat the student away from those peers who create the most auditory and visual stimulation in the classroom.

15. Provide the student with a carrel or divider at his/her desk to reduce auditory and visual stimuli.

16. Make certain that all auditory and visual stimuli in the classroom is reduced as much as possible for all learners.

17. Provide the student with the opportunity to move to a quiet place in the classroom any time that auditory and visual stimuli interferes with his/her ability to function successfully.

18. Provide the student with earphones to wear if auditory stimuli interferes with his/her ability to function. Gradually remove the earphones as the student can more successfully function in the presence of auditory stimuli.

19. Allow the student to close the door or windows in order to reduce auditory and visual stimuli outside of the classroom.

20. Require the student to be productive in the presence of auditory and visual stimuli for short periods of time. Gradually increase the length of time the student is required to be productive as he/she becomes successful.

21. Provide the student with shorter tasks which do not require extended attention in order to be successful. Gradually increase the length of the tasks as the student demonstrates success.

22. Have the student engage in small group activities (e.g., free time, math, reading, etc.) in order to reduce the level of auditory and visual stimuli in the group. Gradually increase group size as the student can function successfully.

23. Model for the student appropriate behavior in the presence of auditory and visual stimuli in the classroom (e.g., continuing to work, asking for quiet, moving to a quieter part of the classroom, etc.).

24. Remove the student from an activity until he/she can demonstrate appropriate on-task behavior.

25. Assign the student shorter tasks but more of them (e.g., modify a 20-problem math activity to 4 activities of 5 problems each to be performed at various times during the day). Gradually increase the number of problems for each activity as the student demonstrates success.

26. Present tasks in the most attractive and interesting manner possible.

27. Assess the degree of task difficulty in relation to the student's ability to successfully perform the task.

28. Interact frequently with the student in order to maintain his/her involvement in the activity (e.g., ask the student questions, ask the student's opinions, stand close to the student, seat the student near the teacher's desk, etc.).

29. Provide the student with a timer which he/she may use to increase the amount of time during which he/she maintains attention (e.g., have the student work on the activity until the timer goes off).

30. Provide the student with a predetermined signal (e.g., hand signal, verbal cue, etc.) when he/she begins to display off-task behaviors.

31. Structure the environment to reduce the opportunity for off-task behavior. Reduce lag time by providing the student with enough activities to maintain productivity.

32. Have the student work with a peer tutor in order to maintain attention to task.

33. Make certain the student has all necessary materials to perform assignments.

34. Make certain the student knows what to do when he/she cannot successfully perform assignments (e.g., raise hand, ask for assistance, go to the teacher, etc.).

35. Maintain visibility to and from the student. The teacher should be able to see the student and the student should be able to see the teacher, making eye contact possible at all times.

36. Make certain to recognize the student when his/her hand is raised in order to convey that assistance will be provided as soon as possible.

37. Teach the student how to manage his/her time until the teacher can provide assistance (e.g., try the problem again, go on to the next problem, wait quietly, etc.).

10. Does not perform academically at his/her ability level

(NOTE: Make certain that the academic programming is appropriate for the student's ability level.)

1. Reinforce the student for improving academic task or homework performance: (a) give the student a tangible reward (e.g., classroom privileges, line leading, passing out materials, five minutes free time, etc.) or (b) give the student an intangible reward (e.g., praise, handshake, smile, etc.).

2. Speak to the student to explain: (a) what he/she is doing wrong (e.g., performing below his/her ability level, failing assignments, etc.) and (b) what he/she should be doing (e.g., improving his/her academic task and homework performance).

3. Establish classroom rules (e.g., work on-task, work quietly, remain in your seat, finish task, meet task expectations). Reiterate rules often and reinforce students for following rules.

4. Reinforce those students in the classroom who show improvement on academic task and homework performance.

5. Write a contract with the student specifying what behavior is expected (e.g., completing an assignment with ____% accuracy) and what reinforcement will be made available when the terms of the contract have been met.

6. Communicate with parents (e.g., notes home, phone calls, etc.) in order to share information concerning the student's progress and so that they may reinforce the student at home for improving his/her academic task and homework performance.

7. Evaluate the appropriateness of the task to determine: (a) if the task is too easy, (b) if the task is too difficult, and (c) if the length of time scheduled to complete the task is appropriate.

8. Have the student question any directions, explanations, instructions he/she does not understand.

9. Assess student performance in a variety of ways (e.g., have the student give verbal explanations, simulations, physical demonstrations, etc.).

10. Give shorter assignments, but more frequently. Increase the length of the assignments as the student demonstrates success.

11. Structure the environment in such a way as to provide the student with increased opportunity for help or assistance on academic or homework tasks (e.g., peer tutors, seat the student near the teacher or aide, etc.).

12. Provide the student with clearly stated written directions for homework in order that someone at home may be able to provide assistance.

13. Teach the student study skills.

14. Reduce distracting stimuli (e.g., place the student in the front row, provide a carrel or "office" space away from distractions, etc.). This is used as a means of reducing distracting stimuli and not as a form of punishment.

15. Interact frequently with the student to monitor his/her task performance.

16. Have the student maintain a chart representing the number of tasks completed and the accuracy rate of each task.

17. Provide time at school for the completion of homework if homework assigned has not been completed or has resulted in failure. (The student's failure to complete homework assignments may be the result of variables in the home over which he/she has no control.)

18. Assess quality and clarity of directions, explanations, and instructions given to the student.

19. Teach the student note-taking skills.

20. Assess the appropriateness of assigning homework to the student.

21. Teach the student direction-following skills: (a) listen carefully, (b) ask questions, (c) use environmental cues, (d) rely on examples provided, etc.

22. Identify resource personnel from whom the student may receive additional assistance (e.g., librarian, special education teacher, other personnel with expertise or time to help, etc.).

23. Establish a level of minimum accuracy which will be accepted as a level of mastery.

24. Deliver reinforcement for any and all measures of improvement.

25. Mastery should not be expected too soon after introducing new information, skills, etc.

26. Provide the student with self-checking materials, requiring correction before turning in assignments.

27. Should the student consistently fail to complete assignments with minimal accuracy, evaluate the appropriateness of tasks assigned.

28. Provide instruction and task format in a variety of ways (e.g., verbal instructions, written instructions, demonstrations, simulations, manipulatives, drill activities with peers, etc.).

29. If the student has difficulty completing homework assignments with minimal accuracy provide a time during the day when he/she can receive assistance at school.

30. Make certain the assignments measure knowledge of content and not related skills such as reading or writing.

31. Have assignments read to the student.

32. Have the student respond to tasks orally.

33. Have the assignments tape recorded, allowing the student to listen to questions as often as necessary.

34. Have the student perform assignments in which he/she experiences difficulty in the resource room where the resource teacher can answer questions.

35. Provide the student with opportunities for review prior to grading assignments.

36. Teach the student to practice basic study skills (e.g., reading for the main idea, note taking, summarizing, highlighting, studying in a good environment, using time wisely, etc.).

37. Arrange a time for the student to study with a peer tutor before completing a graded assignment.

38. Provide multiple opportunities for the student to learn the information covered by assignments (e.g., films, visitors, community resources, etc.).

39. Allow the student to respond to alternative assignment questions (e.g., more generalized questions that represent global understanding).

40. Provide parents with information regarding appropriate ways in which to help their child with homework (e.g., read directions with the student, work a few problems together, answer questions, check the completed assignment, etc.).

41. Modify instruction to include more concrete examples in order to enhance student learning.

42. Monitor student performance in order to detect errors and determine where learning problems exist.

43. Reduce the emphasis on competition. Students who compete academically and fail to succeed may cease to try to do well and do far less than they are able.

44. Allow/require the student to make corrections after assignments have been checked the first time.

45. Provide the student with evaluative feedback for assignments completed (i.e., identify what the student did successfully, what errors were made, and what should be done to correct the errors).

46. Maintain consistency in assignment format and expectations so as not to confuse the student.

47. Provide adequate repetition and drill to assure minimal accuracy of assignments presented (i.e., require mastery/minimal accuracy before moving to the next skill level).

48. It is not necessary to grade every assignment performed by the student. Assignments may be used to evaluate student ability or knowledge and provide feedback. Grades may not need to be assigned until mastery/minimal accuracy has been attained.

49. Provide the student with a selection of assignments and require him/her to choose a minimum number from the total amount (e.g., present the student with 10 academic tasks from which he/she must finish 6 that day).

50. Allow the student to put an assignment away and return to it at a later time if he/she could be more successful.

51. Have the student practice an assignment with the teacher, aide, or peer before performing the assignment for a grade.

52. Monitor the first problem or part of the assignment in order to make certain the student knows what is expected of him/her.

53. Provide frequent interactions and encouragement to support the student's confidence and optimism for success (e.g., make statements such as, "You're doing great", "Keep up the good work", "I'm really proud of you", etc.).

54. Build varying degrees of difficulty into assignments in order to ensure the student's self-confidence and at the same time provide a challenge (e.g., easier problems are intermingled with problems designed to measure knowledge gained).

55. Work the first few problems of an assignment with the student in order to make certain that he/she knows what to do, how to perform the assignment, etc.

56. Modify academic tasks (e.g., format, requirements, length, etc.).

57. Provide the student with clearly stated step-by-step directions for homework in order that someone at home may be able to provide assistance.

58. Make certain that homework relates to concepts already taught rather than introducing a new concept.

(Please note: If the student continues to fail in spite of the above interventions and is not being served by special education personnel, he/she should be referred for consideration for special education services.)

11 Does not follow written directions

1. Reinforce the student for following written directions: (a) give the student a tangible reward (e.g., classroom privileges, line leading, passing out materials, five minutes free time, etc.) or (b) give the student an intangible reward (e.g., praise, handshake, smile, etc.).

2. Speak to the student to explain: (a) what he/she is doing wrong (e.g., ignoring written directions) and (b) what he/she should be doing (e.g., following written directions).

3. Establish classroom rules (e.g., work on-task, work quietly, remain in your seat, finish task, meet task expectations). Reiterate rules often and reinforce students for following rules.

4. Reinforce those students in the classroom who follow written directions.

5. Reinforce the student for following written direction based on the length of time he/she can be successful. Gradually increase the length of time required for reinforcement as the student demonstrates success.

6. Write a contract with the student specifying what behavior is expected (e.g., following written directions) and what reinforcement will be made available when the terms of the contract have been met.

7. Communicate with parents (e.g., notes home, phone calls, etc.) in order to share information concerning the student's progress and so that they may reinforce the student at home for following written directions at school.

8. Evaluate the appropriateness of the task to determine: (a) if the task is too easy, (b) if the task is too difficult, and (c) if the length of time scheduled to complete the task is appropriate.

9. Identify a peer to act as a model for the student to imitate appropriate written direction following.

10. Have the student question any written directions, explanations, instructions he/she does not understand.

11. Assign a peer to work with the student to help him/her follow written directions.

12. Teach the student written direction-following skills (e.g., read carefully, write down important points, ask for clarification, wait until all directions are received before beginning, etc.).

13. Give directions in a variety of ways to increase the probability of understanding (e.g., if the student fails to understand written directions, present them in verbal form).

14. Provide clearly stated written directions (e.g., make the directions as simple and concrete as possible).

15. Reduce distracting stimuli in order to increase the student's ability to follow written directions (e.g., place the student on the front row, provide a carrel or "office" space away from distractions, etc.). This is used as a means of reducing distracting stimuli and not as a form of punishment.

16. Interact frequently with the student in order to help him/her follow written directions.

17. Structure the environment in such a way as to provide the student with increased opportunity for help or assistance on academic tasks (e.g., peer tutoring, directions for work sent home, frequent interactions, etc.).

18. Provide alternatives for the traditional format of presenting written directions (e.g., tape record, summarize directions, directions given by peers, etc.).

19. Assess the quality and clarity of written directions, explanations, and instructions given to the student.

20. Practice written direction following on nonacademic tasks (e.g., recipes, games, etc.).

21. Have the student repeat written directions orally to the teacher.

22. Reduce written directions to individual steps (e.g., give the student each additional step after completion of the previous step).

23. Deliver a predetermined signal (e.g., clapping hands, turning lights off and off, etc.) before giving written directions.

24. Deliver written directions before handing out materials.

25. Require that assignments done incorrectly, for any reason, be redone.

26. Make certain the student achieves success when following written directions.

27. Reduce the emphasis on competition. Competitive activities may cause the student to hurry to begin the task without following written directions.

28. Have the student maintain a record (e.g., chart or graph) of his/her performance in following written directions.

29. Follow a less desirable task with a highly desirable task, making the completion of the first necessary to perform the second.

30. Prevent the student from becoming over stimulated by an activity (e.g., frustrated, angry, etc.).

31. Require the student to wait until the teacher gives him/her a signal to begin an activity after receiving written directions (e.g., hand signal, bell ringing, etc.).

32. Make certain that the student is attending to the teacher (e.g., eye contact, hands free of writing materials, looking at assignment, etc.) before giving written directions.

33. Maintain visibility to and from the student. The teacher should be able to see the student and the student should be able to see the teacher, making eye contact possible at all times in order to make certain the student is attending to written directions.

34. Make certain that written directions are presented on the student's reading level.

35. Present directions in both written and verbal form.

36. Provide the student with a copy of written directions at his/her desk rather than the chalkboard, posted in the classroom, etc.

37. Tape record directions for the student to listen to individually and repeat as necessary.

38. Develop written direction-following assignments/activities (e.g., informal activities designed to have the student carry out directions in steps, increasing the degree of difficulty).

39. Maintain consistency in the format of written directions.

40. Have a peer help the student with any written directions he/she does not understand.

41. Seat the student close to the source of the written directions (e.g., chalkboard, projector, etc.).

42. Make certain that the print is large enough to increase the likelihood of following written directions.

43. Transfer directions from texts and workbooks when pictures or other stimuli make it difficult to attend to or follow written directions.

44. Work the first problem or problems with the student to make certain that he/she follows the written directions accurately.

45. Work through the steps of written directions as they are delivered in order to make certain the student follows the directions accurately.

46. Have the student carry out written directions one step at a time, checking with the teacher to make certain that each step is successfully followed before attempting the next.

47. Make certain that directions are given at the level at which the student can be successful (e.g., two-step or three-step directions should not be given to students who can only successfully follow one-step directions).

48. Use visual cues such as green dot to start, red dot to stop, arrows, etc., in written directions.

49. Highlight, circle, or underline key words in written directions (e.g., key words such as match, circle, underline, etc.).

12 Does not follow verbal directions

1. Reinforce the student for following verbal directions: (a) give the student a tangible reward (e.g., classroom privileges, line leading, passing out materials, five minutes free time, etc.) or (b) give the student an intangible reward (e.g., praise, handshake, smile, etc.).

2. Speak to the student to explain: (a) what he/she is doing wrong (e.g., ignoring verbal directions) and (b) what he/she should be doing (e.g., listening to and following through when given verbal directions).

3. Establish classroom rules (e.g., work on-task, work quietly, remain in your seat, finish task, meet task expectations). Reiterate rules often and reinforce students for following rules.

4. Reinforce those students in the classroom who follow verbal directions.

5. Reinforce the student for following verbal directions based on the length of time he/she can be successful. Gradually increase the length of time required for reinforcement as the student demonstrates success.

6. Write a contract with the student specifying what behavior is expected (e.g., following verbal directions) and what reinforcement will be made available when the terms of the contract have been met.

7. Communicate with parents (e.g., notes home, phone calls, etc.) in order to share information concerning the student's progress and so that they may reinforce the student at home for following verbal directions at school.

8. Evaluate the appropriateness of the task to determine: (a) if the task is too easy, (b) if the task is too difficult, and (c) if the length of time scheduled to complete the task is appropriate.

9. Identify a peer to act as a model for the student to imitate appropriate verbal direction following.

10. Have the student question any verbal directions, explanations, instructions he/she does not understand.

11. Assign a peer to work with the student to help him/her follow verbal directions.

12. Teach the student verbal direction-following skills (e.g., listen carefully, write down important points, use environmental cues, wait until all directions are received before beginning, etc.).

13. Give directions in a variety of ways in order to increase the probability of understanding (e.g., if the student fails to understand verbal directions, present them in written form).

14. Provide clearly stated verbal directions (e.g., make the directions as simple and concrete as possible).

15. Reduce distracting stimuli in order to increase the student's ability to follow verbal directions (e.g., place the student on the front row, provide a carrel or "office" space away from distractions, etc.). This is used as a means of reducing distracting stimuli and not as a form of punishment.

16. Interact frequently with the student in order to help him/her follow verbal directions for the activity.

17. Structure the environment in such a way as to provide the student with increased opportunity for help or assistance on academic tasks (e.g., peer tutoring, directions for work sent home, frequent interactions, etc.).

18. Provide alternatives for the traditional format of presenting verbal directions (e.g., tape record, summarize directions, directions given by peers, etc.).

19. Assess the quality and clarity of verbal directions, explanations, and instructions given to the student.

20. Have the student practice verbal direction-following on nonacademic tasks (e.g., recipes, games, etc.).

21. Have the student repeat directions or give an interpretation after receiving verbal directions.

22. Reduce verbal directions to steps (e.g., give the student each additional step after completion of the previous step).

23. Deliver a predetermined signal (e.g., clapping hands, turning lights off and on, etc.) before giving verbal directions.

24. Give verbal directions before handing out materials.

25. Require that assignments done incorrectly, for any reason, be redone.

26. Make certain the student achieves success when following verbal directions.

27. Reduce emphasis on competition. Competitive activities may cause the student to hurry to begin the task without following verbal directions.

28. Have the student maintain a record (e.g., chart or graph) of his/her performance in following verbal directions.

29. Communicate clearly to the student when it is time to listen to verbal directions.

30. Provide the student with a predetermined signal when he/she is not following verbal directions (e.g., lights turned off and on, hand signals, etc.).

31. Follow a less desirable task with a highly desirable task, making the following of verbal directions and completion of the first task necessary to perform the second.

32. Prevent the student from becoming overstimulated by an activity (e.g., frustrated, angry, etc.).

33. Make certain the student has all the materials needed to perform the assignment/activity.

34. Require the student to wait until the teacher gives him/her a signal to begin the task (e.g., hand signal, ring bell, etc.).

35. Make certain the student is attending to the teacher (e.g., eye contact, hands free of writing materials, looking at assignment, etc.) before giving verbal directions.

36. Stand next to the student when giving verbal directions.

37. Maintain visibility to and from the student. The teacher should be able to see the student and the student should be able to see the teacher, making eye contact possible at all times when giving verbal directions.

38. Make certain that verbal directions are delivered in a nonthreatening manner (e.g., positive voice, facial expression, language used, etc.).

39. Make certain that verbal directions are delivered in a supportive rather than threatening manner (e.g., "Will you please. . .", or "You need. . .", rather than "You better. . .", or "If you don't. . .").

40. Present directions in both written and verbal form.

41. Provide the student with a written copy of verbal directions.

42. Tape record directions for the student to listen to individually and repeat as necessary.

43. Maintain consistency in the format of verbal directions.

44. Develop direction-following assignments/activities (e.g., informal activities designed to have the student carry out verbal directions in steps, increasing degrees of difficulty).

45. Have a designated person be the only individual to deliver verbal directions to the student.

46. Have a peer help the student with any verbal directions he/she does not understand.

47. Seat the student close to the source of the verbal directions (e.g., teacher, aide, peer, etc.).

48. Seat the student far enough away from peers in order to ensure increased opportunities for attending to verbal directions.

49. Work the first problem or problems with the student in order to make certain that he/she follows the verbal directions accurately.

50. Work through the steps of the verbal directions as they are delivered in order to make certain the student follows the directions accurately.

51. Have the student carry out one step of the verbal directions at a time, checking with the teacher to make certain that each step is successfully followed before attempting the next.

52. Make certain that verbal directions are given at the level at which the student can be successful (e.g., two-step or three-step directions are not given to students who can only successfully follow one-step directions).

13 Is reluctant to attempt new assignments or tasks

1. Reinforce the student for attempting a new assignment/task: (a) give the student a tangible reward (e.g., classroom privileges, line leading, passing out materials, five minutes free time, etc.) or (b) give the student an intangible reward (e.g., praise, handshake, smile, etc.).

2. Speak with the student to explain: (a) what he/she is doing wrong (e.g., not attempting a new task) and (b) what he/she should be doing (e.g., asking for assistance or clarification, following directions, starting on time, etc.).

3. Reinforce those students in the classroom who attempt a new assignment/task.

4. Reinforce the student for attempting a new assignment/task within the length of time he/she can be successful. Gradually decrease the amount of time to begin the task in order to be reinforced as the student demonstrates success.

5. Write a contract with the student specifying what behavior is expected (e.g., attempting a new assignment/task) and what reinforcement will be made available when the terms of the contract have been met.

6. Communicate with parents (e.g., notes home, phone calls, etc.) in order to share information concerning the student's progress and so that they may reinforce the student at home for attempting a new assignment/task at school.

7. Evaluate the appropriateness of the task to determine: (a) if the task is too easy, (b) if the task is too difficult, and (c) if the length of time scheduled to complete the task is appropriate.

8. Have the student question any directions, explanations, and instructions he/she does not understand.

9. Assess the quality and clarity of directions, explanations, and instructions given to the student.

10. Assign a peer or volunteer to help the student begin a task.

11. Structure the environment in such a way as to provide the student with increased opportunity for help or assistance.

12. Reduce distracting stimuli (e.g., place the student on the front row, provide a carrel or "office" space away from distractions, etc.). This is used as a means of reducing distracting stimuli and not as a form of punishment.

13. Have the student maintain a record (e.g., chart or graph) of his/her performance in attempting new assignments/tasks.

14. Communicate clearly to the student when it is time to begin.

15. Have the student time his/her activities in order to monitor his/her own behavior and accept time limits.

16. Present the task in the most interesting and attractive manner possible.

17. Maintain mobility in order to provide assistance for the student.

18. Structure time units in order that the student knows exactly how long he/she has to work and when he/she must be finished.

19. Provide the student with more than enough time to finish an activity and decrease the amount of time as the student demonstrates success.

20. Give directions in a variety of ways in order to increase the probability of understanding (e.g., if the student fails to understand verbal directions, present them in written form).

21. Have the student repeat the directions orally to the teacher.

22. Give a signal (e.g., clapping hands, turning lights off and on, etc.) before giving verbal directions.

23. Provide the student with a predetermined signal when he/she is not beginning a task (e.g., verbal cue, hand signal, etc.).

24. Tell the student that directions will only be given once.

25. Rewrite directions at a lower reading level.

26. Deliver verbal directions in a more basic way.

27. Help the student with the first few items on a task and gradually reduce the amount of help over time.

28. Follow a less desirable task with a highly desirable task making the completion of the first necessary to perform the second.

29. Provide the student with a schedule of daily events in order that he/she knows exactly what and how much there is to do in a day. (See Appendix for Schedule of Events.)

30. Prevent the student from becoming overstimulated by an activity (e.g., frustrated, angry, etc.).

31. Specify exactly what is to be done for the completion of a task (e.g., make definite starting and stopping points, a minimum requirement, etc.).

32. Require the student to begin each assignment within a specified period of time (e.g., three minutes, five minutes, etc.).

33. Provide the student with shorter tasks given more frequently.

34. Provide the student with a selection of assignments, requiring him/her to choose a minimum number from the total (e.g., present the student with 10 academic tasks from which he/she must finish 6 that day).

35. Provide the student with a certain number of problems to do on the assignment, requiring him/her to choose a minimum number from the total (e.g., present the student with 10 math problems from which he/she must complete 7).

36. Start with a single problem and add more problems to the task over time.

37. Reduce emphasis on competition (e.g., academic or social). Fear of failure may cause the student to refuse to attempt new assignments/tasks.

38. Provide the student with self-checking materials in order that he/she may check work privately, thus reducing the fear of public failure.

39. Have the student attempt the new assignment/task in a private place (e.g., carrel, "office," quiet study area, etc.) in order to reduce the fear of public failure.

40. Have the student practice a new skill (e.g., jumping rope, dribbling a basketball, etc.) alone, with a peer, or the teacher, before the entire group attempts the activity.

41. Provide the student with the opportunity to perform the assignment/task in a variety of ways (e.g., on tape, with a calculator, orally, etc.).

42. Allow the student to perform new assignments/tasks in a variety of places in the building (e.g., resource room, library, learning center, etc.).

43. Provide the student with a sample of the assignment/task which has been partially completed by a peer or teacher (e.g., book report, project, etc.).

44. Do not require the student to complete the assignment/task in one sitting.

45. Allow the student the option of performing the assignment/task at another time (e.g., earlier in the day, later, another day, etc.).

46. Deliver directions/instructions before handing out materials.

47. Make certain that the student has all the materials he/she needs in order to perform the assignment/task.

48. Have the student explain to the teacher what he/she thinks he/she should do in order to perform the assignment/task.

49. Explain to the student that work not done during work time will have to be made up at other times (e.g., recess, before school, after school, lunch time, etc.).

50. Teach the student direction-following skills: (a) listen carefully, (b) ask questions, (c) use environmental cues, (d) rely on examples provided, and (e) wait until directions are given before beginning.

51. Provide the student with optional courses of action to prevent total refusal to obey teacher directives.

14 Has difficulty with short-term or long-term memory

1. Make certain the student's hearing has been recently checked.

2. Reinforce the student for demonstrating short-term or long-term memory: (a) give the student a tangible reward (e.g., classroom privileges, line leading, passing out materials, five minutes free time, etc.) or (b) give the student an intangible reward (e.g., praise, handshake, smile, etc.).

3. Reinforce the student for demonstrating short-term or long-term memory based on the length of time he/she can be successful. Gradually increase the length of time required for reinforcement as the student demonstrates success.

4. Write a contract with the student specifying what behavior is expected (e.g., following one-step directions, two-step directions, etc.) and what reinforcement will be made available when the terms of the contract have been met.

5. Evaluate the appropriateness of the memory activities to determine if: (a) the task is too difficult and (b) the length of time scheduled to complete the task is appropriate.

6. Have the student question any directions, explanations, or instructions he/she does not understand.

7. Have the student act as a classroom messenger. Give the student a verbal message to deliver to another teacher, secretary, administrator, etc. Increase the length of the messages as the student demonstrates success.

8. Review the schedule of the morning or afternoon activities with the student and have him/her repeat the sequence. Increase the length of the sequence as the student is successful.

9. Have the student engage in concentration game activities with a limited number of symbols. Gradually increase the number of symbols as the student demonstrates success.

10. Reinforce students for remembering to have such materials as pens, pencils, paper, textbooks, notebooks, etc.

11. At the end of the school day, have the student recall three activities in which he/she was engaged during the day. Gradually increase the number of activities the student is required to recall as he/she demonstrates success.

12. After a field trip or special event have the student sequence the activities which occurred.

13. After reading a short story, have the student identify the main characters, sequence the events, and report the outcome of the story.

14. Have the student deliver the schedule of daily events to other students.

15. Use multiple modalities (e.g., auditory, visual, tactile, etc.) when presenting directions, explanations, and instructional content.

16. Assign a peer tutor to engage in short-term memory activities with the student (e.g., concentration games, following directions, etc.).

17. Record a message on tape. Have the student write the message after he/she has heard it. Increase the length of the message as the student demonstrates success.

18. Involve the student in activities in order to enhance his/her short-term memory skills (e.g., carry messages from one location to another or act as group leader, teacher assistant, etc.).

19. Have the student practice short-term memory skills by engaging in activities which are purposeful to him/her (e.g., delivering messages, being in charge of room clean-up, acting as custodian's helper, operating equipment, etc.).

20. Informally assess the student's auditory and visual short-term memory skills in order to determine which is the stronger. Utilize the results when presenting directions, explanations, and instructional content.

21. Have the student practice repetition of information in order to increase short-term memory skills (e.g., repeating names, telephone numbers, dates of events, etc.).

22. Teach the student how to organize information into smaller units (e.g., break the number sequence 132563 into units of 13, 25, 63).

23. Use sentence dictation to develop the student's short-term memory skills (e.g., begin with sentences of three words and increase the length of the sentences as the student demonstrates success).

24. Show the student an object or a picture of an object for a few seconds. Ask the student to recall specific attributes of the object (e.g., color, size, shape, etc.).

25. Deliver directions, explanations, and instructional content in a clear manner and at an appropriate pace.

26. Have the student practice making notes for specific information he/she wants and/or needs to remember.

27. Teach the student to recognize key words and phrases related to information in order to increase his/her short-term or long-term memory skills.

28. Make certain the student is attending (e.g., eye contact is being made, hands are free of materials, student is looking at assignment, etc.) to the source of information.

29. Reduce distracting stimuli when information is being presented, the student is studying, etc.

30. Stop at various points during the presentation of information to check the student's comprehension.

31. Give the student one task to perform at a time. Introduce the next task only when the student has successfully completed the previous task.

32. Have the student memorize the first sentence or line of poems, songs, etc. Require more to be memorized as the student experiences success.

33. Teach the student information-gathering skills (e.g., listen carefully, write down important points, ask for clarification, wait until all information is received before beginning, etc.).

34. Have the student repeat/paraphrase directions, explanations, and instructions.

35. Reduce the emphasis on competition. Competitive activities may cause the student to hurry and begin without listening carefully.

36. Provide the student with environmental cues and prompts designed to enhance his/her success in the classroom (e.g., posted rules, schedule of daily events, steps for performing tasks, etc.). (See Appendix for Schedule of Daily Events.)

37. Provide the student with written lists of things to do, materials he/she will need, etc.

38. Establish a regular routine for the student to follow in performing activities, assignments, etc. (e.g., listen to the person speaking to you, wait until directions are completed, make certain you have all needed materials, etc.).

39. Break the sequence into units and have the student learn one unit at a time.

40. Maintain consistency in sequential activities in order to increase the likelihood of student success (e.g., the student has math every day at one o'clock, recess at two o'clock, etc.).

41. Teach the student to use associative cues or pneumonic devices to remember sequences.

42. Actively involve the student in learning to remember sequences by having the student physically perform sequential activities (e.g., operating equipment, following recipes, solving math problems, etc.).

43. Have the student be responsible for helping a peer remember sequences.

44. Use concrete examples and experiences in sharing information with the student.

45. Teach the student to recognize main points, important facts, etc.

46. Teach the student to rely on resources in the environment to recall information (e.g., notes, textbooks, pictures, etc.).

47. When the student is required to recall information provide him/her with auditory cues to help him/her remember the information (e.g., key words, a brief oral description to cue the student, etc.).

48. Assess the meaningfulness of the material to the student. Remembering is more likely to occur when the material is meaningful and the student can relate it to real experiences.

49. Relate the information being presented to the student's previous experiences.

50. Give the student specific categories and have him/her name as many items as possible within that category (e.g., objects, persons, places, etc.).

51. Give the student a series of words or pictures and have him/her name the category to which they belong (e.g., objects, persons, places, etc.).

52. Describe objects, persons, places, etc., and have the student name the items described.

53. Help the student employ memory aids in order to recall words (e.g., a name might be linked to another word, for example, "Mr. Green" is a very colorful person).

54. Give the student a series of words describing objects, persons, places, etc., and have him/her identify the opposite of each word.

55. Encourage the student to play word games such as *Hangman*, *Scrabble*, *Password*, etc.

56. Have the student complete "fill-in-the-blank" sentences with appropriate words (e.g., objects, persons, places, etc.).

57. Have the student outline, highlight, underline, or summarize information he/she should remember.

58. Make certain the student has adequate opportunities for repetition of information through different experiences in order to enhance his/her memory.

59. Label objects, persons, places, etc., in the environment in order to help the student be able to recall their names.

60. Make certain the student receives information from a variety of sources (e.g., texts, discussions, films, slide presentations, etc.) in order to enhance the student's memory/recall.

15 Has difficulty understanding abstract concepts

1. Make certain to use terms when speaking to the student which convey concepts to describe tangible objects in the environment (e.g., larger, smaller, square, triangle, etc.).

2. Identify tangible objects in the classroom with signs that convey abstract concepts (e.g., larger, smaller, square, triangle, etc.).

3. Use concrete examples when teaching abstract concepts (e.g., numbers of objects to convey "more than," "less than," rulers and yardsticks to convey concepts of "height," "width," etc.).

4. Play "Simon Says" to enhance the understanding of abstract concepts (e.g., "Find the biggest desk.", "Touch something that is a rectangle.", etc.).

5. Conduct a scavenger hunt. Have the student look for the smallest pencil, tallest boy, etc., in the classroom.

6. Teach shapes using common objects in the environment (e.g., round clocks, rectangle desks, square tiles on the floor, etc.).

7. Evaluate the appropriateness of having the student learn abstract concepts at this time.

8. Teach abstract concepts one at a time before pairing the concepts (e.g., dimensionality, size, shape, etc.).

9. Provide repeated physical demonstrations of abstract concepts (e.g., identify things far away and close to the student, small box in a large room, etc.).

10. Review on a daily basis, those abstract concepts which have been previously introduced. Introduce new abstract concepts only after the student has mastery of those previously presented.

11. When introducing abstract concepts, rely on tangible objects (e.g., boxes for dimensionality, family members for size, distances in the classroom for space, cookie cutters for shape, etc.). Do not introduce abstract concepts by using their descriptive titles such as square, rectangle, triangle, etc.

12. Have the student match the names of abstract concepts with objects (e.g., triangle, square, circle, etc.).

13. Give the student direction-following assignments (e.g., "Go to the swing the farthest away.", "Go to the nearest sandbox.", etc.).

14. Have a peer spend time each day with the student pointing out abstract concepts in the classroom (e.g., the rectangle-shaped light switch plate, the round light fixture, the tallest girl, etc.).

15. Have the student question any directions, explanations, instructions, he/she does not understand.

16. Provide repeated physical demonstrations of abstract concepts.

17. Have the student physically perform spatial relationships (e.g., have the student stand near the teacher, far from the teacher, over a table, under a table, etc.).

18. Call attention to spatial relationships which occur naturally in the environment (e.g., call attention to a bird flying "over" a tree, a squirrel running "under" a bush, etc.).

19. For more abstract concepts such as left and right, north, south, east, and west, have the student follow simple map directions. Begin with a map of the building and progress to a map of the community, state, nation, etc., with more complex directions to follow.

20. To teach the student relationships of left and right, place paper bands labeled "left" and "right" around the student's wrists. Remove the paper bands when the student can successfully identify left and right.

21. Use actual change and dollar bills, clocks, etc., to teach concepts of money, telling time, etc.

22. Use a scale, ruler, measuring cups, etc., to teach abstract concepts using measurement.

23. Make certain to use the terms "right" and "left" as part of the directions you are giving to the student (e.g., refer to the windows on the left side of the room, the chalkboard on the right side of the room, etc.).

24. Have the student practice following directions on paper. Instruct the student to make a mark or picture on the right, left, middle, top and bottom parts of the paper according to the directions given.

25. Avoid the problem of mirror images by standing next to the student when giving right and left directions.

26. Have the student sort left and right gloves, shoes, paper hand and foot cut-outs, etc.

27. Be certain to relate what the student has learned in one setting or situation to other situations (e.g., vocabulary words learned should be pointed out in reading selections, math word problems, story writing, etc.).

16 Does not comprehend what he/she reads

1. Make certain the student is reading material on his/her ability level.

2. Set up a system of motivators, either tangible (e.g., extra computer time, helper of the day, etc.) or intangible (e.g., smile, handshake, praise, etc.) to encourage the student to be more successful in reading.

3. Modify or adjust the student's reading material to his/her level.

4. Outline reading material for the student using words and phrases on his/her ability level.

5. Tape record difficult reading material for the student to listen to as he/she reads along.

6. Teach the student to use related learning experiences in his/her classes (e.g., filmstrips, movies, tape recordings, demonstrations, discussions, lectures, videotapes, etc.). Encourage teachers to provide alternative learning experiences for the student.

7. Arrange for a peer tutor to study with the student for quizzes, tests, etc.

8. Use a sight word vocabulary approach in order to teach the student key words and phrases when reading directions and instructions (e.g., key words such as "circle," "underline," "match," etc.).

9. Maintain mobility in the classroom in order to be frequently near the student to provide reading assistance.

10. Use lower grade level texts as alternative reading material in subject areas.

11. Have lectures tape recorded in order to provide an additional source of information for the student.

12. Make a list of main points from the student's reading material, written on the student's reading level.

13. Make available for the student a learning center area where a variety of information is available for him/her in content areas (e.g., the library may have a section with films, slides, videotapes and taped lectures, on such subjects as Pilgrims, the Civil War, the judicial system, etc.).

14. Reduce distracting stimuli in order to increase the student's ability to concentrate on what he/she is reading (e.g., place the student on the front row, provide a carrel or "office" space away from distractions, etc.). This is used as a means of reducing distracting stimuli and not as a form of punishment.

15. Provide the student with a quiet place (e.g., carrel, study booth, etc.) where he/she may go to engage in reading activities.

16. Have the student verbally paraphrase material he/she has just read in order to assess his/her comprehension.

17. Teach the student to identify main points in material he/she has read in order to assess his/her comprehension.

18. Have the student outline, underline, or highlight important points in reading material.

19. Provide the student with written direction following activities in order to enhance comprehension (e.g., following a recipe, following directions to put together a model, etc.).

20. Provide the student with written one-, two-, and three-step direction-following activities (e.g., sharpen your pencil, open your text to page 121, etc.).

21. Have the student take notes while he/she is reading in order to increase comprehension.

22. Have the student read progressively longer segments of reading material in order to build comprehension skills (e.g., begin with a single paragraph and progress to several paragraphs, chapter, short story, novel, etc.).

23. Have the student tape record what he/she reads in order to enhance comprehension by listening to the material read.

24. Teach the student to use context clues to identify words and phrases he/she does not know.

25. Write paragraphs and short stories requiring skills the student is currently developing. These passages should be of high interest to the student using his/her name, family members, friends, pets, and interesting experiences.

26. Have the student dictate stories which are then written for him/her to read, placing an emphasis on comprehension skills.

27. Have the student read high-interest signs, advertisements, notices, etc., from newspapers, magazines, movie promotions, etc.

28. Make certain the student is practicing comprehension skills which are directly related to high-interest reading activities (e.g., adventures, romance, mystery, sports, etc.).

29. Reduce the emphasis on competition. Competitive activities may make it difficult for the student to comprehend what he/she reads.

30. Underline or highlight important points before the student reads the assigned material silently.

31. Write notes and letters to the student to provide reading material which he/she would want to read for comprehension. Students may be encouraged to write each other notes and letters at a time set aside each day, once a week, etc.

32. Give the student time to read a selection more than once, emphasizing comprehension, rather than speed.

33. Use reading series material with high-interest low vocabulary for the older student.

17 Requies repeated drill and practice to learn what other students master easily

1. Reduce the emphasis on competition. Competitive activities may cause the student to hurry and make mistakes.

2. Give the student fewer concepts to learn at any one time, spending more time on each concept until the student can learn it correctly.

3. Have a peer spend time each day engaged in drill activities with the student.

4. Have the student use new concepts frequently throughout the day.

5. Have the student highlight or underline key words, phrases, and sentences from reading assignments, newspapers, magazines, etc.

6. Develop crossword puzzles which contain only the student's spelling words and have him/her complete them.

7. Write sentences, passages, paragraphs, etc., for the student to read which reinforce new concepts.

8. Have the student act as a peer tutor to teach concepts just learned to another student.

9. Have the student review new concepts each day for a short period of time rather than two or three times per week for longer periods of time.

10. Use wall charts to introduce new concepts with visual images such as pictures for the student to associate with previously learned concepts.

11. Initiate a "learn a concept day" program with the student and incorporate the concept into the assigned activities for the day.

12. Require the student to use resources (e.g., encyclopedia, dictionary, etc.) to provide information to help them be successful when performing tasks.

13. Allow the student to use devices to help him/her successfully perform tasks (e.g., calculator, multiplication tables, abacus, dictionary, a peer, etc.).

14. Provide the student with various times throughout the day when he/she can engage in drill activities with the teacher, aide, peer, etc.

15. Provide the student with opportunities for drill activities in the most interesting manner possible (e.g., computer, using a calculator, playing educational games, watching a film, listening to a tape, etc.).

16. Give the student a list of key words, phrases, or main points to learn for each new concept introduced.

17. Underline, circle, or highlight important information from any material the student is to learn (e.g., science, math, geography, etc.).

18. Provide the student with the information he/she needs to learn in the most direct manner possible (e.g., a list of facts, a summary of important points, outline of important events, etc.).

19. Tape record important information the student can listen to as often as necessary.

18 Fights with other students

1. Reinforce the student for demonstrating appropriate behavior: (a) give the student a tangible reward (e.g., classroom privileges, line leading, passing out materials, five minutes free time, etc.) or (b) give the student an intangible reward (e.g., praise, handshake, smile, etc.).

2. Speak with the student to explain: (a) what he/she is doing wrong (e.g., scratching, hitting, pulling hair, etc.) and (b) what he/she should be doing (e.g., following rules, interacting in appropriate ways, dealing with anger and frustration in appropriate ways, etc.).

3. Establish classroom rules (e.g., work on-task, work quietly, remain in your seat, finish task, meet task expectations). Reiterate rules often and reinforce students for following rules.

4. Reinforce those students in the classroom who demonstrate appropriate behavior when interacting with other students.

5. Reinforce the student for demonstrating appropriate behavior based on the length of time he/she can be successful. Gradually increase the length of time required for reinforcement as the student demonstrates success.

6. Remove the student from the group or activity until he/she can demonstrate appropriate behavior and self-control.

7. Write a contract with the student specifying what behavior is expected (e.g., respecting the norms of physical proximity) and what reinforcement will be made available when the terms of the contract have been met.

8. Communicate with parents (e.g., notes home, phone calls, etc.) in order to share information concerning the student's progress and so that they may reinforce the student at home for respecting the norms of physical proximity at school.

9. Evaluate the appropriateness of the task to determine: (a) if the task is too easy, (b) if the task is too difficult, and (c) if the length of time scheduled for the task is appropriate.

10. Prevent frustrating or anxiety producing situations from occurring (e.g., give the student tasks only on his/her ability level, give the student only the number of tasks that he/she can tolerate in one sitting, reduce social interactions which stimulate the student to become physically aggressive, etc.).

11. Teach the student problem-solving skills: (a) identify the problem, (b) identify goals and objectives, (c) develop strategies, (d) develop a plan for action, and (e) carry out the plan.

12. Provide the student with positive feedback which indicates he/she is successful, important, respected, etc.

13. Structure the environment to reduce opportunities for the student to become physically aggressive toward other students (e.g., seating arrangement, supervision, etc.).

14. Maintain visibility to and from the student. The teacher should be able to see the student and the student should be able to see the teacher, making eye contact possible at all times.

15. Be mobile in order to be frequently near the student.

16. Reduce activities which might be threatening to the student (e.g., announcing test score ranges or test scores aloud, making students read aloud in class, emphasizing the success of a particular student(s), etc.).

17. Try various groupings in order to determine the situation in which the student is most likely to socially succeed.

18. Make the necessary adjustments in the environment that prevent the student from becoming overstimulated by peers.

19. Reduce the emphasis on competition and perfection. Repeated failure and frustration may cause outbursts of physical aggression.

20. Teach the student alternative ways to deal with situations which make him/her frustrated or angry (e.g., withdrawing, talking, etc.).

21. Facilitate on-task behavior by providing a full schedule of activities. Prevent lag time from occurring when the student would be free to engage in inappropriate behavior.

22. Maintain supervision in order that the student is not left alone or unsupervised with other students.

23. Provide the student with as many high interest activities as possible to keep him/her from becoming physically aggressive toward other students.

24. Provide the student with opportunities for social and academic success.

25. Make certain that all school personnel are aware of the student's tendency to become physically aggressive in order that they may monitor his/her behavior.

26. Limit the student's independent movement in the school environment.

27. Provide a quiet place for the student to work independently, away from peer interactions. This is not to be used as a form of punishment, but rather an opportunity to increase the student's success in his/her environment.

28. Place reinforcement emphasis on academic productivity and accuracy in order to reduce the likelihood of the student becoming physically aggressive (i.e., increased productivity and accuracy will reduce the likelihood of inappropriate behavior).

29. Reduce or remove any stimulus in the environment which leads to the student's physically aggressive behavior (e.g., possessions, competition, teasing, etc.).

30. Make certain the student understands the natural consequences of hurting other students (e.g., less freedom, more restrictive environment, assault charges, etc.).

31. Prevent the student from receiving too much stimulation (e.g., monitor or supervise student behavior to limit overexcitement in physical activities, games, parties, etc.).

32. Limit the student's opportunity to enter areas of the school environment in which he/she is more likely to be physically aggressive.

33. Separate the student from the peer(s) who may be encouraging or stimulating the student's inappropriate behavior.

34. Do not force the student to interact or remain in a group when he/she is physically aggressive (e.g., daily reading group, physical education group, etc.).

35. Maintain maximum supervision of the student and gradually decrease supervision over time as the student demonstrates appropriate behavior.

19 Becomes physically aggressive with teachers

1. Reinforce the student for demonstrating appropriate behavior: (a) give the student a tangible reward (e.g., classroom privileges, line leading, passing out materials, five minutes free time, etc.) or (b) give the student an intangible reward (e.g., praise, handshake, smile, etc.).

2. Speak with the student to explain: (a) what he/she is doing wrong (e.g., pushing, pulling away, grabbing, etc.) and (b) what he/she should be doing (e.g., following rules, interacting in appropriate ways, dealing with anger and frustration in appropriate ways, etc.).

3. Establish classroom rules (e.g., work on-task, work quietly, remain in your seat, finish task, meet task expectations). Reiterate rules often and reinforce students for following rules.

4. Reinforce those students in the classroom who demonstrate appropriate behavior when interacting with teachers.

5. Reinforce the student for demonstrating appropriate behavior based on the length of time he/she can be successful. Gradually increase the length of time required for reinforcement as the student demonstrates success.

6. Remove the student from the group or activity until he/she can demonstrate appropriate behavior and self-control.

7. Write a contract with the student specifying what behavior is expected (e.g., respecting the norms of physical proximity) and what reinforcement will be made available when the terms of the contract have been met.

8. Communicate with parents (e.g., notes home, phone calls, etc.) in order to share information concerning the student's progress and so that they may reinforce the student at home for respecting the norms of physical proximity at school.

9. Evaluate the appropriateness of the task to determine: (a) if the task is too easy, (b) if the task is too difficult, and (c) if the length of time scheduled for the task is appropriate.

10. Prevent frustrating or anxiety producing situations from occurring (e.g., give the student tasks only on his/her ability level, give the student only the number of tasks that he/she can tolerate in one sitting, reduce social interactions which stimulate the student to become physically aggressive, etc.).

11. Teach the student problem-solving skills: (a) identify the problem, (b) identify goals and objectives, (c) develop strategies, (d) develop a plan for action, and (e) carry out the plan.

12. Provide the student with positive feedback which indicates he/she is successful, important, respected, etc.

13. Structure the environment to prevent opportunities for the student to become physically aggressive toward teachers (e.g., interact frequently with the student to prevent him/her from becoming frustrated).

14. Maintain maximum supervision of the student and gradually decrease supervision over time as the student demonstrates appropriate behavior.

15. Maintain visibility to and from the student. The teacher should be able to see the student and the student should be able to see the teacher, making eye contact possible at all times.

16. Be mobile in order to be frequently near the student.

17. Reduce activities which might be threatening to the student (e.g., announcing test score ranges or test scores aloud, making students read aloud in class, emphasizing the success of a particular student(s), etc.).

18. Try various groupings in order to determine the situation in which the student is most successful.

19. Make the necessary adjustments in the environment that prevent the student from becoming overstimulated by peers which in turn would make it necessary for the teacher to intervene.

20. Reduce the emphasis on competition and perfection. Repeated failure and frustration may cause outbursts of physical aggression.

21. Teach the student alternative ways to deal with situations which make him/her frustrated or angry (e.g., withdrawing, talking, etc.).

22. Facilitate on-task behavior by providing a full schedule of activities. Prevent lag time from occurring when the student would be free to engage in inappropriate behavior.

23. Provide the student with as many high-interest activities as possible to keep him/her from becoming physically aggressive toward teachers.

24. Provide the student with opportunities for social and academic success.

25. Make certain that all school personnel are aware of the student's tendency to become physically aggressive in order that they may monitor his/her behavior.

26. Limit the student's independent movement in the school environment.

27. Provide a quiet place for the student to work independently, away from peer interactions. This is not to be used as a form of punishment, but rather an opportunity to increase the student's success in his/her environment.

28. Place reinforcement emphasis on academic productivity and accuracy in order to reduce the likelihood of the student becoming physically aggressive (i.e., increased productivity and accuracy will reduce the likelihood of inappropriate behavior) toward teachers.

29. Reduce or remove any stimulus in the environment which leads to the student's physically aggressive behavior (e.g., possessions, competition, teasing, etc.).

30. Make certain the student understands the natural consequences of becoming physically aggressive toward a teacher (e.g., less freedom, more restrictive environment, assault charges, etc.).

31. Prevent the student from receiving too much stimulation (e.g., monitor or supervise student behavior to limit overexcitement in physical activities, games, parties, etc.).

32. Limit the student's opportunity to enter areas of the school environment in which he/she is more likely to be physically aggressive.

33. Do not force the student to interact or remain in a group when he/she is physically aggressive (e.g., daily reading group, physical education group, etc.).

34. Always provide the student with behavioral options (e.g., sitting out of an activity, going to a quiet place in the room, performing another activity, etc.).

35. Avoid arguing with the student (e.g., calmly deliver consequences without reacting to the student's remarks).

36. Maintain consistency in behavioral expectations and consequences in order to reduce the likelihood of the student becoming upset by what he/she considers unfair treatment.

37. Avoid physical contact with the student who is likely to become physically aggressive.

38. Maintain an appropriate physical distance from the student when interacting with him/her in order to avoid stimulation of his/her aggressive behavior.

39. Use language that is pleasant and calming when speaking with the student in order to avoid stimulation of his/her aggressive behavior.

20 Makes inappropriate comments to teachers

1. Reinforce the student for communicating in an appropriate manner with teachers: (a) give the student a tangible reward (e.g., classroom privileges, line leading, passing out materials, five minutes free time, etc.) or (b) give the student an intangible reward (e.g., praise, handshake, smile, etc.).

2. Speak with the student to explain: (a) what he/she is doing wrong (e.g., arguing, threatening, calling names, etc.) and (b) what he/she should be doing (e.g., following rules, staying on-task, attending to his/her responsibilities, etc.).

3. Establish classroom rules (e.g., work on-task, work quietly, remain in your seat, finish task, meet task expectations). Reiterate rules often and reinforce students for following rules.

4. Reinforce those students in the classroom who communicate in an appropriate manner with teachers.

5. Reinforce the student for communicating in an appropriate manner based on the length of time he/she can be successful. Gradually increase the length of time required for reinforcement as the student demonstrates success.

6. Remove the student from the group or activity until he/she can demonstrate appropriate behavior.

7. Write a contract with the student specifying what behavior is expected (e.g., using appropriate language) and what reinforcement will be made available when the terms of the contract have been met.

8. Communicate with parents (e.g., notes home, phone calls, etc.) in order to share information concerning the student's progress and so that they may reinforce the student at home for communicating in an appropriate manner at school.

9. Evaluate the appropriateness of the task to determine: (a) if the task is too easy, (b) if the task is too difficult, and (c) if the length of time scheduled for the task is appropriate.

10. Teach the student appropriate ways to communicate displeasure, anger, etc.

11. Reduce stimuli which contribute to the student's derogatory comments or inappropriate gestures.

12. Provide the student with a quiet place to work. This is to be used as a means of reducing distracting stimuli and not as a form of punishment.

13. Provide the student with the opportunity to work with a peer who will be a model for communicating in an appropriate manner.

14. Make certain the student understands the natural consequences of his/her inappropriate behavior (e.g., teachers choose not to interact with him/her, exclusion from activities, etc.).

15. Require that the student identify alternative appropriate behaviors following an instance of derogatory comments or inappropriate gestures.

16. Facilitate on-task behavior by providing a full schedule of activities. Prevent lag time from occurring when the student would be free to engage in inappropriate behavior.

17. Reduce the emphasis on competition. Repeated failure may result in anger and frustration which may take the form of derogatory comments or inappropriate gestures.

18. Emphasize individual success or progress rather than winning or "beating" other students.

19. Modify or adjust situations which contribute to the student's use of obscene or profane language (e.g., if an assignment causes the student to become upset, modify the assignment to a level at which the student can be successful).

20. Interact frequently with the student in order to monitor language used.

21. Maintain visibility to and from the student. The teacher should be able to see the student and the student should be able to see the teacher, making eye contact possible at all times.

22. Try various groupings in order to determine the situation in which the student is most successful.

23. Prevent frustrating or anxiety producing situations from occurring (e.g., give the student tasks only on his/her ability level, give the student only those number of tasks that he/she can successfully manage in one sitting, reduce social interactions which stimulate the student's use of obscene language, etc.).

24. Reduce activities which might threaten the student (e.g., announcing test score ranges or test scores aloud, making students read aloud in class, emphasizing the success of a particular student(s), etc.).

25. Discuss with the student ways he/she could deal with unpleasant experiences which would typically cause him/her to use obscene language (e.g., talk to the teacher, go to a quiet area in the room, go see a counselor, etc.).

26. Make certain that positive reinforcement is not inadvertently given for inappropriate language (e.g., attending to the student only when he/she is using profane or obscene language).

27. Provide the student with a predetermined signal when he/she begins to use inappropriate language.

28. Deal with the student in a calm and deliberate manner rather than in a manner that would show evidence of shock and surprise.

29. Act as an appropriate role model by using appropriate language at all times (e.g., use appropriate language to convey disappointment, unhappiness, surprise, etc.).

30. Teach the student appropriate words or phrases to use in situations of anger, stress, frustration, etc.

31. Have the student question any directions, explanations, instructions he/she does not understand.

32. Intervene early when inappropriate behavior occurs in order to prevent the behavior from becoming more serious. Deliberate interventions prevent future problems.

33. Avoid arguing with the student.

34. Be consistent in expectations and consequences of behavior.

35. Treat the student with respect. Talk to the student in an objective and professional manner at all times.

36. Avoid ignoring the student's inappropriate behavior. Ignored behavior may increase in frequency and may lead to contagion on the part of other students.

37. Avoid confrontations with the student which lead to inappropriate behavior on the part of the student (e.g., give the student options for alternative tasks, other times to perform assignments, assistance in performing assignments, etc.).

38. Develop a routine schedule of activities and tasks for the student in order that he/she knows what to expect at all times.

39. Evaluate the appropriateness of the task in relation to the student's ability to perform the task.

40. Avoid physical contact with the student who is likely to become verbally abusive (e.g., a pat on the back may cause the student to argue, threaten, call names, curse, etc.).

41. Maintain an appropriate physical distance from the student when interacting with him/her in order to avoid stimulation of his/her inappropriate comments.

42. Use language that is pleasant and calming when speaking with the student in order to avoid stimulation of his/her inappropriate comments.

21 Does not respond appropriately to praise or recognition

1. Reinforce the student for responding appropriately to praise or recognition: (a) give the student a tangible reward (e.g., classroom privileges, line leading, passing out materials, five minutes free time, etc.) or (b) give the student an intangible reward (e.g., praise, handshake, smile, etc.).

2. Speak with the student to explain: (a) what he/she is doing wrong (e.g., behaving inappropriately when recognized by others) and (b) what he/she should be doing (e.g., saying "thank you," smiling, etc.).

3. Reinforce those students in the classroom who respond appropriately to praise or recognition.

4. Reinforce the student for responding appropriately to praise or recognition based on the number of times he/she can be successful. Gradually increase the number of times required for reinforcement as the student demonstrates success.

5. Write a contract with the student specifying what behavior is expected (e.g., saying "thank you" when given praise or recognition) and what reinforcement will be made available when the terms of the contract have been met.

6. Communicate with parents (e.g., notes home, phone calls, etc.) in order to share information concerning the student's progress and so that they may reinforce the student at home for responding appropriately to praise or recognition at school.

7. Model appropriate ways to respond to interactions with other students or teachers.

8. Try various groupings in order to determine the situation in which the student is most comfortable.

9. Praise or recognize the student in private. The public aspect of praise or recognition is often the cause of the inappropriate response.

10. Provide the student with many social and academic successes in order that he/she may learn how to respond appropriately.

11. Assess the appropriateness of the social situation in relation to the student's ability to function successfully.

12. Distribute praise and recognition equally to the members of the class.

13. Provide praise or recognition for smaller increments of success so that the student may become gradually accustomed to the recognition.

14. Provide praise and recognition as a natural consequence for appropriate behavior.

15. Praise or recognize the student when he/she will most likely be able to demonstrate an appropriate response (e.g., when the student is not being singled out in a group).

16. Make certain that reinforcement is not inadvertently given for inappropriate behavior (e.g., attending to the student only when he/she responds inappropriately to praise or recognition).

17. Use alternative forms of praise or recognition which are not threatening to the student (e.g., written notes, telephone calls to parents, display work done well, etc.).

18. Present praise with a matter-of-fact delivery and avoid exaggerated exclamations of success.

19. Use feedback related to performance (e.g., test scores, grades, etc.) in place of praise or recognition. Gradually deliver verbal praise and recognition as the student becomes more capable of accepting praise and recognition.

20. Rather than emphasizing winning or "beating" other students in competition, encourage individual success or progress which may be enjoyed privately rather than publicly.

A Reminder: Do not punish a student for his/her inability to respond appropriately to praise or recognition.

22   Is easily angered, annoyed, or upset

1. Reinforce the student for demonstrating self-control in those situations in which he/she is likely to become angry, annoyed, or upset: (a) give the student a tangible reward (e.g., classroom privileges, line leading, passing out materials, five minutes free time, etc.) or (b) give the student an intangible reward (e.g., praise, handshake, smile, etc.).

2. Speak to the student to explain: (a) what he/she is doing wrong (e.g., hitting, arguing, throwing things, etc.) and (b) what he/she should be doing (e.g., moving away from the situation, asking for assistance from the teacher, etc.).

3. Establish classroom rules (e.g., work on-task, work quietly, remain in your seat, finish task, meet task expectations). Reiterate rules often and reinforce students for following rules.

4. Reinforce those students in the classroom who demonstrate self-control.

5. Reinforce the student for demonstrating self-control based on the length of time he/she can be successful. Gradually increase the length of time required for reinforcement as the student demonstrates success.

6. Write a contract with the student specifying what behavior is expected (e.g., problem solving, moving away from the situation, asking for assistance from the teacher, etc.) and what reinforcement will be made available when the terms of the contract have been met.

7. Communicate with parents (e.g., notes home, phone calls, etc.) in order to share information concerning the student's progress and so that they may reinforce the student at home for demonstrating self-control at school.

8. Communicate with parents, agencies, or appropriate parties in order to inform them of the problem, determine the cause of the problem, and solutions to the problem.

9. Evaluate the appropriateness of the academic task to determine: (a) if the task is too easy, (b) if the task is too difficult, and (c) if the length of time scheduled to complete the task is appropriate.

10. Identify a peer to act as a model for the student to imitate self-control.

11. Have the student question any directions, explanations, or instructions he/she does not understand.

12. Prevent frustrating or anxiety producing situations from occurring (e.g., give the student tasks only on his/her ability level, give the student only the number of tasks that he/she can tolerate in one sitting, reduce social interactions which stimulate the student to become physically abusive, etc.).

13. Teach the student problem-solving skills: (a) identify the problem, (b) identify goals and objectives, (c) develop strategies, (d) develop a plan for action, and (e) carry out the plan.

14. Provide the student with positive feedback which indicates he/she is successful, important, respected, etc.

15. Maintain maximum supervision of the student. Gradually decrease supervision over time as the student demonstrates self-control.

16. Maintain visibility to and from the student. The teacher should be able to see the student and the student should be able to see the teacher, making eye contact possible at all times.

17. Be mobile in order to be frequently near the student.

18. Reduce activities which might threaten the student (e.g., announcing test score ranges or test scores aloud, making students read aloud in class, emphasizing the success of a particular student or students, etc.).

19. Try various groupings in order to determine the situation in which the student is most successful.

20. Make the necessary adjustments in the environment to prevent the student from experiencing stress, frustration, and anger.

21. Reduce the emphasis on competition and perfection. Repeated failure and frustration may cause the student to become angered, annoyed, or upset.

22. Teach the student alternative ways to deal with situations which make him/her frustrated, angry, etc. (e.g., withdrawing, talking, etc.).

23. Facilitate on-task behavior by providing a full schedule of daily events. Prevent lag time from occurring when the student would be likely to become involved in activities which would cause him/her to be angered, annoyed, or upset. (See Appendix for Schedule of Daily Events.)

24. Maintain supervision in order that the student is not left alone or allowed to be unsupervised with other students.

25. Provide the student with as many high-interest activities as possible.

26. Provide the student with opportunities for social and academic success.

27. Make other personnel aware of the student's tendency to become easily angered, annoyed, or upset.

28. Provide a quiet place for the student to work independently, away from peer interactions. This is not to be used as a form of punishment, but rather an opportunity to increase the student's success in his/her environment.

29. Place reinforcement emphasis on academic productivity and accuracy to divert the student's attention away from others which cause him/her to become angered, annoyed, or upset.

30. Make the student aware of the natural consequences for becoming easily angered, annoyed, or upset (e.g., loss of friendships, injury, more restrictive environment, legal action, etc.).

31. Separate the student from the peer(s) who may be encouraging or stimulating the student to become angered, annoyed, or upset.

32. Do not force the student to interact or remain in a group if he/she is likely to become easily angered, annoyed, or upset.

33. Provide the student with a selection of optional activities to be performed if he/she becomes angered, annoyed, or upset by an assigned task.

34. Maintain consistency in expectations.

35. Maintain consistency in daily routine.

36. Remove the student from the group or activity until he/she can demonstrate self-control.

37. Maintain a positive/calm environment (e.g., positive comments, acknowledgement of successes, quiet communications, etc.).

38. Allow flexibility in meeting academic demands when the student becomes angered, annoyed, or upset (e.g., allow more time, modify assignments, provide help with assignments, etc.).

39. Present tasks in the most attractive and interesting manner possible.

40. Make certain to ask the student why he/she becomes easily angered, annoyed, or upset. The student may have the most accurate perception as to why he/she becomes easily angered, annoyed, or upset.

41. Teach the student decision-making steps: (a) think about how others may be influenced, (b) think about consequences, (c) carefully consider the unique situation, (d) think of different courses of action which are possible, (e) think about what is ultimately best for him/her, etc.

42. Avoid topics, situations, etc., that may cause the student to become easily angered, annoyed, or upset (e.g., divorce, death, unemployment, alcoholism, etc.).

43. Discourage the student from engaging in those activities that cause him/her to become easily angered, annoyed, or upset.

44. Teach the student to verbalize his/her feelings before losing self-control (e.g., "The work is too hard," "Please leave me alone, you're making me angry," etc.).

23 Agitates and provokes peers to a level of verbal or physical assault

1. Reinforce the student for communicating in an appropriate manner with peers: (a) give the student a tangible reward (e.g., classroom privileges, line leading, passing out materials, five minutes free time, etc.) or (b) give the student an intangible reward (e.g., praise, handshake, smile, etc.).

2. Speak with the student to explain: (a) what he/she is doing wrong (e.g., calling names, making inappropriate gestures, etc.) and (b) what he/she should be doing (e.g., following rules, staying on-task, attending to his/her responsibilities, etc.).

3. Establish classroom rules (e.g., work on-task, work quietly, remain in your seat, finish task, meet task expectations). Reiterate rules often and reinforce students for following rules.

4. Reinforce those students in the classroom who communicate in an appropriate manner.

5. Reinforce the student for communicating in an appropriate manner based on the length of time he/she can be successful. Gradually increase the length of time required for reinforcement as the student demonstrates success.

6. Remove the student from the group or activity until he/she can demonstrate appropriate behavior.

7. Write a contract with the student specifying what behavior is expected (e.g., communicating with peers in a positive manner) and what reinforcement will be made available when the terms of the contract have been met.

8. Communicate with parents (e.g., notes home, phone calls, etc.) in order to share information concerning the student's progress and so that they may reinforce the student at home for demonstrating appropriate behavior at school.

9. Evaluate the appropriateness of the task to determine: (a) if the task is too easy, (b) if the task is too difficult, and (c) if the length of time scheduled for the task is appropriate.

10. Teach the student appropriate ways to communicate displeasure, anger, etc.

11. Reduce the stimuli that contribute to the student's derogatory comments or inappropriate gestures.

12. Provide the student with a quiet place to work (e.g., study carrel, "private office," etc.). This is used as a means of reducing distracting stimuli and not as a form of punishment.

13. Provide the student with the opportunity to work with a peer who will be an appropriate model.

14. Separate the student from the peer(s) who is the primary stimulus or focus of the derogatory comments or inappropriate gestures.

15. Make certain the student understands the natural consequences of his/her inappropriate behavior (e.g., peers choose not to interact with him/her, exclusion from activities, etc.).

16. Require that the student identify alternative appropriate behaviors following an instance of derogatory comments or inappropriate gestures.

17. Facilitate on-task behavior by providing a full schedule of daily events. Prevent lag time from occurring when the student would be free to engage in inappropriate behavior. (See Appendix for Schedule of Daily Events.)

18. Reduce the emphasis on competition. Repeated failure may result in anger and frustration that may take the form of derogatory comments or inappropriate gestures.

19. Emphasize individual success or progress rather than winning or "beating" other students.

20. Intervene early when the student begins to agitate or provoke peers.

21. Remove the student from the classroom if he/she is unable to demonstrate self-control. The student should not be allowed to remain in the classroom and be abusive to peers.

22. Maintain visibility to and from the student. The teacher should be able to see the student and the student should be able to see the teacher, making eye contact possible at all times.

24 Has little or no interaction with teachers

1. Reinforce the student for interacting with teachers: (a) give the student a tangible reward (e.g., classroom privileges, line leading, passing out materials, five minutes free time, etc.) or (b) give the student an intangible reward (e.g., praise, handshake, smile, etc.).

2. Speak with the student to explain: (a) what he/she is doing wrong (e.g., not talking, making eye contact, etc.) and (b) what he/she should be doing (e.g., talking, looking at the teacher, etc.).

3. Establish classroom rules (e.g., work on-task, work quietly, remain in your seat, finish task, meet task expectations). Reiterate rules often and reinforce students for following rules.

4. Reinforce those students in the classroom who interact appropriately with teachers.

5. Reinforce the student for interacting with teachers based on the length of time he/she can be successful. Gradually increase the length of time required for reinforcement as the student demonstrates success.

6. Write a contract with the student specifying what behavior is expected (e.g., sitting near the teacher, talking to the teacher, etc.) and what reinforcement will be made available when the terms of the contract have been met.

7. Communicate with parents (e.g., notes home, phone calls, etc.) in order to share information concerning the student's progress and so that they may reinforce the student at home for interacting with teachers at school.

8. Give the student the responsibility of acting as a teacher's assistant for an activity (e.g., holding up flash cards, demonstrating the use of equipment, etc.).

9. Give the student the responsibility of tutoring another student.

10. Be certain to greet or recognize the student as often as possible (e.g., hallways, cafeteria, welcome to class, acknowledge a job well done, call the student by name, etc.).

11. Request that the student be the leader of a small group activity if he/she possesses mastery of skills or an interest in that area.

12. Have the student run errands which will require interactions with teachers (e.g., delivering attendance reports, taking messages to other teachers, etc.).

13. Interact with the student from a distance, gradually decreasing the distance until a close proximity is achieved.

14. Arrange for one-to-one, teacher/student interactions.

15. Use an alternative form of communication (e.g., puppet).

16. Provide the student with many social and academic successes.

17. Create situations in which the student must interact (e.g., handing completed assignments to the teacher, delivering a message to a teacher, etc.).

18. Identify a peer to act as a model for the student to imitate appropriate interactions with teachers.

19. Encourage the student to question any directions, explanations, instructions he/she does not understand.

20. Evaluate the appropriateness of expecting the student to communicate his/her needs to teachers.

21. Maintain mobility throughout the classroom in order to determine the student's needs.

22. Offer the student assistance frequently throughout the day.

23. Make certain that directions, explanations, and instructions are delivered on the student's ability level.

24. Structure the environment in order that the student is not required to communicate all needs to teachers (e.g., make certain the student's tasks are on his/her ability level, instructions are clear, and maintain frequent interactions with the student in order to ensure his/her success).

25. In order to detect the student's needs, communicate with the student as often as opportunities permit.

26. Demonstrate accepting behavior and interest in student's needs (e.g., willingness to help others, making criticisms constructive and positive, demonstrating confidentiality in personal matters, etc.).

27. Communicate to the student that he/she is a worthwhile individual.

28. Call on the student often in order to encourage communication.

29. Teach the student communication skills (e.g., hand raising, expressing needs in written and/or verbal form, etc.).

30. Encourage the student to communicate his/her needs to other personnel in the educational environment (e.g., school counselor, school psychologist, principal, etc.).

31. Communicate with parents, agencies, or appropriate parties in order to inform them of the problem, determine the cause of the problem, and solutions to the problem.

32. Recognize the student's attempts to communicate his/her needs (e.g., facial expressions, gestures, inactivity, self-depreciating comments, etc.).

33. Teach the student appropriate positive verbal greetings (e.g., "Hi." "How are you doing?" "Good to see you." "Haven't seen you in a long time." etc.).

34. Teach the student appropriate positive verbal requests (e.g., "Please pass the paper." "May I be excused?" "Will you please help me?" etc.).

35. Teach the student appropriate positive ways to verbally indicate disagreement (e.g., "Excuse me." "I'm sorry, but I don't think that's correct." etc.).

36. Model for the student appropriate positive verbal greetings, requests, and indications of disagreement.

37. Teach the student appropriate verbalization for problem resolution as an alternative (e.g., "Let's talk about it." "Let's compromise." "Let's see what would be fair for both of us." etc.).

38. Require the student to practice positive verbal communications with an identified number of teachers throughout the school day.

39. Make certain that all teachers interact with the student on a regular basis and use positive verbal communication when speaking to him/her.

40. Require the student to interact with several adults (e.g., run errands, request materials, etc.) in order to increase the opportunities for communication with adults.

41. Teach the student appropriate ways to communicate to teachers that a problem exists (e.g., "I do not understand the directions." "I was unable to complete my assignment." "I cannot find all of my materials." etc.).

42. Identify teachers with whom the student most often interacts in order to make certain that they model appropriate verbal communications for the student.

43. Teach the student skills in maintaining positive conversations with teachers (e.g., asking questions, listening while the other person speaks, making eye contact, head nodding, making comments which relate to what the other person has said, etc.).

44. Help the student become aware of his/her tone of voice when greeting, requesting, and/or disagreeing by calling attention to inappropriate voice inflections for the situation.

45. Determine an individual(s) in the school environment with whom the student would most want to converse (e.g., custodian, librarian, resource teacher, principal, older student, etc.). Allow the student to spend time with the individual(s) each day.

46. Spend some time each day talking with the student on an individual basis about his/her interests.

47. Pair the student with an outgoing student who engages in conversation with teachers on a frequent basis.

A Reminder: Do not "force" the student to interact with teachers.

25 Has little or no interaction with peers

1. Reinforce the student for interacting with peers: (a) give the student a tangible reward (e.g., classroom privileges, line leading, passing out materials, five minutes free time, etc.) or (b) give the student an intangible reward (e.g., praise, handshake, smile, etc.).

2. Speak with the student to explain: (a) what he/she is doing wrong (e.g., not talking, sharing, etc.) and (b) what he/she should be doing (e.g., talking, sharing, etc.).

3. Establish classroom rules (e.g., work on-task, work quietly, remain in your seat, finish task, meet task expectations). Reiterate rules often and reinforce students for following rules.

4. Reinforce those students in the classroom who interact appropriately with peers.

5. Reinforce the student for interacting with peers based on the length of time he/she can be successful. Gradually increase the length of time required for reinforcement as the student demonstrates success.

6. Write a contract with the student specifying what behavior is expected (e.g., sitting near another student, talking to another student, etc.) and what reinforcement will be made available when the terms of the contract have been met.

7. Communicate with parents (e.g., notes home, phone calls, etc.) in order to share information concerning the student's progress and so that they may reinforce the student at home for interacting with peers at school.

8. Assign a peer to sit/work directly with the student (e.g., in different settings or activities such as art, music, P.E., on the bus, tutoring, group projects, running errands in the building, recess, etc.). Gradually increase group size when the student has become comfortable working with another student.

9. Encourage or reward others for interacting with the student.

10. Give the student the responsibility of acting as a teacher's aide for an activity (e.g., holding up flash cards, demonstrating the use of equipment, etc.).

11. Give the student the responsibility of tutoring a peer.

12. Ask the student to choose a peer to work with on a specific assignment. If the student has difficulty choosing someone, determine the student's preference by other means such as a class survey.

13. Request that the student be the leader of a small group activity if he/she possesses mastery of skills or an interest in that area.

14. Try various groupings to determine the situation in which the student is most comfortable.

15. Assess the appropriateness of the social setting in relation to the student's ability to interact with peers.

16. Provide the student with many social and academic successes.

17. Assign the student to work with one or two peers on a long-term project (e.g., mural, bulletin board, report, etc.).

18. Create situations in which the student must interact (e.g., returning completed assignments to students, proofreading other students' work, etc.).

19. Have the student work with a peer who is younger or smaller (e.g., choose a peer who would be the least threatening).

20. Establish social rules (e.g., share materials, use a quiet voice in the building, walk indoors, use care in handling materials). Reiterate rules often and reinforce students for following rules.

21. Identify a peer to act as a model for the student to imitate appropriate interactions with peers.

22. Determine the peer(s) the student would most prefer to interact with and attempt to facilitate the interaction.

23. Assign an outgoing, nonthreatening peer to help the student interact more appropriately with peers.

24. Structure the environment so that the student has many opportunities to interact with peers.

25. Have the student run errands with a peer in order to facilitate interaction.

26. Conduct a sociometric activity with the class in order to determine the peer who would most prefer to interact with the student.

27. Make certain that the student understands that interacting with a peer is contingent upon appropriate interactions.

28. Teach the student appropriate ways to interact with another student (e.g., how to greet another student, suggest activities, share materials, problem solve, take turns, converse, etc.).

29. Supervise interaction closely in order that the peer with whom the student interacts does not stimulate the student's inappropriate behavior.

30. Make certain that the interaction is not so stimulating as to make successful interactions with another student difficult.

31. Assign an older peer with desirable social skills to interact with the student (e.g., play area, cafeteria, hallways, etc.).

32. Involve the student in extracurricular activities in order to encourage interactions with peer(s).

33. Reduce the emphasis on competition. Failure may cause the student to be reluctant to interact with peers.

34. Teach the student problem-solving skills in order that he/she may better deal with problems that may occur in interactions with another peer (e.g., talking, walking away, calling upon an arbitrator, compromising, etc.).

35. Find a peer with whom the student is most likely to be able to successfully interact (e.g., a student with similar interests, background, classes, behavior patterns, nonacademic schedule, etc.).

36. Structure the interaction according to the needs/abilities of the student (e.g., establish rules, limit the stimulation of the activity, limit the length of the activity, consider time of day, etc.).

37. Limit opportunities for interaction on those occasions in which the student is not likely to be successful (e.g., the student has experienced academic or social failure prior to the scheduled nonacademic activity).

38. Select nonacademic activities designed to enhance appropriate interaction of the student and a peer (e.g., board games, model building, coloring, etc.).

39. Through interviews with other students and observations, determine those characteristics of the student which interfere with successful interactions in order to determine skills or behaviors the student needs to develop for successful interaction.

40. Have the student practice appropriate interactions with the teacher(s).

41. Make certain that the student understands that failing to interact appropriately with a peer may result in removal from the activity and/or loss of participation in future activities.

42. Have the student interact with a peer for short periods of time in order to enhance success. Gradually increase the length of time as the student experiences success.

A Reminder: Do not "force" the student to interact with peers.

26 Makes inappropriate comments to other students

1. Reinforce the student for communicating in an appropriate manner with other students: (a) give the student a tangible reward (e.g., classroom privileges, line leading, passing out materials, five minutes free time, etc.) or (b) give the student an intangible reward (e.g., praise, handshake, smile, etc.).

2. Speak with the student to explain: (a) what he/she is doing wrong (e.g., calling names, arguing, cursing, etc.) and (b) what he/she should be doing (e.g., following rules, staying on-task, attending to his/her responsibilities, etc.).

3. Establish classroom rules (e.g., work on-task, work quietly, remain in your seat, finish task, meet task expectations). Reiterate rules often and reinforce students for following rules.

4. Reinforce those students in the classroom who communicate in an appropriate manner with other students.

5. Reinforce the student for communicating in an appropriate manner based on the length of time he/she can be successful. Gradually increase the length of time required for reinforcement as the student demonstrates success.

6. Remove the student from the group or activity until he/she can demonstrate appropriate behavior.

7. Write a contract with the student specifying what behavior is expected (e.g., communicating with other students in an appropriate manner) and what reinforcement will be made available when the terms of the contract have been met.

8. Communicate with parents (e.g., notes home, phone calls, etc.) in order to share information concerning the student's progress and so that they may reinforce the student at home for communicating in an appropriate manner with other students at school.

9. Evaluate the appropriateness of the task to determine: (a) if the task is too easy, (b) if the task is too difficult, and (c) if the length of time scheduled for the task is appropriate.

10. Teach the student appropriate ways to communicate displeasure, anger, etc.

11. Reduce the stimuli which contribute to the student's arguing, calling names, cursing, etc.

12. Provide the student with a quiet place to work. This is used as a means of reducing distracting stimuli and not as a form of punishment.

13. Provide the student with the opportunity to work with a peer who will be an appropriate model for interacting with other students.

14. Separate the student from the student(s) who is the primary stimulus or focus of the inappropriate comments.

15. Make certain the student understands the natural consequences of his/her inappropriate behavior (e.g., peers choose not to interact with him/her, exclusion from activities, etc.).

16. Require that the student identify alternative, appropriate behaviors following an instance of inappropriate comments (e.g., walking away from the peer, seeking teacher intervention, etc.).

17. Facilitate on-task behavior by providing a full schedule of daily events. Prevent lag time from occurring when the student would be free to engage in inappropriate behavior. (See Appendix for Schedule of Daily Events.)

18. Reduce the emphasis on competition. Repeated failure may result in anger and frustration which may take the form of inappropriate comments.

19. Emphasize individual success or progress rather than winning or "beating" other students.

20. Teach the student problem-solving skills: (a) identify the problem, (b) identify goals and objectives, (c) develop strategies, (d) develop a plan for action, and (e) carry out the plan.

21. Teach the student positive ways to interact with other students.

22. Make certain the student recognizes the inappropriateness of the inappropriate comments (e.g., call attention to the comments when they occur, record each instance, terminate the activity when the comment occurs, etc.).

23. Interact frequently with the student in order to monitor language used.

24. Maintain visibility to and from the student. The teacher should be able to see the student and the student should be able to see the teacher, making eye contact possible at all times.

25. Try various groupings in order to determine the situation in which the student is most comfortable.

26. Prevent the student from becoming overstimulated by an activity (e.g., monitor or supervise student behavior to limit overexcitement).

27. Prevent frustrating or anxiety producing situations from occurring (e.g., give the student tasks only on his/her ability level, give the student only the number of tasks that he/she can successfully manage in one sitting, reduce social interactions which stimulate the student's use of obscene language, etc.).

28. Reduce activities which might threaten the student (e.g., announcing test score ranges or test scores aloud, making students read aloud in class, emphasizing the success of a particular student or students, etc.).

29. Assess the appropriateness of the social situation in relation to the student's ability to function successfully.

30. Discuss with the student ways he/she could deal with unpleasant experiences which would typically cause him/her to use obscene language (e.g., talk to the teacher, go to a quiet area in the school, go see a counselor, etc.).

31. Make certain that positive reinforcement is not inadvertently given for inappropriate language (e.g., attending to the student only when he/she is using profane or obscene language).

32. Provide the student with a predetermined signal when he/she begins to use inappropriate language.

33. Deal with the student in a calm and deliberate manner rather than in a manner that would show evidence of shock and surprise.

34. Act as an appropriate role model by using appropriate language at all times (e.g., use appropriate language to convey disappointment, unhappiness, surprise, etc.).

35. Teach the student appropriate words or phrases to use in situations of anger, stress, frustration, etc.

36. Intervene early when the student begins to make inappropriate comments to other students in order to help prevent the student from losing control.

37. Make certain the student knows which inappropriate comments will not be tolerated at school.

38. Avoid discussion of topics that are sensitive to the student (e.g., divorce, death, unemployment, alcoholism, etc.).

27 Responds inappropriately to typical physical exchanges with other students

1. Reinforce the student for responding appropriately to typical physical exchanges with other students: (a) give the student a tangible reward (e.g., classroom privileges, line leading, passing out materials, five minutes free time, etc.) or (b) give the student an intangible reward (e.g., praise, handshake, smile, etc.).

2. Speak to the student to explain: (a) what he/she is doing wrong (e.g., hitting other students) and (b) what he/she should be doing (e.g., accepting typical physical exchanges in an appropriate manner).

3. Establish classroom rules (e.g., work on-task, work quietly, remain in your seat, finish task, meet task expectations). Reiterate rules often and reinforce students for following rules.

4. Reinforce those students in the classroom who respond appropriately to typical physical exchanges with other students.

5. Reinforce the student for responding appropriately to typical physical exchanges with other students based on the length of time he/she can be successful. Gradually increase the length of time required for reinforcement as the student demonstrates success.

6. Write a contract with the student specifying what behavior is expected (e.g., responding appropriately to typical physical exchanges with other students) and what reinforcement will be made available when the terms of the contract have been met.

7. Communicate with parents (e.g., notes home, phone calls, etc.) in order to share information concerning the student's progress and so that they may reinforce the student at home for responding appropriately to typical physical exchanges with other students at school.

8. Identify a peer to act as a model for the student to imitate the appropriate manner in which to respond to typical physical exchanges with other students.

9. Have the student question any directions, explanations, instructions he/she does not understand.

10. Make certain that peers are, in fact, accidently bumping, touching, or brushing against the student.

11. Have the student walk on the right hand side of the hallways, stairways, etc.

12. Have the student lead the line, walk beside the line, walk at the end of the line, etc., in order to avoid or reduce typical physical exchanges with other students.

13. Have the student avoid crowded areas. Gradually allow the student access to crowded areas as he/she develops the ability to deal with typical physical exchanges with other students in an appropriate manner.

14. Have the student practice dealing with typical physical exchanges in the classroom (e.g., peers bumping against his/her desk, bumping into peers when forming a line, etc.).

15. Seat the student away from classroom movement in order to reduce typical physical exchanges with other students.

16. Call attention to those times when the student bumps, touches, or brushes against other students. Point out and help the student realize that those physical exchanges were typical and accidental.

17. Have the student practice appropriate verbal exchanges which should be made when typical physical exchanges take place (e.g., "Excuse me." "I'm sorry." etc.).

18. Teach the student to avoid typical physical exchanges by giving peers room to pass, taking turns, watching the movement of others around him/her, etc.

19. Point out the natural consequences of failing to respond appropriately to typical physical exchanges with other students (e.g., other students will avoid him/her, loss of friendship, loss of opportunity to interact with peers, etc.).

20. Have a peer accompany the student in congested areas of the school in order to reduce typical physical exchanges and/or intercede should problems occur.

21. Practice role-playing in the classroom which involves typical physical exchanges (e.g., being bumped, touched, brushed against, etc.).

28 Responds inappropriately to friendly teasing

1. Reinforce the student for responding appropriately to friendly teasing: (a) give the student a tangible reward (e.g., classroom privileges, line leading, passing out materials, five minutes free time, etc.) or (b) give the student an intangible reward (e.g., praise, handshake, smile, etc.).

2. Speak to the student to explain: (a) what he/she is doing wrong (e.g., becoming upset, fighting, etc.) and (b) what he/she should be doing (e.g., laughing, joking in return, etc.).

3. Reinforce those students in the classroom who respond appropriately to friendly teasing.

4. Reinforce the student for responding appropriately to friendly teasing based on the number of times he/she can be successful. Gradually increase the number of times required for reinforcement as the student demonstrates success.

5. Write a contract with the student specifying what behavior is expected (e.g., laughing, joking in return, etc.) and what reinforcement will be made available when the terms of the contract have been met.

6. Communicate with parents (e.g., notes home, phone calls, etc.) in order to share information concerning the student's progress and so that they may reinforce the student at home for responding appropriately to friendly teasing at school.

7. Evaluate the appropriateness of the interaction to determine: (a) if the interaction is appropriate, (b) if the timing of the interaction is appropriate, and (c) if the student is able to handle the interaction successfully.

8. Identify a peer to act as a model to imitate appropriate response to friendly teasing.

9. Point out to the student, when he/she is teasing others, that no harm is meant and that the same holds true when others tease him/her.

10. Explain to the student that friendly teasing is a positive means by which people demonstrate that they like other people and enjoy their company.

11. Act as a model for friendly teasing by joking with the students and laughing when they tease you.

12. Help the student recognize the difference between friendly teasing and unkind, rude remarks in order that the student can accept and appreciate friendly teasing.

13. Help the student learn to deal with teasing which upsets him/her by having the student avoid the teasing, walk away from the situation, move to another location, etc.

14. Teach the student appropriate ways in which to respond to friendly teasing (e.g., laugh, joke in return, etc.).

15. Talk with the student about choosing his/her friends in order to assure that they are friendly and sincere.

16. Help the student understand that if he/she cannot accept friendly teasing then it would be best if he/she avoided the situation.

17. Discuss with the student's peers his/her sensitivity and difficulty in dealing with friendly teasing in order that they may adjust their behavior accordingly.

18. Discuss with the students topics which are not appropriate for friendly teasing (e.g., death, disease, handicaps, poverty, etc.).

29 Is not accepted by other students

1. Reinforce the student for appropriately interacting with other students: (a) give the student a tangible reward (e.g., classroom privileges, line leading, passing out materials, five minutes free time, etc.) or (b) give the student an intangible reward (e.g., praise, handshake, smile, etc.).

2. Speak with the student to explain that he/she may be trying too hard to fit in and should relax and allow friendships to develop naturally.

3. Establish classroom rules (e.g., work on-task, work quietly, remain in your seat, finish task, meet task expectations). Reiterate rules often and reinforce students for following rules.

4. Reinforce the student for demonstrating appropriate behavior based on the length of time he/she can be successful. Gradually increase the length of time required for reinforcement as the student demonstrates success.

5. Remove the student from the group or activity until he/she can demonstrate appropriate behavior and self-control.

6. Reinforce those students in the classroom who appropriately interact with the student.

7. Write a contract with the student specifying what behavior is expected (e.g., sitting near a student, talking to a student, etc.) and what reinforcement will be made available when the terms of the contract have been met.

8. Communicate with parents (e.g., notes home, phone calls, etc.) in order to share information concerning the student's progress and so that they may reinforce the student at home for appropriately interacting with other students at school.

9. Have the student be the leader of a small group activity if he/she possesses mastery of skills or an interest in that area.

10. Give the student the responsibility of tutoring a peer if he/she possesses the skills to be shared.

11. Provide the student with a predetermined signal (e.g., hand signal, verbal cue, etc.) when he/she begins to exhibit an inappropriate behavior(s).

12. Maintain maximum supervision of the student's interactions and gradually decrease the amount of supervision over time.

13. Try various groupings in order to determine the situation in which the student is most comfortable.

14. Modify or adjust situations that cause the student to demonstrate behaviors that are different or extreme.

15. Give the student responsibilities in group situations in order that peers may view him/her in a more positive way.

16. Assess the social situation in relation to the student's ability to function successfully (e.g., number of students in the group, behavior of students in the group, etc.).

17. Provide the student with as many academic and social successes as possible in order that peers may view him/her in a more positive way.

18. Encourage the student to further develop any ability or skill he/she may have in order that peers may view him/her in a more positive way.

19. Model appropriate social behavior for the student at all times.

20. Help the student to identify his/her inappropriate behaviors and teach him/her ways to change those behaviors.

21. Reduce the emphasis on competition. Social interactions may be inhibited if the student's abilities are constantly made public and compared to others.

22. Teach the student to be satisfied with his/her own best effort and not insist on perfection.

23. Encourage and assist the student in joining extracurricular activities, clubs, etc.

24. Help the student develop a friendship by pairing him/her with another student for activities. Gradually increase the number of students in the group as the student is socially successful.

30 Bothers other students who are trying to work, listen, etc.

1. Reinforce the student for demonstrating appropriate behavior: (a) give the student a tangible reward (e.g., classroom privileges, line leading, passing out materials, five minutes free time, etc.) or (b) give the student an intangible reward (e.g., praise, handshake, smile, etc.).

2. Speak to the student to explain: (a) what he/she is doing wrong (e.g., bothering other students who are trying to work, listen, etc.) and (b) what he/she should be doing (e.g., demonstrating appropriate behavior).

3. Establish classroom rules (e.g., work on-task, work quietly, remain in your seat, finish task, meet task expectations). Reiterate rules often and reinforce students for following rules.

4. Reinforce those students in the classroom who demonstrate appropriate behavior.

5. Reinforce the student for demonstrating appropriate behavior based on the length of time he/she can be successful. Gradually increase the length of time required for reinforcement as the student demonstrates success.

6. Write a contract with the student specifying what behavior is expected (e.g., demonstrating appropriate behavior) and what reinforcement will be made available when the terms of the contract have been met.

7. Communicate with parents (e.g., notes home, phone calls, etc.) in order to share information concerning the student's progress and so that they may reinforce the student at home for demonstrating appropriate behavior at school.

8. Evaluate the appropriateness of the task to determine: (a) if the task is too easy, (b) if the task is too difficult, and (c) if the length of time scheduled to complete the task is appropriate.

9. Identify a peer to act as a model for the student to imitate appropriate behavior.

10. Have the student question any directions, explanations, instructions he/she does not understand.

11. Reinforce those students in the classroom who demonstrate on-task behavior.

12. Reduce distracting stimuli (e.g., place the student on the front row, provide a carrel or "office" away from distractions, etc.). This is used as a means of reducing distracting stimuli and not as a form of punishment.

13. Interact frequently with the student in order to maintain his/her involvement in the activity (e.g., ask the student questions, ask the student's opinion, stand close to the student, seat the student near the teacher's desk, etc.).

14. Maintain visibility to and from the student. The teacher should be able to see the student and the student should be able to see the teacher, making eye contact possible at all times.

15. Assess the degree of task difficulty in relation to the student's ability to perform the task successfully.

16. Provide a full schedule of activities. Prevent lag time from occurring when the student can bother other students.

17. Remove the student from the group or activity until he/she can demonstrate appropriate behavior and self-control.

18. Teach the student appropriate ways to communicate his/her needs to others (e.g., waiting a turn, raising his/her hand, etc.).

19. Provide the student with enjoyable activities to perform when he/she completes a task early.

20. Seat the student near the teacher.

21. Provide the student with frequent opportunities to participate, share, etc.

22. Provide students with frequent opportunities to interact with one another (e.g., before and after school, between activities, etc.).

23. Seat the student away from those students he/she is most likely to bother.

31 Responds inappropriately to others' attempts to be friendly, complimentary, sympathetic, etc.

1. Reinforce the student for responding appropriately to others' attempts to be friendly, complimentary, sympathetic, etc.: (a) give the student a tangible reward (e.g., classroom privileges, line leading, passing out materials, five minutes free time, etc.) or (b) give the student an intangible reward (e.g., praise, handshake, smile, etc.).

2. Reinforce other students for responding appropriately to interactions with students or teachers.

3. Write a contract stating appropriate ways to respond to others and identify what reinforcement will be made available when the terms of the contract have been met.

4. Communicate with parents (e.g., notes home, phone calls, etc.) in order to share information concerning the student's progress and so that they may reinforce the student at home for responding appropriately to others' attempts to be friendly, complimentary, sympathetic, etc., at school.

5. Speak with the student to explain: (a) what he/she is doing wrong (e.g., using inappropriate language, responding negatively, calling names, making inappropriate gestures, etc.) and (b) what he/she should be doing (e.g., being positive in response to others).

6. Try various groupings in order to determine the situation in which the student is most comfortable.

7. Assign a peer to sit/work directly with the student (e.g., in different settings or activities such as art, music, P.E., on the bus, tutoring, group projects, running errands in the building, recess, etc.). Gradually increase group size when the student has become comfortable working with one other student.

8. Provide the student with positive feedback which indicates he/she is important.

9. Provide the student with many social and academic successes.

10. Provide opportunities for appropriate interactions within the classroom (e.g., peer models engaged in appropriate interactions).

11. Assess the appropriateness of the social situation in relation to the student's ability to be successful.

12. Reduce stimuli which contribute to the student's inappropriate responses to others' attempts to interact.

13. Intervene early to prevent the student from losing self-control.

14. Limit interactions with the peer(s) who is the primary focus of the student's inappropriate responses.

15. Respect the student's right to a reasonable amount of privacy.

16. Allow the student to be a member of a group without requiring active participation.

17. Teach the student social interaction skills (e.g., ways in which to appropriately respond to others' attempts to be friendly, complimentary, sympathetic, etc.).

18. Help the student develop social awareness (e.g., people may be embarrassed by what you say, feelings can be hurt by comments, tact is the best policy, remember interactions which have made you feel good and treat others in the same manner, etc.).

32 Does not share possessions or materials

1. Reinforce the student for sharing: (a) give the student a tangible reward (e.g., classroom privileges, line leading, passing out materials, five minutes free time, etc.) or (b) give the student an intangible reward (e.g., praise, handshake, smile, etc.).

2. Speak with the student to explain: (a) what he/she is doing wrong (e.g., failing to give others opportunities to use things) and (b) what he/she should be doing (e.g., sharing materials).

3. Reinforce those students in the classroom who share.

4. Write a contract with the student specifying what behavior is expected (e.g., sharing) and what reinforcement will be made available when the terms of the contract have been met.

5. Communicate with parents (e.g., notes home, phone calls, etc.) in order to share information concerning the student's progress and so that they may reinforce the student at home for sharing at school.

6. Assess the appropriateness of the task or social situation in relation to the student's ability to perform successfully.

7. Encourage sharing by giving assignments which require sharing to complete the activity (e.g., making murals, bulletin boards, maps, art projects, etc.).

8. Encourage peers to share with the student.

9. Teach the student the concept of sharing by having the student borrow from others or loan things to others.

10. Have the student work directly with a peer in order to model sharing. Gradually increase the group size as the student demonstrates success.

11. Reduce competitiveness in the school environment (e.g., avoid situations where refusing to share contributes to winning, situations where winning or "beating" someone else becomes the primary objective of a game, activity, or academic exercise, etc.).

12. Create and reinforce activities (e.g., school bulletin board, class project, bake sale, etc.) in which students work together for a common goal rather than individual success or recognition. Point out that larger accomplishments are realized through group effort rather than by individuals.

13. Put the student in charge of communal school items (e.g., rulers, pencils, crayons, etc.) in order that he/she may experience sharing.

14. Allow the student to have many turns and enough materials to satisfy his/her immediate needs. Gradually require sharing and taking turns as the student demonstrates success.

15. Provide special activities for the entire class at the end of the day that are contingent upon sharing throughout the day.

16. Structure the classroom environment in such a way as to take advantage of natural sharing opportunities (e.g., allowing more group activities, pointing out natural consequences when a student shares, etc.).

17. Capitalize on opportunities to share and help (e.g., when there is a spill, assign students different responsibilities for cleaning it up; when a new student enters the classroom, assign students responsibilities for his/her orientation, etc.).

18. Discourage students from bringing personal possessions to school which others desire. Encourage the use of communal school property.

19. Provide enough materials, activities, etc., in order that sharing will not always be necessary.

20. Model sharing behavior by allowing students to use your materials contingent upon return of the items.

21. Provide the student with many opportunities to both borrow and lend in order to help him/her learn the concept of sharing.

22. Make certain that every student gets to use materials, take a turn, etc., and that there is no opportunity for selfishness.

23. Point out to the student the natural rewards of sharing (e.g., personal satisfaction, friendships, having people share in return, etc.).

24. Make certain that those students who are willing to share are not taken advantage of by their peers.

25. Make certain that other students are sharing with the student in order that a reciprocal relationship can be achieved.

26. Maintain a realistic level of expectation for sharing.

27. Practice sharing by having each student work with a particular school material for an established length of time. At the end of each time period (e.g., 10 minutes) have each student pass his/her material to another student.

28. Provide students adequate time to complete activities requiring sharing in order that the selfish use of school materials is not necessary for success. Students are less likely to share if sharing reduces the likelihood of finishing on time, being successful, etc.

29. Reduce the demands for the student to make verbal exchanges when sharing (e.g., shyness may inhibit sharing if the student is required to verbally communicate with others). Materials may be placed in a central location when not in use so that they may be obtained by the students. This will enhance the aspect of sharing which makes materials available to others when not in use.

30. Establish rules for sharing school materials (e.g., ask for materials you wish to use, exchange materials carefully, return materials when not in use, offer to share materials with others, take care of shared materials, call attention to materials that need repair). Reiterate rules often and reinforce students for following rules.

33 Does not allow others to take their turns, participate in activities or games, etc.

1. Reinforce the student for taking turns: (a) give the student a tangible reward (e.g., classroom privileges, line leading, passing out materials, five minutes free time, etc.) or (b) give the student an intangible reward (e.g., praise, handshake, smile, etc.).

2. Speak with the student to explain: (a) what he/she is doing wrong (e.g., failing to give others opportunities to have a turn) and (b) what he/she should be doing (e.g., allowing others to have a turn).

3. Reinforce those students in the classroom who take turns.

4. Write a contract with the student specifying what behavior is expected (e.g., taking turns) and what reinforcement will be made available when the terms of the contract have been met.

5. Communicate with the parents (e.g., notes home, phone calls, etc.) in order to share information concerning the student's progress and so that they may reinforce the student at home for taking turns at school.

6. Assess the appropriateness of the task or social situation in relation to the student's ability to perform successfully.

7. Encourage group participation by giving students assignments which require working together to complete the activity (e.g., making murals, bulletin boards, maps, art projects, etc.).

8. Encourage peers to take turns with the student.

9. Have the student work directly with a peer in order to model taking turns and gradually increase group size over time.

10. Reduce competitiveness in the school environment (e.g., avoid situations where refusing to take turns contributes to winning; situations where winning or "beating" someone else becomes the primary objective of a game, activity, or academic exercise, etc.).

11. Create and reinforce activities (e.g., school bulletin board, class project, bake sale, etc.) in which students work together for a common goal rather than individual success or recognition. Point out that larger accomplishments are realized through group effort rather than by individuals.

12. Allow the student to have many turns and enough materials to satisfy immediate needs and gradually require sharing and taking turns.

13. Provide special activities for the entire class at the end of the day which are contingent upon taking turns throughout the day.

14. Structure the classroom environment in such a way as to take advantage of natural opportunities to take turns (e.g., allowing more group activities, point out natural consequences when a student takes turns, etc.).

15. Capitalize on opportunities to work together (e.g., when there is a spill, assign students different responsibilities for cleaning it up; when a new student enters the classroom, assign different students responsibilities for orientation, etc.).

16. Discourage students from bringing personal possessions to school which others desire. Encourage the use of communal school property.

17. Require the student to practice taking turns if he/she is unable to willingly do so.

18. Provide enough materials, activities, etc., in order that taking turns will not always be necessary.

19. Provide the student with many opportunities to take turns in order to help him/her learn the concept of taking turns.

20. Make certain that every student gets to use materials, take a turn, etc., and that there is no opportunity for selfishness.

21. Point out to the student the natural rewards of taking turns (e.g., personal satisfaction, friendships, companionship, etc.).

22. Make certain that those students who are willing to take turns are not taken advantage of by their peers.

23. Make certain that other students are taking turns with the student in order that a reciprocal relationship can be expected.

24. Maintain a realistic level of expectation for taking turns.

25. Have the student engage in an activity with one peer and gradually increase the size of the group as the student demonstrates success.

26. Determine the peers with whom the student would most prefer to interact and attempt to facilitate the interaction.

27. Assign an outgoing, nonthreatening peer to interact with the student.

28. Assign the student to interact with younger peers.

29. Assign the student to engage in activities in which he/she is likely to interact successfully with peers.

30. Make certain that the student understands that interacting with peers is contingent upon appropriate behavior.

31. Teach the student appropriate ways to interact with peers in group games (e.g., suggest activities, share materials, problem solve, take turns, follow game rules, etc.).

32. Supervise activities closely in order that the peer(s) with whom the student interacts does not stimulate his/her inappropriate behavior.

33. Make certain that activities are not so stimulating as to make successful interactions with peers difficult.

34. Involve the student in extracurricular activities in order to encourage appropriate interaction with peers.

35. Find the peer with whom the student is most likely to be able to successfully interact (e.g., a student with similar interests, background, classes, similar behavior patterns, nonacademic schedule, etc.).

36. Make certain, beforehand, that the student is able to successfully engage in the activity (e.g., the student understands the rules, the student is familiar with the game, the student will be compatible with the other students playing the game, etc.).

37. Make certain that the student understands that failing to interact appropriately with peers during activities may result in termination of the game and/or loss of future opportunities to engage in activities.

38. Establish a set of standard behavior rules for group games (e.g., follow rules of the game, take turns, make positive comments, work as a team member, be a good sport). Reiterate rules often and reinforce students for following the rules.

39. Design activities in which each student takes short turns. Increase the length of each student's turn as the student demonstrates success at taking turns.

40. Allow natural consequences to occur when the student fails to take turns (e.g., other students will not want to interact with him/her, other students will not be willing to take turns, etc.).

34 Makes inappropriate comments or unnecessary noises in the classroom

1. Reinforce the student for making appropriate comments in the classroom: (a) give the student a tangible reward (e.g., classroom privileges, line leading, passing out materials, five minutes free time, etc.) or (b) give the student an intangible reward (e.g., praise, handshake, smile, etc.).

2. Speak with the student to explain: (a) what he/she is doing wrong (e.g., making inappropriate comments or unnecessary noises) and (b) what he/she should be doing (e.g., waiting until it is appropriate to speak, thinking of comments which relate to the situation, etc).

3. Establish classroom rules (e.g., work on-task, work quietly, remain in your seat, finish task, meet task expectations). Reiterate rules often and reinforce students for following rules.

4. Reinforce those students in the classroom who make appropriate comments.

5. Reinforce the student for making appropriate comments based on the length of time he/she can be successful. Gradually increase the length of time required for reinforcement as the student demonstrates success.

6. Remove the student from the group or activity until he/she can demonstrate appropriate behavior and self-control.

7. Write a contract with the student specifying what behavior is expected (e.g., making appropriate comments) and what reinforcement will be made available when the terms of the contract have been met.

8. Communicate with the parents (e.g., notes home, phone calls, etc.) in order to share information concerning the student's progress and so that they may reinforce the student at home for making appropriate comments at school.

9. Evaluate the appropriateness of the task to determine if: (a) the task is too easy, (b) the task is too difficult, and (c) the length of time scheduled for the task is appropriate.

10. Make certain that reinforcement is not inadvertently given for inappropriate behavior (e.g., making inappropriate comments or unnecessary noises).

11. Give adequate opportunities to respond (i.e., enthusiastic students need many opportunities to contribute).

12. Have the student be the leader of a small group activity if he/she possesses mastery of skills or an interest in that area.

13. Provide the student with a predetermined signal if he/she begins to make inappropriate comments of unnecessary noises.

14. Explain to the student that he/she may be trying too hard to fit in and he/she should relax and make more appropriate comments.

15. Structure the environment in such a way as to limit opportunities for inappropriate behaviors (e.g., keep the student engaged in activities, have the student seated near the teacher, etc.).

16. Give the student responsibilities in the classroom (e.g., running errands, opportunities to help the teacher, etc.).

17. Reduce activities which might threaten the student (e.g., announcing test score ranges or test scores aloud, making students read aloud in class, emphasizing the success of a particular student or students, etc.).

18. Provide the student with many social and academic successes.

19. Make the necessary adjustments in the environment to prevent the student from experiencing stress, frustration or anger (e.g., reduce peer pressure, academic failure, teasing, etc.).

20. Maintain visibility to and from the student. The teacher should be able to see the student and the student should be able to see the teacher, making eye contact possible at all times.

21. Interact frequently with the student to reduce the need to make inappropriate comments or unnecessary noises.

22. Assess the appropriateness of the social situation in relation to the student's ability to function successfully.

23. Try various groupings in order to determine the situation in which the student is most comfortable.

24. Reinforce the student for raising his/her hand in order to be recognized.

25. Call on the student when he/she is most likely to be able to respond correctly.

26. Teach the student to recognize and make appropriate comments (e.g., comments within the context of the situation, comments that are a follow-up to what has just been said, etc.).

27. Have the student work in small groups in which he/she would have frequent opportunities to speak. Gradually increase the size of the group as the student learns to wait longer for his/her turn to speak.

28. Make certain that the student's feelings are considered when it is necessary to deal with his/her inappropriate comments (i.e., handle comments in such as way as not to diminish the student's enthusiasm for participation).

29. Encourage the student to model the behavior of peers who are successful.

30. Help the student improve concentration skills (e.g., listening to the speaker, taking notes, preparing comments in advance, making comments in the appropriate context, etc.).

31. Have the student question any directions, explanations, instructions he/she does not understand.

32. Deliver directions, explanations, and instructions in a clear and concise manner in order to reduce the student's need to ask questions.

33. Have the student practice waiting his/her turn to speak for short periods of time. Gradually increase the length of time required for reinforcement as the student demonstrates success.

34. Explain to the student the reasons why making inappropriate comments and unnecessary noise is inappropriate (e.g., impolite, hurt others' feelings, etc.).

35. Attempt to provide equal attention to all students in the classroom.

36. Make the student aware of the number of times he/she makes inappropriate comments and unnecessary noise.

35 Has unexcused absences

1. Reinforce the student for coming to school/class: (a) give the student a tangible reward (e.g., classroom privileges, line leading, passing out materials, five minutes free time, etc.) or (b) give the student an intangible reward (e.g., praise, handshake, smile, etc.).

2. Speak with the student to explain: (a) what he/she is doing wrong (e.g., absent from school/class) and (b) what he/she should be doing (e.g., be in attendance).

3. Establish classroom rules (e.g., work on-task, work quietly, remain in your seat, finish task, meet task expectations). Reiterate rules often and reinforce students for following rules.

4. Reinforce those students who come to school/class.

5. Write a contract with the student specifying what behavior is expected (e.g., being in attendance) and what reinforcement will be made available when the terms of the contract have been met.

6. Communicate with the parents (e.g., notes, home, phone calls, etc.) in order to share information concerning the student's progress and so that they may reinforce the student at home for coming to school and class.

7. Evaluate the appropriateness of the task to determine if: (a) the task is too easy, (b) the task is too difficult, and (c) the length of time scheduled for the task in appropriate.

8. Communicate with the parents, agencies, or appropriate parties in order to inform them of the problem, determine the cause of the problem, and consider possible solutions to the problem.

9. Record or chart attendance with the student.

10. Begin the day or class with a success-oriented activity which is likely to be enjoyable for the student.

11. Give the student a preferred responsibility to be performed at the beginning of each day or each class.

12. Reinforce the student for getting on the bus or leaving home on time.

13. Assess the degree of task difficulty in comparison with the student's ability to perform the task.

14. Provide the student with as many high-interest activities as possible.

15. Involve the student in extra-curricular activities.

16. Provide the student with many social and academic successes.

17. Provide the student with academic activities in the most attractive and interesting manner possible.

18. Require the student's attendance to be documented by his/her teachers (e.g., have teachers sign an attendance card).

19. Interact often with the student in a positive manner throughout the day.

20. Collect anecdotal information on the student's absent behavior. If a trend can be determined, remove the student from the situation, modify the situation, or help the student develop the skills to be more successful in the situation.

21. Have the parent bring the student to school.

22. Have a responsible peer walk to school/class with the student.

23. Establish a time for the student to leave his/her home in the morning.

24. Require that time spent away from school/class be made up at recess, lunch, or after school.

25. Have the student document his/her attendance at the end of each school day (e.g., have the student maintain a record of attendance in the special education classroom, office, etc., and fill in the data at the end of each day).

26. Schedule time in the special education resource room at the beginning, middle, and end of the school day in order to support attendance.

27. Provide the student with the option of going to the special education resource room when he/she would otherwise not attend school and work toward a goal of increased attendance in regular classes.

28. Make certain the student is appropriately placed in those classes in which he/she is enrolled (e.g., the class is not too difficult).

29. Reduce the emphasis on competition. Repeated failure may cause the student to remove himself/herself from the competition by not attending school or classes.

30. Help the student develop friendships which may encourage his/her attendance at school/class.

36 Has unexcused tardiness

1. Reinforce the student for coming to an activity at the specified time: (a) give the student a tangible reward (e.g., classroom privileges, line leading, passing out materials, five minutes free time, etc.) or (b) give the student an intangible reward (e.g., praise, handshake, smile, etc.).

2. Speak to the student to explain: (a) what he/she is doing wrong (e.g., coming late to an activity) and (b) what he/she should be doing (e.g., coming to an activity at the specified time).

3. Establish classroom rules (e.g., come to class on time, work on-task, work quietly, remain in your seat, finish task, meet task expectations). Reiterate rules often and reinforce students for following rules.

4. Reinforce those students in the classroom who come to an activity at the specified time.

5. Reinforce the student for coming to an activity within a given period of time. Gradually reduce the length of time the student has to come to an activity as he/she becomes more successful at being punctual.

6. Write a contract with the student specifying what behavior is expected (e.g., coming to school on time) and what reinforcement will be made available when the terms of the contract have been met.

7. Communicate with parents (e.g., notes home, phone calls, etc.) in order to share information concerning the student's progress and so that they may reinforce the student at home for coming to activities at the specified time at school.

8. Evaluate the appropriateness of the task to determine if: (a) the task is too difficult, and (b) the length of time scheduled to complete the task is appropriate.

9. Identify a peer to act as a model for the student to imitate arriving at an activity at the specified time.

10. Provide the student with a schedule of daily events in order that he/she will know which activities to attend and at what times. (See Appendix for Schedule of Daily Events.)

11. Make certain that the student's daily schedule follows an established routine.

12. Limit the number of interruptions in the student's schedule.

13. Make certain the student has adequate time to get to an activity.

14. Make certain that the student knows how to get from one activity to another.

15. Use a timer to help the student get to activities at specified times.

16. Give the student a specific responsibility to be performed at the beginning of each activity in order to encourage him/her to be on time.

17. Provide the student with verbal cues when it is time to change activities (e.g., "It is time for the red group to have reading." "Now it is time for the red group to put away materials and move to the next activity." etc.).

18. Determine why the student is not arriving at activities at the specified times.

19. Ask the student why he/she is not arriving at activities at the specified times. The student may have the most accurate perception as to why he/she is not arriving at activities at the specified times.

20. Help the student understand that it is permissible to leave work unfinished and return to it at a later time.

21. Determine if there are aspects of activities that the student dislikes. Remove, reduce, or modify the unpleasant aspects of activities in order to encourage the student to be on time for and participate in activities.

22. Make the student responsible for time missed (i.e., if the student misses five minutes of an activity he/she must make the time up during recess, lunch, or other desired activities).

23. Have a peer accompany the student to activities.

24. Make certain that the student is successful at school-related activities. The student will be more likely to be on time for activities in which he/she experiences success.

25. Make the student a leader of the activity or group.

26. Make certain that other students do not make it unpleasant for the student to attend activities.

27. Make certain the student has all necessary materials for activities.

28. Record or chart promptness with the student.

29. Begin activities with a task that is highly reinforcing to the student.

30. Give the student a preferred responsibility to be performed at the beginning of each activity.

31. Assess the appropriateness of the degree of difficulty of the task in comparison with the student's ability to perform the task successfully.

32. Provide the student with as many high interest activities as possible.

33. Provide the student with many social and academic successes.

34. Provide the student academic activities in the most attractive manner possible.

35. Give the student a schedule of daily events that must be signed by each teacher in order to document his/her promptness. (See Appendix for Schedule of Daily Events.)

36. Collect anecdotal information on the student's behavior. If a trend can be determined, remove the student from the situation and/or help the student be prompt.

37. Have the student document his/her attendance at the end of each activity.

38. Make certain the student is appropriately placed according to his/her ability level in those classes in which he/she is enrolled.

39. Reduce the emphasis on competition. Repeated failure may cause the student to avoid being on time for activities which are competitive.

40. Involve the student in extracurricular activities.

41. Interact often with the student in a positive manner throughout the day.

37 Makes unnecessary physical contact with others

1. Reinforce the student for respecting the norms of physical proximity: (a) give the student a tangible reward (e.g., classroom privileges, line leading, passing out materials, five minutes free time, etc.) or (b) give the student an intangible reward (e.g., praise, handshake, smile, etc.).

2. Speak with the student to explain: (a) what he/she is doing wrong (e.g., touching, handholding, etc.) and (b) what he/she should be doing (e.g., talking, exchanging greetings, etc.). Discuss appropriate ways to seek attention.

3. Establish classroom rules (e.g., work on-task, work quietly, remain in your seat, finish task, meet task expectations). Reiterate rules often and reinforce students for following rules.

4. Reinforce those students in the classroom who interact appropriately with other students or teachers.

5. Reinforce the student for respecting the norms of physical proximity based on the length of time he/she can be successful. Gradually increase the length of time required for reinforcement as the student demonstrates success.

6. Remove the student from the group or activity until he/she can demonstrate appropriate behavior and self-control.

7. Write a contract with the student specifying what behavior is expected (e.g., shaking hands rather than hugging) and what reinforcement will be made available when the terms of the contract have been met.

8. Communicate with parents (e.g., notes home, phone calls, etc.) in order to share information concerning the student's progress and so that they may reinforce the student at home for respecting the norms of physical proximity at school.

9. Separate the student from the person who is the primary focus of the student's attempts to gain frequent physical contact.

10. Reduce the opportunity for the student to engage in inappropriate physical contact (e.g., stand an appropriate distance from the student when interacting).

11. Model socially acceptable physical contact for the student (e.g., handshake, pat on the back, etc.).

12. Provide the student with many social and academic successes.

13. Indicate to the student that public displays of frequent physical contact are inappropriate.

14. Work directly with the student only in the presence of others.

15. Provide the student with verbal recognition and reinforcement for social and academic successes.

16. Give the student your full attention when communicating with him/her in order to prevent the student's need for physical contact.

17. Provide the student with social interaction in place of physical interaction (e.g., call the student by name, speak to the student, praise, congratulate, etc.).

18. Provide the student with high-interest activities (e.g., academic activities which are inherently interesting, activities during free time, etc.).

19. Try various groupings to find a situation in which the student's need for physical attention can be satisfied by socially acceptable interactions (e.g., handholding while dancing as an extracurricular activity, a hug for an accomplishment, handshake or "high five" in sports, etc.).

20. Acknowledge the student when he/she seeks attention verbally instead of making it necessary for the student to gain attention through physical contact.

21. Allow natural consequences to occur as a result of the student's inappropriate behavior (e.g., excessive physical contact may cause people to stay away from the student or may result in pushing, shoving, etc.).

22. Make certain that reinforcement is not inadvertently given for inappropriate behavior (e.g., attending to the student only when he/she makes unnecessary physical contact).

23. Prevent the student from becoming overstimulated by an activity (e.g., monitor or supervise student behavior to limit overexcitement in physical activities, games, parties, etc.).

24. Teach the student appropriate ways to interact with others (e.g., verbal and physical introductions, interactions, etc.).

25. Avoid inadvertently stimulating the student's unnecessary physical contact (e.g., attire, language used, physical proximity, etc.).

38 Blames other persons or materials to avoid taking responsibility for his/her mistakes

1. Reinforce the student for accepting responsibility for his/her own behavior: (a) give the student a tangible reward (e.g., classroom privileges, line leading, passing out materials, five minutes free time, etc.) or (b) give the student an intangible reward (e.g., praise, handshake, smile, etc.).

2. Speak with the student to explain: (a) what he/she is doing wrong (e.g., failing to take responsibility for his/her behavior, blaming other persons or materials, etc.) and (b) what he/she should be doing (e.g., accepting responsibility for his/her own behavior, accepting outcomes, etc.).

3. Establish classroom rules (e.g., work on-task, work quietly, remain in your seat, finish task, meet task expectations). Reiterate rules often and reinforce students for following rules.

4. Reinforce those students in the classroom who accept responsibility for their own behavior.

5. Reinforce the student for accepting responsibility for his/her own behavior based on the length of time he/she can be successful. Gradually increase the length of time required for reinforcement as the student demonstrates success.

6. Remove the student from the group or activity until he/she can accept responsibility for his/her behavior.

7. Write a contract with the student specifying what behavior is expected (e.g., accepting responsibility for his/her own mistakes) and what reinforcement will be made available when the terms of the contract have been met.

8. Communicate with parents (e.g., notes home, phone calls, etc.) in order to share information concerning the student's progress and so that they may reinforce the student at home for accepting responsibility for his/her behavior at school.

9. Evaluate the appropriateness of the task to determine: (a) if the task is too easy, (b) if the task is too difficult, and (c) if the length of the time scheduled for the task is appropriate.

10. Explain to the student that he/she should be satisfied with his/her own best effort rather than perfection.

11. Structure the environment in order to reduce peers from interfering with the student (e.g., remove the opportunity to blame others).

12. Teach the student problem-solving skills: (a) identify the problem, (b) identify goals and objectives, (c) develop strategies, (d) develop a plan of action, and (e) carry out the plan.

13. Provide the student with as many social and academic successes as possible.

14. Make the necessary adjustments in the environment to prevent the student from experiencing stress, frustration, anger, etc.

15. Provide the student with positive feedback which indicates he/she is successful, competent, important, valuable, etc.

16. Make certain that excuses are not accepted in place of meeting responsibility.

17. Make certain that all materials are appropriate and in good working order.

18. Be certain to recognize the student when he/she indicates a need for help.

19. Provide the student with all necessary information prior to an activity in order to increase the likelihood of his/her success.

20. Reduce stimuli in the environment which may contribute to the student's failures or difficulties.

21. Provide the student with a quiet place to work. This is to be used as a form of reducing distracting stimuli and not as a form of punishment.

22. Program assignments which will ensure initial success. Gradually increase the degree of difficulty of assignments as the student's ability and responsibility increases.

23. Make certain that instructions and expectations are clearly stated.

24. Reduce the emphasis on competition. Repeated failure may result in the student blaming someone or something for his/her own failure.

25. Encourage the student to begin assignments early in order to have time to deal with problems which may arise.

26. Provide the student with a schedule of daily events in order that he/she may plan his/her time accordingly. (See Appendix for Schedule of Daily Events.)

39 Steals or forcibly takes things from other students, teachers, the school building, etc.

(A Reminder: The problem is not whether the student is willing to admit guilt. The problem here is that the student takes things that belong to others.)

1. Reinforce the student for demonstrating appropriate behavior: (a) give the student a tangible reward (e.g., classroom privileges, line leading, passing out materials, five minutes free time, etc.) or (b) give the student an intangible reward (e.g., praise, handshake, smile, etc.).

2. Speak with the student to explain: (a) what he/she is doing wrong (e.g., taking things which belong to others) and (b) what he/she should be doing (e.g., asking to use things, borrowing, sharing, returning, etc.).

3. Establish classroom rules (e.g., work on-task, work quietly, remain in your seat, finish task, meet task expectations). Reiterate rules often and reinforce students for following rules.

4. Reinforce those students in the classroom who demonstrate appropriate behavior in reference to others' belongings.

5. Reinforce the student for demonstrating appropriate behavior based on the length of time he/she can be successful. Gradually increase the length of time required for reinforcement as the student demonstrates success.

6. Remove the student from the group or activity until he/she can demonstrate appropriate behavior and self-control.

7. Write a contract with the student specifying what behavior is expected (e.g., not taking things which belong to others) and what reinforcement will be made available when the terms of the contract have been met.

8. Communicate with the parents (e.g., notes home, phone calls, etc.) in order to share information concerning the student's progress and so that they may reinforce the student at home for appropriate use or consideration of others' belongings at school.

9. Structure the environment so that time does not permit inappropriate behavior.

10. Teach the student the concept of borrowing by loaning and requiring the return of those things the student has been taking from others.

11. Identify those things the student has been taking from others and provide the student with those items as reinforcers for appropriate behavior.

12. Reduce the opportunity to steal by restricting students from bringing unnecessary items to school.

13. Maintain visibility to and from the student. The teacher should be able to see the student and the student should be able to see the teacher, making eye contact possible at all times.

14. Supervise the student in order to monitor behavior.

15. Encourage all students to monitor their own belongings.

16. Make certain the student has necessary school-related items (e.g., pencil, ruler, paper, etc.).

17. Label all property brought to school by students and teachers with a permanent marker.

18. Secure all school items of value (e.g., cassette tapes, lab materials, industrial arts and home economics supplies, etc.).

19. Make certain the student understands the natural consequences of his/her inappropriate behavior (e.g., the student must make restitution for taking things which belong to others).

20. Communicate with the student's family to establish procedures whereby the student may earn those things he/she would otherwise take.

21. Teach the student to share (e.g., schedule activities daily which require sharing).

22. Help the student build or create a prized possession to satisfy his/her need for ownership (e.g., this can be done in art, home economics, industrial arts, etc.).

23. Deal with the taking of belongings privately rather than publicly.

24. Provide multiples of the items which are being taken in order to have enough for all or most students to use (e.g., pencils, erasers, rulers etc).

(Please note: Do not rely on or encourage students in the classroom to be informants. Do not use peer pressure in the classroom to solve incidents of stealing.)

40 Behaves inappropriately when others do well or receive praise or attention

1. Reinforce the student for behaving appropriately when others do well or receive praise or attention: (a) give the student a tangible reward (e.g., classroom privileges, line leading, passing out materials, five minutes free time, etc.) or (b) give the student an intangible reward (e.g., praise, handshake, smile, etc.).

2. Speak to the student to explain: (a) what he/she is doing wrong (e.g., getting angry, tantruming, etc.) and (b) what he/she should be doing (e.g., making positive comments, continuing to participate appropriately, etc.).

3. Reinforce those students in the classroom who behave appropriately when others do well or receive praise or attention.

4. Reinforce the student for behaving appropriately based on the length of time he/she can be successful. Gradually increase the length of time required for reinforcement as the student demonstrates success.

5. Write a contract with the student specifying what behavior is expected (e.g., making a positive comment) and what reinforcement will be made available when the terms of the contract have been met.

6. Communicate with parents (e.g., notes home, phone calls, etc.) in order to share information concerning the student's progress and so that they may reinforce the student at home for behaving appropriately at school.

7. Evaluate the appropriateness of the task or situation to determine: (a) if the task is too easy, (b) if the task is too difficult, and (c) if the length of time scheduled to complete the task is appropriate.

8. Identify a peer to act as a model for the student to imitate behaving appropriately when others do well or receive praise or attention.

9. Have the student question any directions, explanations, instructions he/she does not understand.

10. Do not allow the student to participate if the task or situation is too stimulating.

11. Make certain to help the student achieve a level of success in an activity in order that he/she will do well and receive praise or attention.

12. Make certain that the student is assigned a role in an activity in which he/she can be successful in order that he/she can be a participant and enjoy the activity (e.g., banker in Monopoly, scorekeeper in a game, teacher assistant, note taker in discussions, etc.).

13. Make certain that some attention is given to the student when others do well or receive praise or attention. Gradually reduce the attention given to the student as he/she demonstrates appropriate behavior when others do well or receive praise or attention.

14. Deliver praise or attention as privately as possible in order to reduce the likelihood of upsetting any students in the classroom.

15. Reduce the emphasis on competition. Encourage and reinforce participation, team work, good sportsmanship, personal improvement, etc.

16. Gradually increase the degree of difficulty of the task or activity as the student demonstrates success.

17. Make certain that the student succeeds or receives attention often enough to create a balance with those times when other students succeed or receive praise or attention.

18. Have the student take part in activities with other students who are appropriate models for behavior when others do well or receive praise or attention.

19. Establish rules and go over them at the beginning of an activity in order to reduce the likelihood of misunderstanding.

20. Encourage the student to remove himself/herself from situations which may cause him/her to become upset, angry, embarrassed, etc.

21. Encourage an atmosphere of students helping one another, congratulating each other, finding something about each other to compliment, etc.

22. Make certain that the teacher is a good role model by participating in games, demonstrating good sportsmanship, complimenting others, etc.

23. If the student becomes frustrated or upset by the task or activity remove him/her from the situation, stop the activity, or provide an alternative activity.

24. Make certain that the student understands that an inability to behave appropriately during a game or activity will result in the termination of the activity.

25. Be certain to provide close supervision of the student in tasks and activities in order to intervene early and provide problem-solving alternatives should inappropriate behaviors occur.

26. Help the student find activities (e.g., reading, creating, peer tutoring, etc.) with which he/she can achieve personal satisfaction and success.

27. Do not require the student to participate in games and activities which may be threatening or cause him/her to demonstrate inappropriate behavior.

28. Make certain the student does not participate in activities with another student(s) who is likely to stimulate his/her inappropriate behavior.

29. Provide the student with several activities throughout the day in which he/she can do well and receive praise and attention.

30. Be aware of the student's strengths and limitations in order to have him/her participate in activities in which he/she will succeed rather than fail.

31. Have the student engage in games or activities with a younger student with whom he/she will not have a competitive relationship. Gradually have the student participate in games or activities with older, more skilled peers as he/she demonstrates appropriate behavior.

32. Call on the student when he/she is most likely to be able to respond correctly (e.g., something in which the student is interested, when the teacher is certain he/she knows the answer, etc.).

41 Engages in inappropriate behaviors while seated

1. Reinforce the student for sitting appropriately in his/her seat: (a) give the student a tangible reward (e.g., classroom privileges, line leading, passing out materials, five minutes free time, etc.) or (b) give the student an intangible reward (e.g., praise, handshake, smile, etc.).

2. Speak to the student to explain: (a) what he/she is doing wrong (e.g., tipping chair) and (b) what he/she should be doing (e.g., sitting appropriately in his/her chair).

3. Establish classroom rules (e.g., work on-task, work quietly, remain in your seat, finish task, meet task expectations). Reiterate rules often and reinforce students for following rules.

4. Reinforce those students in the classroom who sit appropriately in their seats.

5. Reinforce the student for sitting appropriately in his/her seat based on the length of time he/she can be successful. Gradually increase the length of time required for reinforcement as the student demonstrates success.

6. Write a contract with the student specifying what behavior is expected (e.g., sitting appropriately in his/her seat) and what reinforcement will be made available when the terms of the contract have been met.

7. Communicate with parents (e.g., notes home, phone calls, etc.) in order to share information concerning the student's progress and so that they may reinforce the student at home for sitting appropriately in his/her seat at school.

8. Evaluate the appropriateness of the task to determine: (a) if the task is too easy, (b) if the task is too difficult, and (c) if the length of time scheduled to complete the task is appropriate.

9. Identify a peer to act as a model for the student to imitate appropriate ways in which to sit in his/her seat.

10. Have the student question any directions, explanations, instructions he/she does not understand.

11. Have desks and/or chairs that can be fastened to the floor or which are designed to prevent tipping.

12. Provide the student with a specific description of appropriate in-seat behavior (e.g., face forward, feet on floor, back straight, etc.).

13. Implement logical consequences for students who fail to sit appropriately in their seats (e.g., the student would have to sit on the floor, stand next to his/her desk to work, sit in a chair without a desk, etc.).

14. Maintain consistency of expectations for having the student sit appropriately in his/her seat.

15. Make certain the student is aware of the natural consequences that may occur from sitting inappropriately in his/her seat (e.g., injury, damaging property, hurting others, etc.).

16. Place the student in a carrel in order to reduce distracting stimuli which may cause him/her to sit inappropriately in his/her seat.

17. Seat the student next to a peer who sits appropriately in his/her seat.

18. Deliver a predetermined signal (e.g., hand signal, ring a bell, etc.) when the student begins to sit inappropriately in his/her seat.

19. Model for the student appropriate ways in which to sit in a chair or at a desk.

20. Provide activities which are interesting to the student in order to keep him/her on-task and sitting appropriately in his/her seat.

21. Seat the student near the teacher.

22. Seat the student away from peers in order to reduce the likelihood that he/she will sit inappropriately in his/her seat.

23. Evaluate the necessity of having the student sit facing forward, feet on floor, back straight, etc.

24. Make certain that the chair or desk the student is assigned to use is appropriate and/or comfortable for him/her (e.g., the desk is not too high, the chair is not too big, etc.).

25. Remove any materials the student uses to make noises while seated.

26. Use natural consequences when the student touches others as they walk by (e.g., move the student to another location in the room, have others walk away from the student, etc.).

42 Behaves in a manner inappropriate for the situation

1. Reinforce the student for demonstrating appropriate behaviors related to the situation: (a) give the student tangible rewards (e.g., classroom privileges, line leading, passing out materials, five minutes free time, etc.) or (b) give the student an intangible reward (e.g., praise, handshake, smile, etc.).

2. Speak with the student to explain: (a) what he/she is doing wrong (e.g., laughing when a peer hurts himself) and (b) what he/she should be doing (e.g., helping the peer).

3. Establish classroom rules (e.g., work on-task, work quietly, remain in your seat, finish task, meet task expectations). Reiterate rules often and reinforce students for following rules.

4. Reinforce those students in the classroom who demonstrate appropriate behaviors related to the situation.

5. Reinforce the student for demonstrating appropriate behaviors related to the situation based on the length of time he/she can be successful. Gradually increase the length of time required for reinforcement as the student demonstrates success.

6. Remove the student from the group or activity until he/she can demonstrate appropriate behavior and self-control.

7. Write a contract with the student specifying what behavior is expected (e.g., demonstrating appropriate behavior related to the situation) and what reinforcement will be made available when the terms of the contract have been met.

8. Communicate with the parents (e.g., notes home, phone calls, etc.) in order to share information concerning the student's progress and so that they may reinforce the student at home for demonstrating appropriate behaviors related to situations at school.

9. Evaluate the appropriateness of the task to determine: (a) if the task is too easy, (b) if the task is too difficult, and (c) if the length of time scheduled for the task is appropriate.

10. Reduce stimuli which would contribute to unrelated or inappropriate behavior (e.g., testing situations, peers, physical activities, etc.).

11. Interact frequently with the student to maintain involvement.

12. Structure the environment so that time does not permit unrelated or inappropriate behavior from occurring.

13. Give the student responsibilities to keep him/her actively involved in the activity.

14. Modify or adjust situations which cause the student to demonstrate unrelated or inappropriate behavior (e.g., keep the student from becoming overstimulated in activities).

15. Make the necessary adjustments in the environment to prevent the student from experiencing stress, frustration, anger, etc., as much as possible.

16. Reduce distracting stimuli (e.g., place the student in the front row, provide a carrel or quiet place away from distractions, etc.). This is used as a means of reducing distracting stimuli and not as a form of punishment.

17. Try various groupings in order to determine the situations in which the student demonstrates appropriate behavior.

18. Interact frequently with the student in order to maintain his/her attention to the activity (e.g., ask the student questions, ask the student's opinions, stand close to the student, seat the student near the teacher's desk, etc.).

19. Maintain a consistent routine.

20. Model socially acceptable behavior for the student (e.g., pat on the back, handshake, etc.).

21. Make certain that reinforcement is not inadvertently given to the student's inappropriate comments or behaviors (e.g., attending to the student only when he/she demonstrates behaviors which are inappropriate to the situation).

22. Prevent the student from becoming overstimulated by an activity (e.g., monitor or supervise student behavior to limit overstimulation in physical activities, games, parties, etc.).

23. Help the student develop attention-maintaining behaviors (e.g., maintain eye contact, take notes on the subject, ask questions related to the subject, etc.).

24. Assign a peer to work with the student in order to model on-task behavior.

25. Reduce the emphasis on competition. Repeated failure may result in behaviors which are inappropriate for the situation.

26. Make the student aware of activities or events well in advance in order that he/she may prepare for them.

27. Deliver a predetermined signal (e.g., hand signal, verbal cue, etc.) when the student begins to display behaviors which are inappropriate to the situation.

A Reminder: Do not "force" the student to participate in any activity he/she finds unpleasant, embarrassing, etc.

43 Tries to avoid situations, assignments, responsibilities

1. Determine whether physical discomfort is being used as an excuse to escape situations and not the result of a medical problem, neglect, or abuse.

2. Reinforce the student for participating, performing assignments, or taking responsibilities: (a) give the student a tangible reward (e.g., classroom privileges, line leading, passing out materials, five minutes free time, etc.) or (b) give the student an intangible reward (e.g., praise, handshake, smile, etc.).

3. Speak to the student to explain: (a) what he/she is doing wrong (e.g., complaining, asking to leave the room, etc.) and (b) what he/she should be doing (e.g., reporting only legitimate discomfort or needs).

4. Establish classroom rules (e.g., work on-task, work quietly, remain in your seat, finish task, meet task expectations). Reiterate rules often and reinforce students for following rules.

5. Reinforce those students in the classroom who are participating, performing assignments, or taking responsibilities.

6. Reinforce the student for participating, performing assignments, or taking responsibilities based on the length of time he/she can be successful. Gradually increase the length of time required for reinforcement as the student demonstrates success.

7. Write a contract with the student specifying what behavior is expected (e.g., participating, performing assignments, or taking responsibilities) and what reinforcement will be made available when the terms of the contract have been met.

8. Communicate with parents (e.g., notes home, phone calls, etc.) in order to share information concerning the student's progress and so that they may reinforce the student at home for appropriate behavior at school.

9. Communicate with parents, agencies, or appropriate parties in order to inform them of the problem, determine the cause of the problem, and solutions to the problem.

10. Evaluate the appropriateness of the task to determine: (a) if the task is too easy, (b) if the task is too difficult, and (c) if the length of time scheduled to complete the task is appropriate.

11. Identify a peer to act as a model for the student to imitate appropriate participation, performance of assignments, or acceptance of responsibilities.

12. Have the student question any directions, explanations, instructions he/she does not understand.

13. Give the student assignments and responsibilities he/she would enjoy performing (e.g., acting as teacher assistant, line leading, chores in the classroom, etc.). Gradually introduce less desirable assignments and responsibilities as the student demonstrates success.

14. Follow a less desirable activity with a more desirable activity, requiring the student to complete the first in order to perform the second.

15. Make certain the student understands that leaving the classroom may only be done at regularly scheduled intervals (e.g., recess, break time, lunch, class changes, etc.).

16. Provide the student with many academic and social successes.

17. Assess the appropriateness of the social setting in relation to the student's ability to function successfully (i.e., do not place the student with peers who are threatening to him/her).

18. Program alternative activities for the student to perform or engage in if he/she has difficulty performing assigned activities. Gradually remove the alternative activities as the student demonstrates success.

19. Allow the student to leave the classroom to get materials from his/her locker, use the restroom, go to the nurse's office, go to the counselor's office, etc., after he/she has performed assignments or taken care of responsibilities.

20. Provide the student with positive feedback that indicates that he/she is successful, competent, important, valuable, etc.

21. Have the student record and chart his/her own appropriate behavior (e.g., participating in classroom activities, performing assignments, taking responsibilities, etc.).

22. Make certain that reinforcement is not inadvertently given for complaints of physical discomfort (e.g., allowing the student to leave the room, avoid assignments, leave school, etc.).

23. Seek student input in planning the curriculum, extracurricular activities, etc.

24. Reduce the emphasis on competition. Repeated failure may cause the student to avoid situations, assignments, or responsibilities.

25. Provide the student with a selection of assignments and require him/her to choose a minimum number from the total amount (e.g., present the student with 10 academic tasks from which he/she must finish 6 that day).

26. Explain to the student that work not done during work time must be done during other times (e.g., recreational time, break time, after school, etc.).

27. Give the student a preferred responsibility to be performed at various times throughout the day.

28. Present assignments and responsibilities in the most attractive and interesting manner possible.

29. Interact frequently with the student in order to maintain his/her involvement in assignments, responsibilities, etc.

30. Make the necessary adjustments in the environment to prevent the student from experiencing stress, frustration, anger, etc., as much as possible.

31. Identify variables in the environment which cause the student to avoid situations, assignments, or responsibilities and reduce or remove these variables from the environment.

A Reminder: Do not "force" the student to participate in any activity.

44 Behaves impulsively, without self-control

1. Reinforce the student for acting in a deliberate and responsible manner: (a) give the student a tangible reward (e.g., classroom privileges, line leading, passing out materials, five minutes free time, etc.) or (b) give the student an intangible reward (e.g., praise, handshake, smile, etc.).

2. Speak with the student to explain: (a) what he/she is doing wrong (e.g., taking action before thinking about what he/she is doing) and (b) what he/she should be doing (e.g., considering consequences, thinking about the correct response, considering others, etc.).

3. Establish classroom rules (e.g., work on-task, work quietly, remain in your seat, finish task, meet task expectations). Reiterate rules often and reinforce students for following rules.

4. Reinforce those students in the classroom who act in a deliberate and responsible manner.

5. Reinforce the student for demonstrating appropriate behavior based on the length of time he/she can be successful. Gradually increase the length of time required for reinforcement as the student demonstrates success.

6. Remove the student from the group or activity until he/she can demonstrate appropriate behavior and self-control.

7. Write a contract with the student specifying what behavior is expected (e.g., acting in a deliberate and responsible manner) and what reinforcement will be made available when the terms of the contract have been met.

8. Communicate with parents (e.g., notes home, phone calls, etc.) in order to share information concerning the student's progress and so that they may reinforce the student at home for acting in a deliberate and responsible manner at school.

9. Evaluate the appropriateness of the task to determine: (a) if the task is too easy, (b) if the task is too difficult, and (c) if the length of time scheduled for the task is appropriate.

10. Reduce the opportunity to act impulsively by limiting decision-making. Gradually increase opportunities for decision-making as the student demonstrates success.

11. Maintain supervision at all times and in all areas of the school environment.

12. Maintain visibility to and from the student. The teacher should be able to see the student and the student should be able to see the teacher, making eye contact possible at all times.

13. Be mobile in order to be frequently near the student.

14. Give the student additional responsibilities (e.g., chores, errands, etc.) to give him/her a feeling of success or accomplishment.

15. Prevent the student from becoming overstimulated by an activity (e.g., monitor or supervise student behavior to limit overexcitement in physical activities, games, parties, etc.).

16. Provide the student with adequate time to perform activities in order to reduce his/her impulsive behavior.

17. Provide the student with a routine to be followed when making decisions (e.g., place a list of decision-making strategies on the student's desk).

18. Explain to the student that he/she should be satisfied with his/her own best effort rather than perfection.

19. Provide the student with clear, simply stated explanations, instructions, and directions so that he/she knows exactly what is expected.

20. Assist the student in beginning each task in order to reduce impulsive responses.

21. Have a peer work with the student in order to model deliberate and responsible behavior in academic and social settings.

22. Reduce distracting stimuli (e.g., place the student on the front row, provide a carrel or quiet place away from distractions, etc.). This is used as a means of reducing distracting stimuli and not as a form of punishment.

23. Teach the student decision-making steps: (a) think about how other persons may be influenced, (b) think about consequences, (c) carefully consider the unique situation, (d) think of different courses of action which are possible, and (e) think about what is ultimately best for him/her.

24. Make the student aware of the reasons we all must practice responsibility (e.g., others' rights are not infringed upon, others are not hurt, order is not lost, property is not damaged or destroyed, etc.).

25. Reduce the emphasis on competition. Competition may result in impulsive behavior in order to win or be first.

26. Emphasize individual success or progress rather than winning or "beating" other students.

27. Make certain that all students get equal opportunities to participate in activities (e.g., students take turns, everyone has an equal opportunity to be first, etc.).

28. Allow natural consequences to occur in order that the student can learn that persons who take their turn and act in a deliberate fashion are more successful than those who act impulsively (e.g., if you begin an activity before understanding the directions you will finish early, but may perform the assignment incorrectly and receive a failing grade, may have to repeat the assignment, etc.).

29. Deliver a predetermined signal (e.g., hand signal, verbal cue, etc.) when the student begins to demonstrate impulsive behaviors.

30. Make certain the student has an adequate amount or number of activities scheduled in order to prevent the likelihood of impulsively engaging in unplanned activities. (See Appendix for Schedule of Daily Events.)

31. Assign the student to an area of the classroom where he/she is to remain at any one time.

32. Maintain consistency in the daily routine of activities.

33. Make certain the student knows which areas or activities in the classroom are "off limits" to him/her.

A Reminder: Do not confuse impulsive behavior with enthusiasm. Impulsive behavior should be controlled while enthusiasm should be encouraged.

45 Exhibits extreme mood changes

1. Reinforce the student for demonstrating consistent and appropriate behavior: (a) give the student a tangible reward (e.g., classroom privileges, line leading, passing out materials, five minutes free time, etc.) or (b) give the student an intangible reward (e.g., praise, handshake, smile, etc.).

2. Speak with the student to explain: (a) what he/she is doing wrong (e.g., becoming angry or upset easily, etc.) and (b) what he/she should be doing (e.g., following rules, considering others, controlling impulsive behavior, etc.).

3. Establish classroom rules (e.g., work on-task, work quietly, remain in your seat, finish task, meet task expectations). Reiterate rules often and reinforce students for following rules.

4. Write a contract with the student specifying what behavior is expected (e.g., consistent and appropriate behavior) and what reinforcement will be made available when the terms of the contract have been met.

5. Communicate with the parents (e.g., notes home, phone calls, etc.) in order to share information concerning the student's progress and so that they may reinforce the student at home for demonstrating consistent and appropriate behavior at school.

6. Reinforce the student for demonstrating appropriate behavior (academic or social) based on the length of time he/she can be successful. Gradually increase the length of time required for reinforcement as the student demonstrates success.

7. Evaluate the appropriateness of the task to determine if: (a) the task is too easy, (b) the task is too difficult, and (c) the time scheduled to complete the task is appropriate.

8. Communicate with parents, agencies, or appropriate parties in order to inform them of the problem, determine the cause of the problem, and consider possible solutions to the problem.

9. Provide the student with as many social and academic successes as possible.

10. Make the necessary adjustments in the environment to prevent the student from experiencing stress, frustration, anger, etc.

11. Provide a consistent routine for the student in order to enhance stability.

12. Try various groupings in order to determine the situation in which the student is most comfortable.

13. Allow flexibility in meeting academic demands when the student demonstrates sudden or dramatic mood changes (e.g., allow more time, modify assignments, provide help with assignments, etc.).

14. Separate the student from the peer who stimulates the sudden or dramatic mood changes.

15. Teach the student problem-solving skills: (a) identify the problem, (b) identify goals and objectives, (c) develop strategies, (d) develop a plan for action, and (e) carry out the plan.

16. Teach the student to recognize a mood change in order that he/she may deal with it appropriately.

17. Provide a pleasant/calm atmosphere which would lessen the possibility of sudden or dramatic mood changes.

18. Inform the student in advance when a change at school is going to occur (e.g., change in routine, special events, end of one activity and beginning of another, etc.).

19. Give the student adequate time to make adjustments to activity changes, situations, etc. (e.g., provide the student with several minutes to move from one activity to another).

20. Prevent the occurrence of specific stimuli that cause the student to demonstrate sudden or dramatic mood changes (e.g., demanding situations, interruptions, competition, announcing test scores, abrupt changes, etc.).

21. Avoid discussions or prevent stimuli in the environment that remind the student of unpleasant experiences/sensitive topics (e.g., divorce, death, unemployment, alcoholism, etc.).

46 Is unpredictable in behavior

1. Reinforce the student for demonstrating appropriate behaviors: (a) give the student tangible rewards (e.g., classroom privileges, line leading, passing out materials, five minutes free time, etc.) or (b) give the student an intangible reward (e.g., praise, handshake, smile, etc.).

2. Speak with the student to explain: (a) what he/she is doing wrong and (b) what he/she should be doing.

3. Establish classroom rules (e.g., work on-task, work quietly, remain in your seat, finish task, meet task expectations). Reiterate rules often and reinforce students for following rules.

4. Reinforce those students in the classroom who demonstrate appropriate behaviors related to the situation.

5. Reinforce the student for demonstrating appropriate behaviors related to the situation based on the length of time he/she can be successful. Gradually increase the length of time required for reinforcement as the student demonstrates success.

6. Remove the student from the group or activity until he/she can demonstrate appropriate behavior and self-control.

7. Write a contract with the student specifying what behavior is expected (e.g., demonstrating appropriate behaviors related to the situation) and what reinforcement will be made available when the terms of the contract have been met.

8. Communicate with the parents (e.g., notes home, phone calls, etc.) in order to share information concerning the student's progress and so that they may reinforce the student at home for demonstrating appropriate behaviors related to situations at school.

9. Evaluate the appropriateness of the task to determine if: (a) the task is too easy, (b) the task is too difficult, and (c) the length of time scheduled for the task is appropriate.

10. Reduce stimuli which would contribute to unrelated or inappropriate behavior (e.g., testing situations, peers, physical activities, etc.).

11. Structure the environment so that time does not permit unrelated or inappropriate behavior from occurring.

12. Modify or adjust situations that cause the student to demonstrate unrelated or inappropriate behavior (e.g., keep the student from becoming overstimulated in activities).

13. Make the necessary adjustments in the environment to prevent the student from experiencing stress, frustration, anger, etc., as much as possible.

14. Reduce distracting stimuli (e.g., place the student in the front row, provide a carrel or quiet place away from distractions, etc.). This is used as a means of reducing distracting stimuli and not as a form of punishment.

15. Try various groupings in order to determine the situation in which the student demonstrates appropriate behavior.

16. Maintain a consistent routine.

17. Model socially acceptable behavior for the student (e.g., pat on the back, handshake, etc.).

18. Make certain that reinforcement is not inadvertently given to the inappropriate comments or behaviors.

19. Prevent the student from becoming overstimulated by an activity (i.e., monitor or supervise student behavior to limit overstimulation in physical activities, games, parties, etc.).

20. Assign a peer to work with the student in order to model appropriate behavior.

21. Reduce the emphasis on competition. Repeated failure may result in unpredictable behaviors.

22. Make the student aware of activities or events well in advance in order that he/she may prepare for them.

23. Discuss concerns with other professionals to determine if further investigation is warranted (e.g., abuse or neglect).

24. Explain that the concerns or worries, while legitimate, are not unusual for students (e.g., everyone worries about tests, grades, etc.).

25. Provide the student with opportunities for social and academic success.

26. Separate the student from the peer(s) who may be encouraging or stimulating the inappropriate behavior.

27. Provide praise and recognition of appropriate behavior as often as possible.

28. Structure the environment in such a way that time does not permit opportunities for the student to demonstrate inappropriate behavior.

29. Provide the student with alternative approaches to testing (e.g., test the student orally, make tests shorter, let the student respond orally, let the student take the test in the resource room, etc.).

30. Avoid discussion of topics sensitive to the student (e.g., divorce, death, unemployment, alcoholism, etc.).

31. Provide as many enjoyable and interesting activities as possible.

32. Provide a consistent routine for the student in order to enhance stability.

33. Allow flexibility in meeting academic demands when the student demonstrates sudden or dramatic mood changes (e.g., allow more time, modify assignments, provide help with assignments).

34. Teach the student to recognize a sudden or dramatic change in behavior in order that he/she may deal with it appropriately.

35. Inform the student in advance when a change at school is going to occur (e.g., change in routine, special events, end of one activity and beginning of another, etc.).

36. Give the student adequate time to make adjustments to activity changes, situations, etc. (e.g., provide the student with several minutes to move from one activity to another).

37. Prevent the occurrence of specific stimuli that cause the student to demonstrate sudden or dramatic changes in behavior (e.g., demanding situations, interruptions, competition, abrupt changes, etc.).

38. Provide the student with a selection of assignments and require him/her to choose a minimum number from the total amount (e.g., present the student with 10 academic tasks from which he/she must finish 6 that day).

39. Provide the student with a schedule of daily events in order that he/she will know what is expected of him/her. (See Appendix for Schedule of Daily Events.)

40. Provide the student with a predetermined signal (e.g., quiet sign, hand signal, verbal cue, etc.) when he/she begins to demonstrate an inappropriate behavior.

41. Provide a pleasant/calm atmosphere which would lessen the possibility of sudden or dramatic changes in behavior.

42. Reduce distracting stimuli (e.g., place the student in the front row, provide a carrel or quiet place away from distractions, etc.). This is used as a means of reducing stimuli and not as a form of punishment.

A Reminder: Do not "force" the student to participate in any activity he/she finds unpleasant, embarrassing, etc.

47 Does not follow directives from teachers or other school personnel

1. Reinforce the student for following directives from teachers or other school personnel: (a) give the student a tangible reward (e.g., classroom privileges, line leading, passing out materials, five minutes free time, etc.) or (b) give the student an intangible reward (e.g., praise, handshake, smile, etc.).

2. Speak with the student to explain: (a) what he/she is doing wrong (e.g., failing to follow directions or observe rules) and (b) what he/she should be doing (e.g., following established guidelines or expectations).

3. Establish classroom rules (e.g., work on-task, work quietly, remain in your seat, finish task, meet task expectations). Reiterate rules often and reinforce students for following rules.

4. Reinforce those students in the classroom who follow directives from teachers and other school personnel.

5. Reinforce the student for following the directives of teachers and other school personnel based on the length of time he/she can be successful. Gradually increase the amount of time required for reinforcement as the student demonstrates success.

6. Remove the student from the group or activity until he/she can demonstrate appropriate behavior and self-control.

7. Write a contract with the student specifying what behavior is expected (e.g., following teacher directives) and what reinforcement will be made available when the terms of the contract have been met.

8. Communicate with the parents (e.g., notes home, phone calls, etc.) in order to share information concerning the student's progress and so that they may reinforce the student at home for following directives from teachers and other school personnel.

9. Evaluate the appropriateness of the task to determine if: (a) the task is too easy, (b) the task is too difficult, and (c) the length of time scheduled for the task is appropriate.

10. Structure the environment in such a way that the student remains active and involved in appropriate behavior.

11. Maintain visibility to and from the student. The teacher should be able to see the student and the student should be able to see the teacher, making eye contact possible at all times.

12. Give the student preferred responsibilities.

13. Present the tasks in the most interesting and attractive manner possible.

14. Maintain maximum supervision of the student and gradually decrease supervision as the student becomes successful at following directives.

15. Have the student maintain a chart representing the amount of time spent following teacher directives or rules, with reinforcement for increasing appropriate behavior.

16. Be mobile in order to be frequently near the student.

17. Provide the student with many social and academic successes.

18. Provide the student with positive feedback that indicates he/she is successful.

19. Post rules in various places, including the student's desk.

20. Make certain the student receives the information necessary to perform activities (e.g., written information, verbal directions, reminders, etc.).

21. Teach the student direction-following skills: (a) listen carefully, (b) ask questions, (c) use environmental cues, (d) rely on examples provided, (e) wait until all directions are given before beginning, etc.

22. Maintain the most positive, professional relationship with the student (i.e., an adversary relationship is likely to result in failure to follow directions).

23. Be a consistent authority figure (e.g., be consistent in relationship with student).

24. Provide the student with optional courses of action in order to prevent total refusal to obey directives from teachers and other school personnel.

25. Intervene early to prevent the student's behavior from leading to contagion for other students.

26. Deliver directions in a step-by-step sequence.

27. Have a peer act as a model for following teacher directives.

28. Interact with the student frequently to determine if directives are being followed.

29. Maintain consistency in rules, routine, and general expectations of conduct and procedure.

30. Allow natural consequences to occur as a result of not following directives from teachers and other school personnel (e.g., assignments are performed incorrectly, accidents will occur, detention will be assigned, etc.).

31. Limit the student's opportunity to engage in activities in which he/she will not follow directives from teachers and other school personnel (e.g., recess, industrial arts activities, field trips, etc.).

32. Do not allow the student to be unsupervised anywhere in the school environment.

48 Ignores consequences of his/her behavior

1. Reinforce the student for engaging in appropriate behavior: (a) give the student a tangible reward (e.g., classroom privileges, line leading, passing out materials, five minutes free time, etc.) or (b) give the student an intangible reward (e.g., praise, handshake, smile, etc.).

2. Speak with the student to explain: (a) what he/she is doing wrong (e.g., taking action before thinking about what he/she is doing) and (b) what he/she should be doing (e.g., considering consequences, thinking about the correct response, considering other persons, etc.).

3. Establish classroom rules (e.g., work on-task, work quietly, remain in your seat, finish task, meet task expectations). Reiterate rules often and reinforce students for following rules.

4. Reinforce those students in the classroom who engage in appropriate behavior.

5. Reinforce the student for demonstrating appropriate behavior based on the length of time he/she can be successful. Gradually increase the length of time required for reinforcement as the student demonstrates success.

6. Remove the student from the group or activity until he/she can demonstrate appropriate behavior and self-control.

7. Write a contract with the student specifying what behavior is expected (e.g., acting in a deliberate and responsible manner) and what reinforcement will be made available when the terms of the contract have been met.

8. Communicate with parents (e.g., notes home, phone calls, etc.) in order to share information concerning the student's progress and so that they may reinforce the student at home for engaging in appropriate behaviors at school.

9. Evaluate the appropriateness of the task to determine: (a) if the task is too easy, (b) if the task is too difficult, and (c) if the length of time scheduled for the task is appropriate.

10. Make certain that consequences are delivered consistently for behavior demonstrated (e.g., appropriate behavior results in positive consequences and inappropriate behavior results in negative consequences).

11. Provide the student with many social and academic successes.

12. Structure the environment in such a way as to limit opportunities for inappropriate behavior (e.g., keep the student engaged in activities, have the student seated near the teacher, maintain visibility to and from the student, etc.).

13. Prevent the student from becoming overstimulated by an activity (e.g., monitor or supervise student behavior to limit overexcitement in physical activities, games, parties, etc.).

14. Provide the student with natural consequences for inappropriate behavior (e.g., for disturbing others during group activities, the student would have to leave the activity).

15. Provide the student with a clearly identified list of consequences for inappropriate behavior.

16. Teach the student problem-solving skills: (a) identify the problem, (b) identify goals and objectives, (c) develop strategies, (d) develop a plan for action, and (e) carry out the plan.

17. Clarify for the student that it is his/her behavior which determines consequences (e.g., positive or negative).

18. Provide a learning experience which emphasizes the cause-and-effect relationship between behavior and the inevitability of some form of consequence (e.g., both negative and positive behaviors and consequences).

19. Point out consequences of other students' behavior as they occur (e.g., take the opportunity to point out that consequences occur for all behavior and for all persons).

20. Supervise the student closely in situations in which he/she is likely to act impulsively (e.g., maintain close physical proximity, maintain eye contact, communicate frequently with the student, etc.).

21. Prevent peers from engaging in those behaviors that would cause the student to fail to consider or regard consequences of his/her behavior (e.g., keep other students from upsetting the student).

22. Make the consequences of a behavior obvious by identifying the consequence as it occurs and discussing alternative behavior which would have prevented the particular consequence.

23. Call on the student when he/she can answer successfully.

24. Avoid competition. Failure may cause the student to ignore consequences of his/her behavior.

25. Allow the student more decision-making opportunities relative to class activities and assignments.

26. Present tasks in the most attractive and interesting manner possible.

27. Give the student responsibilities in the classroom (e.g., teacher assistant, peer tutor, group leader, etc.).

28. Evaluate the appropriateness of the task in relation to the student's ability to perform the task successfully.

29. Show an interest in the student (e.g., acknowledge the student, ask the student's opinion, spend time working one-on-one with the student, etc.).

49 Makes sexually-related comments or engages in behavior with sexual overtones

1. Reinforce the student for engaging in socially appropriate individual or group behavior: (a) give the student a tangible reward (e.g., classroom privileges, line leading, passing out materials, five minutes free time, etc.) or (b) give the student an intangible reward (e.g., praise, handshake, smile, etc.).

2. Speak with the student to explain: (a) what he/she is doing wrong (e.g., making sexual references, touching others, making gestures, etc.) and (b) what he/she should be doing (e.g., following rules, working on-task, attending to responsibilities, etc.).

3. Reinforce those students in the classroom who engage in appropriate behavior.

4. Reinforce the student for demonstrating appropriate behavior based on the length of time he/she can be successful. Gradually increase the length of time required for reinforcement as the student demonstrates success.

5. Remove the student from the group or activity until he/she can demonstrate appropriate behavior and self-control.

6. Write a contract with the student specifying what behavior is expected (e.g., communicating with others in an appropriate manner) and what reinforcement will be made available when the terms of the contract have been met.

7. Communicate with the parents (e.g., notes home, phone calls, etc.) in order to share information concerning the student's progress and so that they may reinforce the student at home for engaging in appropriate behavior at school.

8. Establish classroom rules (e.g., work on-task, work quietly, remain in your seat, finish task, meet task expectations). Reiterate rules often and reinforce students for following rules.

9. Communicate with parents, agencies or appropriate parties in order to inform them of the problem, determine the cause of the problem, and consider possible solutions to the problem.

10. Indicate to the student that public displays of sexually-related behavior are inappropriate.

11. Supervise the student closely in order to prevent inappropriate sexually-related behaviors from occurring.

12. Structure the environment so that time does not permit the student to engage in inappropriate behaviors (e.g., maintain a full schedule of activities).

13. Seat the student close to the teacher in order to provide more direct supervision.

14. Maintain visibility to and from the student. The teacher should be able to see the student and the student should be able to see the teacher, making eye contact possible at all times.

15. Be mobile in order to be frequently near the student.

16. Do not allow the student to be left alone or unsupervised with other students.

17. Make certain the student understands the natural consequences of his/her inappropriate behavior (e.g., peers will not want to interact with him/her, removal from the group may be necessary, etc.).

18. Model socially-acceptable behavior for the student (e.g., pat on the back, appropriate verbal communications, handshake, etc.).

19. Separate the student from the peer(s) who stimulates the inappropriate sexually-related behavior.

20. Make certain the student knows exactly which sexually-related behaviors are unacceptable at school (e.g., words, gestures, comments, touching, exposing, etc.).

21. Do not inadvertently reinforce the student for demonstrating sexually-related behaviors (e.g., attending to the student only when he/she demonstrates sexually-related behaviors, demonstrating shock, etc.).

22. Maintain a professional relationship with students at all times and in all settings making certain that your behavior does not stimulate sexually-related behaviors.

50 Becomes overexcited

1. Reinforce the student for demonstrating self-control in the presence of visual and auditory stimuli in the classroom: (a) give the student a tangible reward (e.g., classroom privileges, line leading, passing out materials, five minutes free time, etc.) or (b) give the student an intangible reward (e.g., praise, handshake, smile, etc.).

2. Speak to the student to explain: (a) what he/she is doing wrong (e.g., becoming easily angered or upset) and (b) what he/she should be doing (e.g., following rules, considering others, controlling impulsive behavior, etc.).

3. Establish classroom rules (e.g., work on-task, work quietly, remain in your seat, finish task, meet task expectations). Reiterate rules often and reinforce students for following rules.

4. Reinforce those students in the classroom who demonstrate self-control in the presence of visual and auditory stimuli in the classroom.

5. Reinforce the student for demonstrating self-control in the presence of visual and auditory stimuli in the classroom based on the length of time he/she can be successful. Gradually increase the length of time required for reinforcement as the student demonstrates success.

6. Write a contract with the student specifying what behavior is expected (e.g., maintaining self-control in the presence of visual and auditory stimuli in the classroom) and what reinforcement will be made available when the terms of the contract have been met.

7. Communicate with parents (e.g., notes home, phone calls, etc.) in order to share information concerning the student's progress and so that they may reinforce the student at home for demonstrating self-control in the presence of visual and auditory stimuli in the classroom.

8. Identify a peer to act as a model for the student to imitate demonstrating self-control in the presence of visual and auditory stimuli in the classroom.

9. Have the student question any directions, explanations, instructions he/she does not understand.

10. Evaluate the visual and auditory stimuli in the classroom in order to determine what level of stimuli the student can respond to appropriately.

11. Reduce visual and auditory stimuli to a level at which the student can successfully function. Gradually allow visual and auditory stimuli to increase as the student demonstrates that he/she can successfully tolerate the increased levels.

12. Seat the student so that he/she experiences the least amount of visual and auditory stimuli possible.

13. Provide the student with a quiet place in which to work where visual and auditory stimuli are reduced. This is used to reduce distracting stimuli and not as a form of punishment.

14. Place the student away from those peers who create the most visual and auditory stimulation in the classroom.

15. Provide the student with a carrel or divider at his/her desk to reduce visual and auditory stimuli.

16. Make certain that all visual and auditory stimuli in the classroom are reduced as much as possible for all learners.

17. Provide the student with the opportunity to move to a quiet place in the classroom any time that visual and auditory stimuli interfere with his/her ability to function successfully.

18. Provide the student with earphones to wear if auditory stimuli interfere with his/her ability to function. Gradually remove the earphones as the student can more successfully function in the presence of auditory stimuli.

19. Allow the student to close the door or windows in order to reduce visual and auditory stimuli outside of the classroom.

20. Require the student to be productive in the presence of visual and auditory stimuli for short periods of time. Gradually increase the length of time the student is required to be productive as he/she becomes successful.

21. Provide the student with shorter tasks that do not require extended attention in order to be more successful. Gradually increase the length of the tasks as the student demonstrates he/she can be successful in the presence of visual and auditory stimuli.

22. Have the student engage in small group activities (e.g., free time, math, reading, etc.) in order to reduce the level of visual and auditory stimuli in the group. Gradually increase group size as the student can function successfully in the presence of visual and auditory stimuli.

23. Teach the student appropriate ways to respond to visual and auditory stimuli in the classroom (e.g., moving to another part of the room, asking others to be quiet, leaving the group, etc.).

24. Model for the student appropriate behavior in the presence of visual and auditory stimuli in the classroom (e.g., continuing to work, asking for quiet, moving to a quieter part of the classroom, etc.).

25. Remove the student from an activity in the classroom if he/she is unable to demonstrate self-control in the presence of the visual and auditory stimuli involved in the activity.

26. Make the necessary adjustments in the environment in order to prevent the student from experiencing stress, frustration, anger, etc.

27. Provide a consistent routine for the student in order to enhance stability.

28. Allow flexibility in meeting academic demands when the student becomes overexcited (e.g., allow more time, modify assignments, provide help with assignments, etc.).

29. Teach the student to recognize when he/she is becoming overexcited in order that he/she may deal with it appropriately.

30. Provide a pleasant/calm atmosphere which would lessen the possibility of the student becoming overexcited.

31. Post classroom rules in various locations in the classroom in order to enhance the student's ability to remember the rules.

32. Avoid discussion or prevent stimuli in the environment which remind the student of unpleasant experiences/sensitive topics (e.g., divorce, death, unemployment, alcoholism, etc.).

51 Lies, denies, exaggerates, distorts the truth

1. Reinforce the student for making accurate statements: (a) give the student a tangible reward (e.g., classroom privileges, line leading, passing out materials, five minutes free time, etc.) or (b) give the student an intangible reward (e.g., praise, handshake, smile, etc.).

2. Speak with the student to explain: (a) what he/she is doing wrong (e.g., lying, denying his/her behavior, etc.) and (b) what he/she should be doing (e.g., reporting accurately what has occurred or will occur).

3. Write a contract with the student specifying what behavior is expected (e.g., making accurate statements) and what reinforcement will be made available when the terms of the contract have been met.

4. Communicate with parents (e.g., notes home, phone calls, etc.) in order to share information concerning the student's progress and so that they may reinforce the student at home for making accurate statements at school.

5. Avoid putting the student in a situation in which he/she has the opportunity to lie, deny, exaggerate, etc. (e.g., highly competitive activities, situations with limited supervision, etc.).

6. Avoid making accusations which would increase the probability of the student making inaccurate statements in response. If it is known that the student is responsible, an admission of guilt is not necessary to deal with the situation.

7. Supervise the student closely in order to monitor the accuracy of statements made.

8. Explain to the student that he/she should be satisfied with his/her own best effort rather than perfection.

9. Provide the student with many social and academic successes.

10. Provide the student with positive feedback which indicates he/she is successful.

11. Reduce competitiveness in information sharing in order that the student will not feel compelled to make inaccurate statements about his/her experiences.

12. Try various groupings in order to determine the situation in which the student is most comfortable and does not feel compelled to lie, deny, exaggerate the truth, etc.

13. Provide the student with experiences which can be shared if the absence of such experiences has been causing the student to fabricate information.

14. Reduce or remove punishment for accidents, forgetting, and situations with inadequate evidence. Punishment in these situations often causes students to lie.

15. Develop a system of shared responsibility (e.g., instead of trying to determine who is guilty, classmates work together to help clean up, return materials, make repairs, etc.).

16. Teach the student that making inaccurate statements does not prevent consequences (e.g., the student has to re-do tasks even though he/she claims the task was completed and lost).

17. Take no action in situations where conclusive evidence does not exist.

18. Help the student learn that telling the truth as soon as possible prevents future problems (e.g., admitting that he/she made a mistake, forgot, etc., means that the necessary steps can be taken to correct the situation instead of waiting until the truth is determined in some other way).

19. Allow natural consequences to occur when the student lies, denies, exaggerates, etc. (e.g., work not completed must be completed, lying to others will cause them not to believe you, etc.).

52 Brings inappropriate or illegal materials to school

1. Reinforce the student for demonstrating appropriate behavior: (a) give the student a tangible reward (e.g., classroom privileges, line leading, passing out materials, five minutes free time, etc.) or (b) give the student an intangible reward (e.g., praise, handshake, smile, etc.).

2. Speak with the student to explain: (a) what he/she is doing wrong (e.g., bringing inappropriate or illegal materials to school) and (b) what he/she should be doing (e.g., following an established code of conduct, following rules, taking care of responsibilities, etc.).

3. Establish classroom rules (e.g., work on-task, work quietly, remain in your seat, finish task, meet task expectations). Reiterate rules often and reinforce students for following rules.

4. Reinforce those students in the classroom who demonstrate appropriate behavior.

5. Reinforce the student for demonstrating appropriate behavior based on the length of time he/she can be successful. Gradually increase the length of time required for reinforcement as the student demonstrates success.

6. Remove the student from the group or activity until he/she can demonstrate appropriate behavior and self-control.

7. Write a contract with the student specifying what behavior is expected (e.g., not bringing alcohol to school) and what reinforcement will be made available when the terms of the contract have been met.

8. Communicate with parents (e.g., notes home, phone calls, etc.) in order to share information concerning the student's progress and so that they may reinforce the student at home for demonstrating appropriate behavior at school.

9. Communicate with parents, agencies, or appropriate parties in order to inform them of the problem, determine the cause of the problem, and consider possible solutions to the problem.

10. Provide a drug information program for the individual student, the class, or the student body.

11. Provide an orientation to penalties for possession or use of alcohol and drugs at school.

12. Involve the student in extracurricular activities to help him/her develop appropriate interests.

13. Identify individuals the student may contact with his/her concerns (e.g., guidance counselor, school nurse, social worker, school psychologist, etc.).

14. Share concerns with the administration and seek referral to an agency for investigation of alcohol or drug abuse.

15. Encourage the student to become involved in athletic activities.

16. Assign the student activities which would require interactions with a respected role model (e.g., older student, high school student, college student, community leader, someone held in esteem, etc.).

17. Provide the student with intelligent, accurate information concerning drugs and alcohol rather than sensationalized scare tactic information.

18. Provide many opportunities for social and academic success.

19. Encourage the student to excel in a particular area of interest (e.g., provide information for him/her, provide personal and professional support, sponsor the student, etc.).

20. Maintain frequent contact with the student during school hours (e.g., follow up on details of earlier communications, maintain a direction for conversation, etc.).

21. Lead and direct the student. Do not lecture and make demands.

22. Maintain anecdotal records of the student's behavior to check patterns or changes in behavior.

23. When natural consequences from peers occur (e.g., criticism, loss of friendship, etc.) as the result of the use of drugs or alcohol at school bring the consequences to the attention of the student.

24. Encourage the student's parents to be positive and helpful with the student as opposed to being negative and threatening.

25. Act as a resource for parents by providing information on agencies, counseling programs, etc.

26. Teach the student to be satisfied with his/her own best effort rather than perfection.

27. Reduce the emphasis on competition and help the student realize that success is individually defined.

28. Be willing to take the time to listen, share, and talk with the student.

29. Increase your own professional knowledge of laws and treatment concerning drug or alcohol use and abuse.

30. Teach the student alternative ways to deal with demands, challenges, and pressures of the school-age experience (e.g., deal with problems when they arise, practice self-control at all times, share problems or concerns with others, etc.).

31. Maintain adequate supervision at all times and in all areas of the school (e.g., hallways, bathrooms, between classes, before and after school, school grounds, etc.).

32. Provide appropriate reading material (e.g., magazines, novels, etc.) at school, which is of interest to the student, so that he/she will not bring inappropriate reading material to school

53 Destroys school or other students' property

1. Reinforce the student for demonstrating appropriate care and handling of others' property: (a) give the student a tangible reward (e.g., classroom privileges, line leading, passing out materials, five minutes free time, etc.) or (b) give the student an intangible reward (e.g., praise, handshake, smile, etc.).

2. Speak to the student to explain: (a) what he/she is doing wrong (e.g., defacing property, destroying property, etc.) and (b) what he/she should be doing (e.g., putting property away, returning property, etc.).

3. Establish classroom rules (e.g., work on-task, work quietly, remain in your seat, finish task, meet task expectations). Reiterate rules often and reinforce students for following rules.

4. Reinforce those students in the classroom who demonstrate appropriate care and handling of others' property.

5. Reinforce the student for demonstrating appropriate care and handling of others' property based on the length of time he/she can be successful. Gradually increase the length of time required for reinforcement as the student demonstrates success.

6. Write a contract with the student specifying what behavior is expected (e.g., putting property away, returning property, etc.) and what reinforcement will be made available when the terms of the contract have been met.

7. Communicate with parents (e.g., notes home, phone calls, etc.) in order to share information concerning the student's progress and so that they may reinforce the student at home for demonstrating appropriate care and handling of others' property at school.

8. Evaluate the appropriateness of the task to determine: (a) if the task is too easy, (b) if the task is too difficult, and (c) if the length of time scheduled to complete the task is appropriate.

9. Identify a peer to act as a model for the student to imitate appropriate care and handling of others' property.

10. Have the student question any directions, explanations, instructions he/she does not understand.

11. Provide time at the beginning of each day to help the student organize the materials he/she will use throughout the day.

12. Provide the student with adequate work space (e.g., a large desk or table at which to work).

13. Provide storage space for materials the student is not using at any particular time.

14. Reduce distracting stimuli (e.g., place the student on the front row, provide a carrel or quiet place away from distractions, etc.). Overstimulation may cause the student to misuse others' property.

15. Interact frequently with the student in order to prompt organizational skills and appropriate use of materials.

16. Assign the student organizational responsibilities in the classroom (e.g., equipment, software materials, etc.).

17. Limit the student's use of materials (e.g., provide the student with only those materials necessary at any given time).

18. Act as a model for organization and appropriate use of work materials (e.g., putting materials away before getting others out, having a place for all materials, maintaining an organized desk area, following a schedule for the day, etc.).

19. Provide adequate time for the completion of activities. Inadequate time for completion of activities may result in the student's misuse of others' property.

20. Allow natural consequences to occur as the result of the student's inability to appropriately care for and handle others' property (e.g., property not maintained appropriately will be lost or not serviceable).

21. Assess the quality and clarity of directions, explanations, and instructions given to the student for use in the care and handling of others' property.

22. Assist the student in beginning each task in order to reduce impulsive behavior.

23. Provide the student with structure for all academic activities (e.g., specific directions, routine format for tasks, time units, etc.).

24. Give the student a checklist of materials necessary for each activity.

25. Minimize materials needed.

26. Provide an organizer for materials inside the student's desk.

27. Teach the student appropriate care and handling of others' property (e.g., sharpening pencils, keeping books free of marks and tears, etc.).

28. Make certain that all personal property is labeled with the students' names.

29. Point out to the student that borrowing personal property from others does not reduce his/her responsibility for the property.

30. Teach the student how to conserve rather than waste materials (e.g., amount of glue, paper, tape, etc., to use; putting lids, caps, and tops on such materials as markers, pens, bottles, jars, cans, etc.).

31. Teach the student appropriate ways to deal with anger and frustration rather than destroying others' property (e.g., pencils, pens, workbooks, notebooks, textbooks, etc.).

32. Teach the student to maintain property belonging to others (e.g., keep property with him/her, know where property is at all times, secure property in locker, etc.).

33. Provide the student with an appropriate place to store/secure others' property (e.g., desk, locker, closet, etc.) and require the student to store all property when not in use.

34. Teach the student that the failure to care for others' property will result in the loss of freedom to use others' property.

35. Provide reminders (e.g., a list of property or materials) to help the student maintain and care for school property.

36. Limit the student's freedom to take property from school if he/she is unable to remember to return such items.

37. Limit the student's opportunity to use others' property if he/she is unable to care for his/her own personal property.

38. Reduce the number of materials the student is responsible to care for or handle. Increase the number as the student demonstrates appropriate care of property.

39. Teach the student safety rules in the care and handling of others' property and materials (e.g., pencils, scissors, compass; and biology, industrial arts, and home economics materials, etc.).

40. Require that lost or damaged property be replaced by the student. If the student cannot replace the property, restitution can be made by working at school.

41. Make certain the student is not inadvertently reinforced for losing or damaging property by providing him/her with new materials. Provide the student with used or damaged materials, copies of the materials, etc., rather than new materials.

42. Teach the student rules for the care and handling of others' property (e.g., always ask to use other's property, treat the property with care, inform the teacher if the property becomes damaged, return the property in the same or better condition, etc.).

43. Do not permit peers to allow the student to use their property if he/she is not able to care for it properly.

44. Remove others' property from the student if he/she is unable to appropriately care for and handle the property.

45. Maintain mobility throughout the classroom in order to supervise the student's care and handling of others' property.

46. Remove the student from the group or activity until he/she can demonstrate appropriate behavior and self-control.

47. Structure the environment to reduce free or unplanned time which is likely to contribute to the student's inappropriate behavior.

48. Maintain visibility to and from the student. The teacher should be able to see the student and the student should be able to see the teacher, making eye contact possible at all times.

49. Make the necessary adjustments in the environment to prevent the student from experiencing stress, frustration, anger, etc., as much as possible.

50. Prevent the student from becoming overstimulated by an activity.

51. Make the student responsible for specific materials (e.g., tape recorder, overhead projector, microscope, etc.) in the school environment, in order to enhance a sense of responsibility and obligation to use the materials with care.

54 Cheats

1. Reinforce the student for doing his/her own work: (a) give the student a tangible reward (e.g., classroom privileges, line leading, passing out materials, five minutes free time, etc.) or (b) give the student an intangible reward (e.g., praise, handshake, smile, etc.).

2. Speak to the student to explain: (a) what he/she is doing wrong (e.g., cheating, copying, etc.) and (b) what he/she should be doing (e.g., doing his/her own work).

3. Establish classroom rules (e.g., work on-task, work quietly, remain in your seat, finish task, meet task expectations). Reiterate rules often and reinforce students for following rules.

4. Reinforce those students in the classroom who do their own work.

5. Reinforce the student for doing his/her own work based on the length of time he/she can be successful. Gradually increase the length of time required for reinforcement as the student demonstrates success.

6. Write a contract with the student specifying what behavior is expected (e.g., doing his/her own work) and what reinforcement will be made available when the terms of the contract have been met.

7. Communicate with parents (e.g., notes home, phone calls, etc.) in order to share information concerning the student's progress and so that they may reinforce the student at home for doing his/her own work at school.

8. Evaluate the appropriateness of the task to determine: (a) if the task is too easy, (b) if the task is too difficult, and (c) if the length of time scheduled to complete the task is appropriate.

9. Identify a peer to act as a model for the student to imitate performing his/her own work.

10. Have the student question any directions, explanations, instructions he/she does not understand.

11. Review prior to administering tests and quizzes in order to better prepare the student.

12. Reduce the emphasis on test and quiz scores by grading the student's daily performance.

13. Maintain mobility in order to be frequently near the student when he/she takes tests and quizzes or performs daily assignments.

14. Reduce the emphasis on competition. Fear of failure may cause the student to resort to cheating or copying others' work in order to be successful.

15. Seat the student away from others if he/she is prone to cheating and/or copying others' work.

16. Seat the student near the teacher when he/she takes tests and quizzes.

17. Make certain that other students do not allow the student to look at their work during tests and quizzes and while performing assignments.

18. Make certain the student is aware of the consequences for cheating and/or copying others' work (e.g., assignments will be taken away, failing grades will be recorded, etc.).

19. Arrange to have a peer help the student study for tests and quizzes and perform daily assignments.

20. Evaluate the level of difficulty in relation to the student's ability to perform the task.

21. Make certain the student understands all directions, explanations, and instructions prior to taking test and quizzes and performing assignments.

22. Make certain the student knows that he/she can ask questions when taking tests and quizzes or performing assigned activities.

23. Communicate with parents or guardians in order that they may help the student study for tests and quizzes (e.g., send home directions, explanations, and instructions relating to content covered on tests and quizzes, material to review, etc.).

24. Have the student take tests and quizzes elsewhere in the building under the individual supervision of an instructor (e.g., library, resource room, counselor's office, etc.).

25. Check the student for obvious attempts to cheat prior to taking a test or quiz (e.g., "cheat sheet," answers written on hands and cuffs, etc.).

26. Help the student accept the fact that self-improvement is more important than getting the highest grade in the class, making all A's, being the first one done with an assignment, etc., by reinforcing and grading on the basis of self-improvement.

55 Demonstrates inappropriate behavior when moving with a group

1. Reinforce the student for demonstrating appropriate behavior when moving with a group: (a) give the student a tangible reward (e.g., classroom privileges, line leading, passing out materials, five minutes free time, etc.) or (b) give the student an intangible reward (e.g., praise, handshake, smile, etc.).

2. Speak to the student to explain: (a) what he/she is doing wrong (e.g., running, pushing peers, etc.) and (b) what he/she should be doing (e.g., walking without touching peers).

3. Reinforce those students who demonstrate appropriate behavior when moving with a group.

4. Reinforce the student for moving appropriately with a group based on the length of time he/she can be successful. Gradually increase the length of time required for reinforcement as the student demonstrates success.

5. Write a contract with the student specifying what behavior is expected (e.g., walking in the halls) and what reinforcement will be made available when the terms of the contract have been met.

6. Communicate with parents (e.g., notes home, phone calls, etc.) in order to share information concerning the student's progress and so that they may reinforce the student at home for moving appropriately with a group at school.

7. Evaluate the appropriateness of the expectation of moving with a group to determine: (a) if the task is too easy, (b) if the task is too difficult, and (c) if the length of time scheduled to complete the task is appropriate.

8. Identify a peer to act as a model for the student to imitate appropriate movement with a group.

9. Have the student question any directions, explanations, instructions he/she does not understand.

10. Reinforce the student for waiting appropriately in line (e.g., standing against the wall, talking quietly, standing near others without making physical contact, etc.).

11. Reinforce the student for walking at the same pace as other students when moving with a group.

12. Have the student walk with his/her arms crossed, arms against his/her side, hands in pockets, etc., if touching others is a problem.

13. Form a second line or group for those students who move at a slower pace.

14. Separate the student from the peer(s) who stimulates his/her inappropriate behavior when moving with a group.

15. Have the student walk alone, behind the group, beside the teacher, etc., when he/she displays inappropriate behavior when moving with a group.

16. Provide the student with a demonstration/model for moving appropriately with a group.

17. Have the student act as a line leader, line monitor, etc., when moving with a group.

18. Have the students walk in pairs when moving as a group.

19. Stop the line frequently in order to assure student success when moving with a group.

20. Provide the student with rules for moving appropriately with a group (e.g., walk in the halls, go directly from one area to another, talk quietly in the halls, walk on the right side of the hall, use the appropriate stairway). Reiterate rules often and reinforce the student for following rules.

56 Responds inappropriately to redirection in academic and social situations

1. Reinforce the student for responding appropriately to redirection in academic and social situations: (a) give the student a tangible reward (e.g., classroom privileges, line leading, passing out materials, five minutes free time, etc.) or (b) give the student an intangible reward (e.g., praise, handshake, smile, etc.).

2. Speak to the student to explain: (a) what he/she is doing wrong (e.g., not correcting errors on an assignment, failing to return to seat when told to do so, etc.) and (b) what he/she should be doing (e.g., correcting errors on an assignment, returning to seat when told to do so, etc.).

3. Establish classroom rules (e.g., work on-task, work quietly, remain in your seat, finish task, correct errors, meet task expectations). Reiterate rules often and reinforce students for following rules.

4. Reinforce those students in the classroom who respond appropriately to redirection in academic and social situations.

5. Reinforce the student for responding appropriately to redirection within a given period of time based on the number of times he/she can be successful. Gradually increase the number of times required for reinforcement as the student demonstrates success.

6. Write a contract with the student specifying what behavior is expected (e.g., returning to seat when told to do so) and what reinforcement will be made available when the terms of the contract have been met.

7. Communicate with parents (e.g., notes home, phone calls, etc.) in order to share information concerning the student's progress and so that they may reinforce the student at home for responding appropriately to redirection in academic and social situations at school.

8. Evaluate the appropriateness of the task to determine: (a) if the task is too easy, (b) if the task is too difficult, and (c) if the length of time scheduled to complete the task is appropriate.

9. Identify a peer to act as a model for the student to imitate appropriate response to redirection in academic and social situations.

10. Have the student question any directions, explanations, instructions he/she does not understand.

11. Allow natural consequences to occur when the student fails to respond appropriately to redirection in academic and social situations (e.g., make highly reinforcing activities contingent upon responding appropriately to redirection in academic and social situations).

12. Remove the student from the activity if he/she fails to respond appropriately to redirection in academic and social situations.

13. Make certain that attention is not inadvertently given to the student for failing to respond appropriately to redirection in academic and social situations (e.g., remove attention from the student when he/she fails to respond appropriately to redirection in academic and social situations in those instances when attention is reinforcing the inappropriate behavior).

14. Provide adequate time for the student to respond appropriately to redirection in academic and social situations.

15. Make certain that redirection in academic and social situations is delivered in the most positive manner possible.

16. Deliver redirection to the student as privately as possible.

17. Deliver instructions in a clear and concise manner.

18. Assist the student in responding appropriately to redirection in academic situations (e.g., help the student correct one or two items in order to get him/her started).

19. Develop subsequent tasks based on errors the student makes rather than requiring an immediate correction of work done incorrectly.

20. Make certain that the student's failure to respond to redirection in social situations results in loss of opportunity to engage in that activity for some period of time (e.g., one day).

21. Make certain the student understands the assignment or activity by having him/her rephrase the directions.

22. Make certain the student understands the communication regarding redirection by having the student rephrase the redirection.

23. Determine the reason for errors made by the student.

24. Evaluate the demands made on the student in academic and social situations in order to make certain that expectations are within the student's level of ability.

25. In order to reduce the need for redirection in academic situations, require the student to check all work for errors prior to handing in assignments.

26. Make certain the student understands that natural consequences may occur as a result of failing to appropriately respond to redirection in a social situation (e.g., peers will not include him/her in activities, peers will not want to share materials with him/her, etc.).

27. When redirection is delivered to the student in academic and social situations, make certain that an explanation as to why the redirection has been made is also given (e.g., "You need to return to your seat because we are ready to begin a new activity.").

28. Make certain that the activity is not so overstimulating as to result in the student's inability to respond appropriately to redirection in academic and social situations.

29. Be consistent in expectations when redirecting the student in academic and social situations (e.g., require the student to immediately correct errors after work has been checked, require the student to return to his/her seat within three minutes, etc.).

30. Base expectations for student response to redirection in academic and social situations on his/her ability level (e.g., one student may be expected to return to his/her seat immediately upon redirection while another student may be given three minutes to respond appropriately).

31. Avoid those circumstances under which the student demonstrates difficulty in responding appropriately to redirection in academic and social situations (e.g., highly competitive situations, situations in which the student is embarrassed by his/her errors, etc.).

32. Make certain that redirection does not become a pervasive aspect of everything the student does by allowing redirection to become a necessary part of every academic and social situation in which the student engages.

33. Monitor the student's behavior in order to provide redirection before the student's errors or inappropriate behavior exceeds his/her ability to respond appropriately.

34. Make certain that the student understands that redirection is designed to help him/her succeed rather than as a form of punishment (e.g., use statements such as, "This sentence would be much easier to read if it was written with correct capitalization and punctuation. Please write it again and I'll check it for you.").

35. Make certain that communications with the student regarding redirection are appropriate to that student's ability to respond (e.g., match the form in which redirection is delivered to the student's most likely successful response such as, "Would you please go to your seat." rather than "You need to go to your seat immediately.").

57 Does not accept changes in established routine

1. Reinforce the student for accepting changes in an established routine: (a) give the student a tangible reward (e.g., classroom privileges, line leading, passing out materials, five minutes free time, etc.) or (b) give the student an intangible reward (e.g., praise, handshake, smile, etc.).

2. Speak to the student to explain: (a) what he/she is doing wrong (e.g., tantruming, refusing to accept the change, etc.) and (b) what he/she should be doing (e.g., accepting the change in routine).

3. Establish classroom rules (e.g., work on-task, work quietly, remain in your seat, finish task, meet task expectations). Reiterate rules often and reinforce students for following rules.

4. Reinforce those students in the classroom who accept changes in an established routine.

5. Reinforce the student for accepting changes in an established routine based on the number of times he/she can be successful. Gradually increase the number of times required for reinforcement as the student demonstrates success.

6. Write a contract with the student specifying what behavior is expected (e.g., accepting a change in routine) and what reinforcement will be made available when the terms of the contract have been met.

7. Communicate with parents (e.g., note home, phone calls, etc.) in order to share information concerning the student's progress and so that they may reinforce the student at home for accepting changes in an established routine at school.

8. Evaluate the appropriateness of the change in routine in order to determine if the change is too difficult and if the length of time scheduled is appropriate.

9. Identify a peer to act as a model for the student to imitate appropriate acceptance of changes in an established routine.

10. Have the student question any directions, explanations, instructions he/she does not understand concerning the change in an established routine.

11. Have the student work near a peer in order to follow change in an established routine.

12. Provide the student with a schedule of revised daily events which identifies the activities for the day and the times at which they will occur. (See Appendix for Schedule of Daily Events.)

13. Revisions in the schedule for the day's events should be attached to the student's desk and/or carried with the student throughout the day.

14. Post the revised routine throughout the classroom (e.g., on the student's desk, chalkboard, bulletin board, etc.).

15. Attempt to limit the number of times that changes must occur in the student's routine.

16. Discuss any necessary changes in the student's routine well in advance of the occurrence of the changes.

17. Teach the student to tell time in order to enhance his/her ability to accept change in an established routine.

18. Have the student rely on a predetermined signal (e.g., turn lights off and on, hand signal, etc.) in order to enhance his/her ability to accept change in an established routine.

19. Have the student use a timer to remind him/her of changes in an established routine.

20. Reduce distracting stimuli which might cause the student to be unable to accept change in an established routine (e.g., movement, noise, peers, etc.).

21. Model acceptance of change in an established routine.

22. Have a peer remind the student of changes in his/her routine.

23. Have the student rely on environmental cues to remind him/her when to change activities in his/her revised routine (e.g., other students changing activities, bells, lights, buses arriving, etc.).

24. Remind the student when it is time to change activities.

25. Have a peer accompany the student to other locations in the building when change in an established routine has occurred.

26. Allow the student an appropriate amount of time to accept changes in an established routine.

27. Explain changes in routine to the student personally.

28. Provide activities similar to those canceled in the student's routine (e.g., if an art activity is canceled due to the art teacher's absence, provide an art activity in the classroom for the student).

29. Provide the student with highly desirable activities to perform when changes in his/her routine are necessary.

30. If change in the student's routine proves too difficult, have the student remain with his/her established routine (e.g., if an assembly is too overstimulating for the student, have him/her continue to work in his/her established routine).

31. Initially limit the number/degrees of change(s) in the student's established routine. Gradually increase the number/degree of change(s) in the routine as the student demonstrates success.

32. In order to help the student accept change in an established routine, implement environmental changes within the classroom in order to provide the student experience with change (e.g., change in seating, instructional delivery, task format, etc.).

33. Prepare a substitute teacher information packet that includes all information pertaining to the classroom (e.g., student roster, class schedule, class rules, behavior management techniques, class helpers, etc.).

34. Make certain that the student understands that classroom rules and consequences are in effect when a substitute teacher is in the classroom.

35. Indicate the name of several teachers and where they can be found in case the substitute teacher should need their assistance.

36. Inform the substitute teacher of the classroom rules and consequences if the rules are not followed by the student.

37. Have the student work on practice work (work that has already been taught to the student and that he/she knows how to do) in order to reduce frustration and feelings of failure when a substitute teacher is in the classroom.

38. Make an attempt to use a substitute teacher who has skills necessary to deal with problem behavior and special needs students.

39. Make certain that the substitute teacher is familiar with the behavioral support system used in the classroom (e.g., rules, point system, reinforcers, etc.).

40. Provide the substitute teacher with detailed information on the activities and assignments.

41. Assign the student specific activities to perform on any day when a substitute teacher may be responsible for the classroom (e.g., assistant to the substitute teacher, errands to run, line leading, class monitor, etc.).

42. Make certain the substitute teacher follows all procedures indicated by the classroom teacher (e.g., academic activities, behavioral support system, etc.).

43. Have special or unique responsibilities performed by other personnel in the building (e.g., administering medication, feeding, toileting, etc.).

44. Assign a peer to work with the student to act as a model for appropriate behavior and provide information necessary for success when changes are made in an established routine.

45. If an aide works in the classroom, have the aide monitor the student's behavior, provide reinforcement, deliver instructions, etc., when a substitute teacher is in the classroom.

46. Provide a quiet place for the student to work.

47. Inform the students in advance when it will be necessary for a substitute teacher to be in the classroom and establish expectations for behavior and academic performance.

58 Does not follow school rules

1. Reinforce the student for following school rules: (a) give the student a tangible reward (e.g., classroom privileges, line leading, passing out materials, five minutes free time, etc.) or (b) give the student an intangible reward (e.g., praise, handshake, smile, etc.).

2. Speak to the student to explain: (a) what he/she is doing wrong (e.g., failing to follow school rules) and (b) what he/she should be doing (e.g., following school rules).

3. Establish school rules (e.g., walk in halls, arrive to class on time, respect the privacy of others, talk quietly in the halls). Reiterate rules often and reinforce students for following rules.

4. Reinforce those students in the classroom who follow school rules.

5. Reinforce the student for following school rules based on the length of time he/she can be successful. Gradually increase the length of time required for reinforcement as the student demonstrates success.

6. Write a contract with the student specifying what behavior is expected (e.g., walking in the halls) and what reinforcement will be made available when the terms of the contract have been met.

7. Communicate with parents (e.g., notes home, phone calls, etc.) in order to share information concerning the student's progress and so that they may reinforce the student at home for following school rules.

8. Evaluate the appropriateness of the task to determine: (a) if the task is too easy, (b) if the task is too difficult, and (c) if the length of time scheduled to complete the task is appropriate.

9. Have the student question any directions, explanations, instructions he/she does not understand.

10. Structure the environment in such a way that the student remains active and involved.

11. Maintain visibility to and from the student. The teacher should be able to see the student and the student should be able to see the teacher, making eye contact possible at all times.

12. Maintain maximum supervision of the student and gradually decrease supervision as the student is able to follow school rules.

13. Have the student maintain a chart representing the amount of time spent following school rules, with reinforcement for increasing acceptable behavior.

14. Practice mobility to be frequently near the student.

15. Provide the student with many social and academic successes.

16. Provide the student with positive feedback that indicates he/she is successful.

17. Post school rules in various places, including on the student's desk, in the hallways, etc.

18. Be a consistent authority figure (e.g., be consistent in relationship with students).

19. Provide the student with optional courses of action in order to prevent total refusal to obey school rules (e.g., return to the classroom).

20. Intervene early to prevent the student's behavior from leading to contagion for other students.

21. Require the student to verbalize the school rules at designated times throughout the day (e.g., before school, recess, lunch, at the end of the day, etc.).

22. Have a peer act as a model for following school rules.

23. Interact with the student frequently to determine if school rules are being followed.

24. Make certain that all educators maintain consistent enforcement of school rules.

25. Have the student question any school rules he/she does not understand.

26. Provide the student with a list of school rules and/or behavior expectations to carry at all times in the school environment.

27. Help the student identify specific school rules he/she has difficulty following and make these rules goals for behavior improvement.

28. Separate the student from the peer(s) who stimulates his/her inappropriate behavior.

29. Make certain that rules and behavior expectations are consistent throughout the school and classrooms.

30. Model for the student those behaviors he/she is expected to display in the school environment.

31. Have a peer accompany the student in nonacademic settings.

32. Make certain the behavioral demands are appropriate for the student's ability level (e.g., staying in line, waiting a turn, moving with a group, sitting at a table with a group, moving about the building alone, etc.).

33. Make certain the student is actively involved in the environment (i.e., give the student responsibilities, activities, and errands to run in order to provide purposeful behavior).

34. Reinforce the student for moving from one place to another in an appropriate length of time.

35. Have the student carry a point card at all times so that he/she can be reinforced anywhere in the school environment for following rules.

36. Inform other personnel of any behavior problems the student may have in order that supervision and assistance may be provided.

37. Reinforce the student for going directly from one location to another.

38. Be consistent in applying consequences for behavior (e.g., appropriate behavior receives positive consequences while inappropriate behavior receives negative consequences).

39. Reinforce the student for remaining in assigned areas (e.g., play areas, student lounge, recreational area, etc.).

40. Use related consequences for the student's inappropriate behavior (e.g., running in the halls results in having to walk with an adult, throwing food in the cafeteria results in having to sit next to an adult when eating, disruption in the library requires additional adult supervision, etc.).

59 Indicates that he/she does not care or is not concerned about performance, grades, report cards, graduating, consequences of behavior, etc.

1. Reinforce the student for showing an interest and participating in school activities: (a) give the student a tangible reward (e.g., classroom privileges, line leading, passing out materials, five minutes free time, etc.) or (b) give the student an intangible reward (e.g., praise, handshake, smile, etc.).

2. Speak with the student to explain: (a) what he/she is doing wrong (e.g., failing to show an interest and participate in school activities) and (b) what he/she should be doing (e.g., showing an interest and participating in school activities).

3. Establish classroom rules (e.g., work on-task, work quietly, remain in your seat, finish task, meet task expectations). Reiterate rules often and reinforce students for following rules.

4. Reinforce those students in the classroom who show an interest and participate in school activities.

5. Reinforce the student for showing an interest and participating in school activities based on the length of time he/she can be successful. Gradually increase the length of time required for reinforcement as the student demonstrates success.

6. Write a contract with the student specifying what behavior is expected (e.g., showing an interest and participating in school activities) and what reinforcement will be made available when the terms of the contract have been met.

7. Communicate with parents (e.g., notes home, phone calls, etc.) in order to share information concerning the student's progress and so that they may reinforce the student at home for showing an interest and participating in school activities.

8. Communicate with parents, agencies, or appropriate parties in order to inform them of the problem, determine the cause of the problem, and consider possible solutions to the problem.

9. Evaluate the appropriateness of the task to determine: (a) if the task is too easy, (b) if the task is too difficult, and (c) if the length of time scheduled to complete the task is appropriate.

10. Call on the student when he/she can answer successfully.

11. Avoid competition. Failure may cause the student to lose interest or not participate in school activities.

12. Allow the student more decision-making opportunities relative to class activities and assignments.

13. Present tasks in the most attractive and interesting manner possible.

14. Give the student responsibilities in the classroom (e.g., teacher assistant, peer tutor, group leader, etc.).

15. Provide a full schedule of daily events to keep the student actively involved. (See Appendix for Schedule of Daily Events.)

16. Provide the student with as many academic and social successes as possible.

17. Evaluate the appropriateness of the task in relation to the student's ability to perform the task successfully.

18. Determine the student's preferred activities, interests, etc., and incorporate them into his/her daily schedule, program, etc., at various points throughout the day.

19. Provide the student with "real life" experiences from the environment. Have individuals from the work force (e.g., mechanic, draftsman, secretary, etc.) visit the class to relate the importance of school-to-work experiences that involve math, reading, writing, etc.

20. Show an interest in the student (e.g., acknowledge the student, ask the student's opinion, spend time working one-on-one with the student, etc.).

60 Needs immediate rewards/reinforcement in order to demontrate appropriate behavior

1. Reinforce the student as often as necessary while gradually increasing the amount of time between reinforcement: (a) give the student a tangible reward (e.g., classroom privileges, line leading, passing out materials, five minutes free time, etc.) or (b) give the student an intangible reward (e.g., praise, handshake, smile, etc.).

2. Speak with the student to explain: (a) what he/she is doing wrong (e.g., asking for reinforcement as soon as a task is completed) and (b) what he/she should be doing (e.g., waiting until the end of the activity or until an established time, saving tokens or points for reinforcement at a later time, etc.).

3. Establish classroom rules (e.g., work on-task, work quietly, remain in your seat, finish task, meet task expectations). Reiterate rules often and reinforce students for following the rules.

4. Reinforce those students who can accept extended time periods between reinforcement.

5. Write a contract with the student specifying what behavior is expected (e.g., working five minutes without asking for reinforcement) and what reinforcement will be made available when the terms of the contract have been met.

6. Communicate with parents (e.g., notes home, phone calls, etc.) in order to share information concerning the student's progress and so that they may reinforce the student at home for tolerating extended time periods between reinforcement at school.

7. Evaluate the appropriateness of the task to determine: (a) if the task is too easy, (b) if the task is too difficult, and (c) if the length of time scheduled for the task is appropriate.

8. Have the student maintain a chart representing his/her own appropriate behavior in order that his/her success is recognized.

9. Provide the student with positive feedback which indicates he/she is successful, competent, important, valuable, etc. (e.g., provide social reinforcement in place of tangible reinforcement).

10. Make certain that natural consequences follow appropriate behavior (e.g., recognition from the group for success, compliments, congratulations, etc.).

11. Reduce the emphasis on material rewards and increase the emphasis on intrinsic rewards (e.g., emphasize a job well done, improvement, personal success, etc.).

12. Provide the student with an abundance of tangible reinforcement in order that it may satisfy his/her need for gratification.

13. Present the task in an attractive and interesting manner with as much success built in as possible (e.g., the task should be inherently reinforcing).

14. Be certain to greet and acknowledge the student as often as possible rather than providing recognition only as a reinforcer.

15. Encourage the student to save tokens, points, etc., over time for delayed reinforcement (e.g., make tangible reinforcement a goal rather than an immediate need satisfaction).

16. Make certain that reinforcement is not inadvertently given for inappropriate behavior (e.g., responding to the student only when he/she makes errors, responding to the student when he/she misrepresents a need for help, etc.).

17. Interact frequently with the student in order to replace tangible reinforcement with social reinforcement.

18. Reinforce with tangibles less often as the student experiences more satisfaction with a job well done (i.e., intrinsic satisfaction begins to replace tangibles as reinforcement).

19. Make certain that reinforcement is used as a natural consequence for a job well done or for appropriate behavior.

20. Provide reinforcement at routine intervals in order that the student learns that reinforcement is delayed, but forthcoming (e.g., free time, end of the day, Friday afternoon, etc.).

61 Does not care for personal appearance

*Evidence of inappropriate care for personal appearance would include such things as dirt on body and under fingernails, dirty hair, body odor, unbrushed teeth, offensive breath, failure to use a handkerchief appropriately, and toileting accidents.

1. Reinforce the student for caring for his/her personal appearance: (a) give the student a tangible reward (e.g., classroom privileges, line leading, passing out materials, five minutes free time, etc.) or (b) give the student an intangible reward (e.g., praise, handshake, smile, etc.).

2. Speak to the student to explain: (a) what he/she is doing wrong (e.g., wearing dirty clothing, failing to wash hair or clean fingernails, etc.) and (b) what he/she should be doing (e.g., wearing clean clothing, washing hair, cleaning fingernails, etc.).

3. Reinforce those students in the classroom who care for their personal appearance.

4. Reinforce the student for caring for his/her personal appearance based on the length of time he/she can be successful. Gradually increase the length of time required for reinforcement as the student demonstrates success.

5. Write a contract with the student specifying what behavior is expected (e.g., wearing clean clothing, washing hair, cleaning fingernails, etc.) and what reinforcement will be made available when the terms of the contract have been met.

6. Communicate with parents (e.g., notes home, phone calls, etc.) in order to share information concerning the student's progress and so that they may reinforce the student at home for caring for his/her personal appearance.

7. Identify a peer to act as a model for the student to imitate appropriate hygiene (e.g., wearing clean clothing, washing hair, cleaning fingernails, etc.).

8. Have the student question any hygiene expectations he/she does not understand.

9. Establish hygiene rules (e.g., bathe regularly, brush teeth, wash hair, launder clothing after wearing, clean and trim nails, maintain personal cleanliness after using restroom, and use handkerchief). Reiterate rules often and reinforce students for following the rules.

10. Evaluate the demands of the responsibility of the student for his/her own hygiene in order to determine if the expectations are too high. If expectations are too difficult for the student, assistance should be provided.

11. Designate one adult in the educational environment to work directly with the student to help him/her care for his/her personal appearance.

12. Provide the student with training in the use of personal grooming and related materials (e.g., washcloth, soap, shampoo, toothbrush, toothpaste, hairbrush, comb, nail clippers, toilet paper, handkerchief, etc.).

13. Allow the student to attend to personal hygiene needs at school if the opportunity is not available elsewhere (e.g., launder clothing, bathe, wash hair, etc.).

14. Maintain personal hygiene materials at school for the student's use.

15. Provide a comprehensive unit of information and instruction on personal hygiene. The unit should include health and appearance aspects. Classroom visitors can include dentist, nurse, doctor, cosmetologist, etc.

16. Communicate with parents, agencies, or appropriate parties in order to inform them of the problem, determine the cause of the problem, and consider possible solutions to the problem.

17. Require the student to maintain a daily routine of grooming and attending to personal hygiene at school.

18. Have the student keep a change of clean clothing at school.

19. As part of instruction on interviewing and job placement, emphasize the importance of personal hygiene and grooming (e.g., have a representative of business or industry visit the class to make a presentation on the importance of personal appearance).

20. Provide the student with a checklist of personal hygiene activities and have the student complete the checklist daily.

21. Provide visual reminders of personal hygiene in appropriate locations (e.g., picture of washing hands and brushing teeth at sink, picture of deodorant in restroom, etc.).

22. Teach the student to launder clothing.

23. Reinforce the student for gradually improving personal hygiene over time rather than expecting total mastery of personal hygiene skills immediately.

24. Make certain that all communications with the student concerning personal hygiene are conducted in a private manner.

25. Provide the student with scheduled times during the day to attend to personal hygiene needs.

26. Allow the student to arrive early at school in order to care for his/her personal appearance.

62 Engages in inappropriate behaviors related to bodily functions

1. Reinforce the student for demonstrating appropriate behavior related to bodily functions: (a) give the student a tangible reward (e.g., classroom privileges, line leading, passing out materials, five minutes free time, etc.) or (b) give the student an intangible reward (e.g., praise, handshake, smile, etc.).

2. Speak to the student to explain: (a) what he/she is doing wrong (e.g., urinating on floor, masturbating, etc.) and (b) what he/she should be doing (e.g., demonstrating appropriate social behavior).

3. Reinforce those students in the classroom who demonstrate appropriate social behavior.

4. Reinforce the student for demonstrating appropriate social behavior based on the length of time he/she can be successful. Gradually increase the length of time required for reinforcement as the student demonstrates success.

5. Write a contract with the student specifying what behavior is expected (e.g., talking about topics which are appropriate for social situations) and what reinforcements will be made available when the terms of the contract have been met.

6. Communicate with parents (e.g., notes home, phone calls, etc.) in order to share information concerning the student's progress and so that they may reinforce the student at home for demonstrating appropriate social behavior at school.

7. Communicate with parents, agencies, or appropriate parties in order to inform them of the problem, determine the cause of the problem, and consider possible solutions to the problem.

8. Evaluate the appropriateness of the task to determine: (a) if the task is too easy, (b) if the task is too difficult, and (c) if the length of time scheduled to complete the task is appropriate.

9. Identify a peer to act as a model for the student to imitate appropriate social behavior.

10. Discuss appropriate social behavior with the student and make certain he/she understands which behaviors are appropriate for public places and which are not.

11. Provide adequate supervision throughout the school environment in order to prevent the student from talking about bodily functions, masturbating, etc.

12. Make certain that the student is not inadvertently reinforced for engaging in inappropriate behavior related to bodily functions (e.g., deal with the problem privately; avoid reacting in a shocked, disgusted or angry manner, etc.).

13. Make certain that natural consequences follow the student's inappropriate behavior related to bodily functions (e.g., others will not want to interact with the student; require the student to clean up urine, feces, etc.).

14. Do not leave the student unsupervised.

15. Remove the student from the group or activity until he/she demonstrates appropriate behavior.

16. Remove the student from the peer or situation which stimulates him/her to engage in inappropriate behavior related to bodily functions.

17. Inform other school personnel in order to make them aware of the problem.

18. Make certain the student knows how to use restroom facilities appropriately.

19. Provide the student with accurate information regarding bodily functions in order to answer questions and clear up misunderstandings.

20. Teach the student alternative ways to deal with his/her anger (e.g., talk with the teacher, move away from the situation, talk to other school personnel, etc.).

21. Share concerns with administration and seek referral to an agency for investigation of possible abuse and neglect.

22. Provide the student with a full schedule of daily events in order to increase active involvement in the environment. (See Appendix for Schedule of Daily Events.)

23. Provide the student with a quiet place to work in order to reduce overstimulation. This is to be used to reduce stimulation and not as a form of punishment.

24. Maintain visibility to and from the student. The teacher should be able to see the student and the student should be able to see the teacher, making eye contact possible at all times.

63 Does not change behavior from one situation to another

1. Reinforce the student for changing his/her behavior from one situation to another without difficulty: (a) give the student a tangible reward (e.g., classroom privileges, line leading, passing out materials, five minutes free time, etc.) or (b) give the student an intangible reward (e.g., praise, handshake, smile, etc.).

2. Speak to the student to explain: (a) what he/she is doing wrong (e.g., failing to stop one activity and begin another) and (b) what he/she should be doing (e.g., changing from one activity to another).

3. Establish classroom rules (e.g., work on-task, work quietly, remain in your seat, finish task, meet task expectations). Reiterate rules often and reinforce students for following rules.

4. Reinforce those students in the classroom who change their behavior from one situation to another without difficulty.

5. Reinforce the student for demonstrating acceptable behavior based on the length of time he/she can be successful. Gradually increase the length of time required for reinforcement as the student demonstrates success.

6. Write a contract with the student specifying what behavior is expected (e.g., putting materials away and getting ready for another activity) and what reinforcement will be made available when the terms of the contract have been met.

7. Communicate with parents (e.g., notes home, phone calls, etc.) in order to share information concerning the student's progress and so that they may reinforce the student at home for demonstrating acceptable behavior at school.

8. Evaluate the appropriateness of the task to determine: (a) if the task is too easy, (b) if the task is too difficult, and (c) if the length of time scheduled to complete the task is appropriate.

9. Have the student question any directions, explanations, instructions he/she does not understand.

10. Assign a peer to work with the student to provide an appropriate model.

11. Explain to the student that he/she should be satisfied with his/her best effort rather than insist on perfection.

12. Prevent the student from becoming overstimulated by an activity. Supervise student behavior in order to limit overexcitement in physical activities, games, parties, etc.

13. Have the student time his/her activities in order to monitor his/her own behavior and accept time limits.

14. Convince the student that work not completed in one sitting can be completed later. Provide the student ample time to complete earlier assignments in order to guarantee closure.

15. Provide the student with more than enough time to finish an activity and decrease the amount over time as the student demonstrates success.

16. Structure time limits in order that the student knows exactly how long he/she has to work and when he/she must be finished.

17. Allow a transition period between activities in order that the student can make adjustments in his/her behavior.

18. Employ a signal technique (e.g., turning the lights off and on) to warn that the end of an activity is near.

19. Establish definite time limits and provide the student with this information before the activity begins.

20. Assign the student shorter activities and gradually increase the length of the activities as the student demonstrates success.

21. Maintain consistency in daily routine.

22. Maintain consistency of expectations and keep expectations within the ability level of the student.

23. Allow the student to finish the activity unless it will be disruptive to the schedule.

24. Schedule activities so the student has more than enough time to finish the activity if he/she works consistently.

25. Provide the student with a list of materials needed for each activity (e.g., pencil, paper, textbook, workbook, etc.).

26. Present instructions/directions prior to handing out necessary materials.

27. Collect the student's materials (e.g., pencil, paper, textbook, workbook, etc.) when it is time to change from one situation to another.

28. Provide the student with clearly stated expectations for all situations.

29. Prevent the student from becoming so stimulated by an event or activity that he/she cannot control his/her behavior.

30. Establish rules that are to be followed in various parts of the school building (e.g., lunchroom, music, art, gymnasium, library, playground, etc.).

31. Identify the expectations of different environments and help the student develop the skills to be successful in those environments.

32. In conjunction with other school personnel, develop as much consistency across the various environments as possible (e.g., rules, criteria for success, behavioral expectations, consequences, etc.).

33. Reduce the student's involvement in activities which prove too stimulating for him/her.

34. Have the student engage in relaxing transitional activities designed to reduce the effects of stimulating activities (e.g., put head on desk, listen to the teacher read a story, put head phones on and listen to relaxing music, etc.).

35. Provide the student with more than enough time to adapt or modify his/her behavior to different situations (e.g., have the student stop recess activities five minutes prior to coming into the building).

36. Communicate clearly to the student when it is time to begin an activity.

37. Communicate clearly to the student when it is time to stop an activity.

38. Provide the student with a schedule of daily events in order that he/she will know what activity comes next and can prepare for it. (See Appendix for Schedule of Daily Events.)

39. Reduce the emphasis on competition (e.g., academic or social). Fear of failure may cause the student to fail to adapt or modify his/her behavior to different situations.

40. Have the student begin an activity in a private place (e.g., carrel, "office," quiet study area, etc.) in order to reduce his/her difficulty in adapting or modifying his/her behavior to different situations.

41. Allow the student the option of performing the activity at another time (e.g., earlier in the day, later in the day, another day, etc.).

42. Do not allow the student to begin a new activity until he/she has gained self-control.

43. Evaluate the appropriateness of the situation in relation to the student's ability to successfully adapt or modify his/her behavior.

64 Does not participate in classroom activities or special events that are interesting to other students

1. Reinforce the student for participating in group activities or special events: (a) give the student a tangible reward (e.g., classroom privileges, line leading, passing out materials, five minutes free time, etc.) or (b) give the student an intangible reward (e.g., praise, handshake, smile, etc.).

2. Speak with the student to explain: (a) what he/she is doing wrong, (e.g., failing to take part) and (b) what he/she should be doing (e.g., talking, taking turns, playing, sharing, etc.).

3. Establish classroom rules (e.g., work on-task, work quietly, remain in your seat, finish task, meet task expectations). Reiterate rules often and reinforce students for following rules.

4. Reinforce other students in the classroom for participating in group activities or special events.

5. Write a contract with the student specifying what behavior is expected (e.g., taking part in group activities) and what reinforcement will be made available when the terms of the contract have been met.

6. Communicate with parents (e.g., notes home, phone calls, etc.) in order to share information concerning the student's progress and so that they may reinforce the student at home for participating in group activities or special events at school.

7. Evaluate the appropriateness of the task to determine: (a) if the task is too easy, (b) if the task is too difficult, and (c) if the length of time scheduled for the task is appropriate.

8. Assign a peer to sit/work directly with the student (e.g., in different settings or activities such as art, music, P.E., on the bus, tutoring, group projects, running errands in the building, recess, etc.). Gradually increase group size when the student has become comfortable working with one other student.

9. Encourage or reward others for participation in the group or special activities.

10. Give the student the responsibility of helping another student in the group.

11. Give the student responsibilities in a group in order that others might view him/her in a positive light.

12. Ask the student questions that cannot be answered yes or no.

13. Call on the student when he/she is most likely to be able to respond successfully (e.g., something in which the student is interested, when the teacher is certain the student knows the answer, etc.).

14. Try various groupings in order to determine the situation in which the student is most successful.

15. Have peers invite the student to participate in school or extracurricular activities.

16. Request that the student be the leader of a small group activity if he/she possesses mastery or an interest in the activity.

17. Allow the student to be present during group activities without requiring active participation.

18. Reduce the emphasis on competition. Frequent or continuous failure is likely to result in embarrassment which will cause reluctance to participate.

19. Demonstrate respect for the student's opinions, responses, suggestions, etc.

20. Provide the student with many social and academic successes.

21. Provide the student with positive feedback which indicates he/she is successful.

22. Present tasks in the most attractive and interesting manner possible.

23. Determine the student's interests in order that activities which require participation might be presented through his/her interests.

24. Allow the student to choose a special event or interesting activity for the class.

25. Provide the student with success-oriented special events or activities in order that he/she may develop an interest in them.

26. Modify or adjust situations that cause the student to be reluctant to participate (e.g., degree of difficulty, competition, fear of failure, threat of embarrassment, etc.).

27. Emphasize individual success or progress rather than winning or "beating" other students.

28. Provide the student with opportunities for small group participation as opposed to large group participation.

29. Encourage the student to participate in small groups. Gradually increase group size as the student demonstrates success.

30. Encourage the student to share things of special interest with other members of the class.

31. Identify a peer to act as a model for the student to imitate appropriate interactions in classroom activities.

32. Have the student question any directions, explanations, instructions he/she does not understand.

33. Allow the student to choose a group of peers with whom he/she feels comfortable.

34. Determine the peers the student would most prefer to interact with in classroom activities and attempt to facilitate the interaction.

35. Assign outgoing, nonthreatening peers to help the student participate in classroom activities.

36. Structure the environment so that the student has many opportunities to interact with other peers in classroom activities.

37. Assign the student to classroom activities in which he/she is likely to interact successfully with peers.

38. Conduct a sociometric activity with the class in order to determine those peers who would most prefer to interact with the student in classroom activities.

39. Make certain that the student understands that interacting with peers in classroom activities is contingent upon appropriate behavior.

40. Teach the student appropriate ways to interact with peers in classroom activities (e.g., share materials, problem solve, take turns, converse, etc.).

41. Supervise classroom activities closely in order that the peers with whom the student interacts do not stimulate inappropriate behavior.

42. Make certain that the classroom activity is not so stimulating as to make successful interactions with peers difficult.

43. Teach the student problem-solving skills in order that he/she may better deal with problems that may occur in interactions with peers in classroom activities (e.g., talking, walking away, calling upon an arbitrator, compromising, etc.).

44. Limit opportunities for interaction in classroom activities on those occasions in which the student is not likely to be successful (e.g., the student has experienced academic or social failure prior to the scheduled classroom activity).

45. Select nonacademic activities designed to enhance appropriate social interaction of the student and peers during classroom activities (e.g., board games, model building, coloring, etc.).

46. Through interviews with other students and observations, determine those characteristics of the student which interfere with successful interactions during classroom activities. Use information gained to determine skills or behaviors the student needs to develop for successful interactions.

47. Have the student practice appropriate interactions with the teacher(s) in classroom activities (e.g., simulations, role playing, etc.).

48. Make certain, beforehand, that the student is able to successfully engage in the classroom activity (e.g., the student understands the rules, is familiar with the activity, will be compatible with peers engaged in the activity, etc.).

49. Make certain the student has the necessary materials for the classroom activity.

50. Assign the student responsibilities to perform during classroom activities in order to enhance peer interaction (e.g., being a leader, passing out materials, acting as a peer tutor, etc.).

51. Make certain the student knows how to use all materials for the classroom activity.

A Reminder: Do not "force" the student to take part in any activity or special event.

65 Blames self for situations beyond his/her control

1. Explain to the student that he/she should be happy with his/her own best effort rather than perfection.

2. Reinforce the student for accepting errors that he/she makes.

3. Speak with the student to explain: (a) what he/she is doing wrong (e.g., being overly critical of himself/herself) and (b) what he/she should be doing (e.g., being more constructive in self-criticism when evaluating himself/herself).

4. Reward others for accepting errors they make.

5. Write a contract with the student specifying what behavior is expected (e.g., accepting his/her own best effort) and what reinforcement will be made available when the terms of the contract have been met.

6. Evaluate the appropriateness of the task to determine: (a) if the task is too easy, (b) if the task is too difficult, and (c) if the length of time scheduled for the task is appropriate.

7. Reinforce the student for improvement rather than expecting excellence.

8. Recognize the student often and in various settings (e.g., hallways, cafeteria, etc.).

9. Provide the student with positive feedback which indicates he/she is successful, competent, important, valuable, etc.

10. Provide the student with success-oriented tasks (i.e., the expectation is that success will result in more positive attitudes and perceptions toward self and environment).

11. Provide the student with as many social and academic successes as possible.

12. Make the necessary adjustments in the environment to prevent the student from experiencing stress, frustration, etc.

13. Assign a peer to help the student with class assignments, homework, etc.

14. Emphasize individual differences and that everyone has strengths and weaknesses.

15. Reduce emphasis on competition and perfection. Repeated failure may result in unwarranted self-blame or self-criticism.

16. Encourage the student to refrain from comparing his/her performance to other students' performances and emphasize personal improvement (e.g., maintain records of own progress rather than comparing work to others).

17. Provide the student with evidence of his/her ability in order that he/she might better understand that self-blame/criticism is unwarranted.

18. Have the student regularly record his/her own progress in order to have tangible evidence of success.

19. Deliver praise and constructive criticism consistently to all students.

20. When accidents occur, make "clean up" a group responsibility in order to convey the idea that we all make mistakes and accidents are common to all of us.

21. Call on the student when he/she will most likely be able to answer correctly.

22. Encourage the student to act as a peer tutor in order that he/she may recognize his/her own strengths and abilities.

23. Reduce activities which might threaten the student (e.g., announcing test score ranges or test scores aloud, making students read aloud in class, emphasizing the success of a particular student(s), etc.).

A Reminder: Make certain that the self-blame or self-criticism is in fact unwarranted.

66 Becomes upset when a suggestion or constructive criticism is given

1. Reinforce the student for responding in an appropriate manner to constructive criticism: (a) give the student a tangible reward (e.g., classroom privileges, line leading, passing out materials, five minutes free time, etc.) or (b) give the student an intangible reward (e.g., praise, handshake, smile, etc.).

2. Speak with the student to explain: (a) what he/she is doing wrong (e.g., yelling, cursing, making derogatory comments, crying, etc.) and (b) what he/she should be doing (e.g., asking for directions, help, clarification, etc.).

3. Establish classroom rules (e.g., work on-task, work quietly, remain in your seat, finish task, meet task expectations). Reiterate rules often and reinforce students for following rules.

4. Reinforce those students in the classroom who respond appropriately to constructive criticism.

5. Reinforce the student for responding in an appropriate manner to constructive criticism based on the number of times he/she can be successful. Gradually increase the number of times required for reinforcement as the student demonstrates success.

6. Remove the student from the group or activity until he/she can demonstrate appropriate behavior or self-control.

7. Write a contract with the student specifying what behavior is expected (e.g., responding appropriately to constructive criticism) and what reinforcement will be made available when the terms of the contract have been met.

8. Communicate with parents (e.g., notes home, phone calls, etc.) in order to share information concerning the student's progress and so that they may reinforce the student at home for responding in an appropriate manner to constructive criticism at school.

9. Evaluate the appropriateness of the task to determine: (a) if the task is too easy, (b) if the task is too difficult, and (c) if the length of time scheduled for the task is appropriate.

10. Demonstrate appropriate ways to respond to constructive criticism.

11. Try various groupings in order to determine the situation in which the student is most comfortable.

12. Provide the student with positive feedback which indicates he/she is successful, competent, important, valuable, etc.

13. Provide the student with many social and academic successes.

14. Structure the environment in such a way that the teacher is the only one providing constructive criticism. As the student learns to accept constructive criticism from the teacher, allow input from others.

15. Assess the appropriateness of the social situation in relation to the student's ability to function successfully.

16. Provide constructive criticism in private.

17. Provide constructive criticism equally to all members of the class.

18. Provide constructive criticism when the student is most likely to demonstrate an appropriate response.

19. Make certain that positive reinforcement is not inadvertently given for inappropriate behavior (e.g., lowering expectations because the student becomes upset when criticism is delivered).

20. Make certain the student receives adequate, positive reinforcement any time he/she is behaving in an appropriate manner.

21. Assess criticism to make certain it is constructive and positive.

22. Have the student question anything he/she does not understand while performing assignments.

23. Encourage the student to check and correct his/her own work.

24. Explain to the student that constructive criticism is meant to be helpful, not threatening.

25. Reduce the emphasis on competition and perfection. A highly competitive atmosphere or repeated failure may cause the student to react in inappropriate ways to constructive criticism from others.

26. Make the necessary adjustments in the environment to prevent the student from experiencing stress, frustration, anger, etc.

27. Provide the student with academic tasks which can be self-checked.

28. Supervise the student while he/she is performing tasks in order to monitor quality.

29. Provide the student with clearly stated criteria for acceptable work.

30. Make certain that constructive criticism is tactfully conveyed.

31. Make certain that an offer of assistance is made at the same time constructive criticism is delivered.

32. Require a demonstration of ability rather than having the student perform the entire assignment or activity again (e.g., work a few problems correctly rather than repeating the entire assignment).

33. Identify a peer to act as a model for the student to imitate appropriate response to constructive criticism.

34. Have the student question any directions, explanations, instructions he/she does not understand.

35. Allow natural consequences to occur when the student fails to respond appropriately to constructive criticism (e.g., make highly reinforcing activities contingent upon responding appropriately to redirection in academic and social situations).

36. Make certain that attention is not inadvertently given to the student for failing to respond appropriately to constructive criticism (i.e., remove attention from the student when he/she fails to respond appropriately to redirection in academic and social situations in those instances when attention is reinforcing inappropriate behavior).

37. Provide adequate time for the student to respond appropriately to constructive criticism.

38. Deliver instructions in a clear and concise manner.

39. Assist the student in responding appropriately to constructive criticism (e.g., help the student correct one or two items in order to get him/her started).

40. Develop subsequent tasks to be performed the next day based on errors the student makes rather than requiring an immediate correction of work done incorrectly.

67 Threatens to hurt self or commit suicide

1. Reinforce the student for engaging in appropriate behavior: (a) give the student a tangible reward (e.g., classroom privileges, line leading, passing out materials, five minutes free time, etc.) or (b) give the student an intangible reward (e.g., praise, handshake, smile, etc.).

2. Speak with the student to explain: (a) what he/she is doing wrong (e.g., threatening to hurt self) and (b) what he/she should be doing (e.g., talking about the situation, self-controlling, problem-solving, etc.).

3. Establish classroom rules (e.g., work on-task, work quietly, remain in your seat, finish task, meet task expectations). Reiterate rules often and reinforce students for following rules.

4. Reinforce those students in the classroom who engage in appropriate behavior.

5. Reinforce the student for demonstrating appropriate behavior based on the length of time he/she can be successful. Gradually increase the amount of time required for reinforcement as the student demonstrates success.

6. Remove the student from the group or activity until he/she can demonstrate appropriate behavior and self-control.

7. Communicate with the parents (e.g., notes home, phone calls, etc.) in order to share information concerning the student's progress and so that they may reinforce the student at home for appropriate behavior at school.

8. Evaluate the appropriateness of the task to determine if: (a) the task is too easy, (b) the task is too difficult, and (c) the length of time scheduled for the task is appropriate.

9. Prevent frustrating or anxiety producing situations from occurring (e.g., give the student tasks on his/her ability level, give the student the number of tasks that he/she can tolerate in one sitting, stop social interactions that stimulate the student to threaten self-harm, etc.).

10. Interact frequently with the student to prevent self-abusive behavior by meeting the student's needs as they occur.

11. Maintain visibility to and from the student. The teacher should be able to see the student and the student should be able to see the teacher, making eye contact possible at all times.

12. Facilitate on-task behavior by providing a full schedule of daily events. Prevent lag time from occurring when the student would be free to engage in self-abusive behavior. (See Appendix for Schedule of Daily Events.)

13. Remove from the environment any object that the student may use to hurt himself/herself.

14. Provide the student with positive feedback that indicates he/she is successful, important, respected, etc.

15. Maintain a positive/calm environment (e.g., positive comments, acknowledgement of successes, quiet communications, etc.).

16. Provide the student with a quiet place to work (e.g., carrel, study area).

17. Reduce the emphasis on competition. Repeated failure may result in anger and frustration that may cause the student to try to hurt himself/herself.

18. Maintain consistency in expectations.

19. Allow the student input relative to making decisions (e.g., changing activities, choosing activities, length of activities, etc.).

20. Provide the student with a selection of optional activities to be performed (e.g., if an activity results in harmful behaviors, an optional activity can be substituted).

21. Teach the student appropriate ways to deal with anxiety, frustration, and anger (e.g., move away from the stimulus, verbalize unhappiness, choose another activity, etc.).

22. Teach the student problem-solving skills: (a) identify the problem, (b) identify goals and objectives, (c) develop strategies, (d) develop a plan for action, and (e) carry out the plan.

23. Maintain consistency in daily routine.

24. Do not allow the student to be unsupervised anywhere in the school environment.

25. Avoid discussions or prevent stimuli in the environment that remind the student of unpleasant experiences/sensitive topics (e.g., divorce, death, unemployment, alcoholism, etc.).

NOTE: All references to suicide should be considered serious, and steps should be taken to respond to the situation.

68 Indicates that no one likes him/her, no one cares about him/her, etc.

1. Reinforce the student for interacting with others: (a) give the student a tangible reward (e.g., classroom privileges, line leading, passing out materials, five minutes free time, etc.) or (b) give the student an intangible reward (e.g., praise, handshake, smile, etc.).

2. Establish classroom rules (e.g., work on-task, work quietly, remain in your seat, finish task, meet task expectations). Reiterate rules often and reinforce students for following rules.

3. Reinforce those students in the classroom who make positive, supportive comments to the student.

4. Reinforce the student for interacting with others based on the length of time he/she can be successful. Gradually increase the length of time required for reinforcement as the student demonstrates success.

5. Remove the student from the group until he/she can interact appropriately with others.

6. Write a contract with the student specifying what behavior is expected (e.g., interacting appropriately with others) and what reinforcement will be made available when the terms of the contract have been met.

7. Communicate with the parents (e.g., notes home, phone calls, etc.) in order to share information concerning the student's progress and so that they may reinforce the student at home for interacting appropriately with others at school.

8. Record or chart the number of times the student verbally expresses that others do not like or care about him/her in order to make the student aware of the frequency.

9. Teach the student problem-solving skills: (a) identify the problem, (b) identify goals and objectives, (c) develop strategies, (d) develop a plan for action, and (e) carry out the plan.

10. Provide the student with as many academic and social successes as possible in order that peers may view him/her in a more positive way.

11. Make the necessary adjustments in the environment to prevent the student from experiencing stress, frustration, anger, etc.

12. Give the student additional responsibilities (e.g., chores, errands, etc.) to give him/her a feeling of success or accomplishment.

13. Structure the environment so that the student does not have time to dwell on real or imagined problems.

14. Take the time to listen in order that the student realizes your concern and interest in him/her.

15. Identify for the student more appropriate ways to express his/her feelings.

16. Reduce stimuli that contributes to the student's verbal expression of unhappiness (e.g., seek input from the student as to what upsets him/her).

17. Separate the student from the peer(s) who stimulates the verbal expressions of unhappiness.

18. Try various groupings in order to determine the situation in which the student is most comfortable.

19. Encourage the student to participate in extracurricular activities that will help him/her develop those skills necessary to interact appropriately with others at school.

20. Make certain that reinforcement (e.g., attention, getting his/her way, etc.) is not inadvertently given for verbal expressions of unhappiness.

21. Provide the student with alternative activities to perform in case some activities prove upsetting.

22. Reduce the emphasis on competition. Repeated failure may cause the student to feel that others do not like or care about him/her.

23. Reinforce those students in the classroom who deal with unhappiness in an appropriate manner.

24. Encourage and help the student to make friends (e.g., pair the student with a peer; when that relationship is successful, introduce other students).

25. When natural consequences occur as a result of the student's displays of unhappiness, point them out to him/her (e.g., peers prefer not to interact with the student).

26. Provide the student with as many positive interactions as possible (e.g., recognize the student, greet the student, compliment attire, etc.).

27. Discourage the student from engaging in those activities that cause him/her unhappiness.

28. Help the student identify how he/she wishes things were in the environment and work with him/her toward those goals.

29. Teach the student alternative ways to deal with unpleasant social interactions during the school-age experience (e.g., deal with problems when they arise, practice self-control at all times, share problems or concerns with others, etc.).

30. Teach the student alternative ways to communicate unhappiness (e.g., written, spoken, etc.).

31. Speak with the student to explain that he/she may be trying too hard to fit in and should relax and allow friendships to develop naturally.

32. Reinforce those students in the classroom who appropriately interact with other students.

33. Have the student be the leader of a small group activity if he/she possesses mastery of skills or an interest in that area.

34. Give the student the responsibility of tutoring a peer if he/she possesses the skills to be shared.

35. Provide the student with a predetermined signal (e.g., verbal cue, hand signal, etc.) when he/she begins to demonstrate inappropriate behaviors when interacting with others (e.g., whining, fighting, throwing objects, refusing to share, etc.).

36. Maintain maximum supervision of the student's interactions and gradually decrease the amount of supervision over time.

37. Give the student responsibilities in group situations in order that peers may view the student in a more positive way.

38. Encourage the student to further develop any ability or skill he/she may have in order that peers may view him/her in a more positive way.

39. Help the student to identify his/her inappropriate behaviors and teach him/her ways to change those behaviors.

40. Ask the student to choose a peer to work with on a specific assignment. Encourage the student and peer to interact with each other in nonacademic areas (e.g., recess, lunch, break time, etc.).

A Reminder: Do not "force" the student to interact with others with whom he/she is uncomfortable.

69 Does not smile, laugh, or demonstrate happiness

1. Reinforce the student for demonstrating happiness when appropriate: (a) give the student a tangible reward (e.g., classroom privileges, line leading, passing out materials, five minutes free time, etc.) or (b) give the student an intangible reward (e.g., praise, handshake, smile, etc.).

2. Encourage the student to engage in classroom activities or special events.

3. Reinforce those students in the classroom who engage in classroom activities or special events.

4. Communicate with the parents, agencies, or appropriate parties in order to inform them of the problem, determine the cause of the problem, and consider possible solutions to the problem.

5. Evaluate the appropriateness of the task to determine if: (a) the task is too easy, (b) the task is too difficult, and (c) the length of time scheduled for the task is appropriate.

6. Present tasks in the most attractive and interesting manner possible.

7. Determine those activities the student prefers and provide them often.

8. Reduce or discontinue competitive activities. Repeated failure reduces enjoyment of the activity.

9. Make every attempt to create a positive atmosphere in the classroom (e.g., cooperative group activities, positive motivation strategies, positive communications, etc.).

10. Provide the student with as many social and academic successes as possible.

11. Include the student in classroom/group activities (e.g., invite the student to join a group, assign the student a part or responsibility in an activity, etc.).

12. Indicate a need for the student's involvement in an activity (e.g., the student is a part of the class/activities, is valued and needed, etc.).

13. Include fun and enjoyable activities as part of the daily curriculum.

14. Have peers invite the student to participate in school and extracurricular activities.

15. Avoid discussions of topics sensitive to the student (e.g., divorce, death, unemployment, alcoholism, etc.).

16. Be certain to greet or recognize the student as often as possible (e.g., hallways, cafeteria, welcome to class, acknowledge a job well done, etc.).

17. Call attention to the student's accomplishments (e.g., publicly or privately depending on which is most appropriate).

18. Interact frequently with the student.

19. Try various groupings in order to determine the situation in which the student is most comfortable.

20. Make certain that interactions with the student are natural and not contrived.

21. Help the student develop a friendship by assigning him/her to work with a peer on an activity, project, etc.

22. Have the student complete a reinforcer survey in order to determine his/her interests, favorite activities, what is rewarding to him/her, etc., and use the information obtained to create a pleasant atmosphere at school for the student. (See Appendix for Reinforcer Survey.)

23. Speak to the student to explain: (a) that you recognize he/she is unhappy and (b) appropriate ways to deal with unhappiness.

24. Reinforce those students in the classroom who deal with unhappiness in an appropriate manner.

25. Take time to talk with the student in order that he/she realizes that the teacher's interest in him/her is genuine.

26. Make certain that reinforcement is not inadvertently given when the student does not smile, laugh, or demonstrate happiness (e.g., attending to the student only when he/she demonstrates unhappiness).

27. Discourage the student from engaging in those activities which cause him/her unhappiness.

28. Give the student additional responsibilities (e.g., chores, errands, etc.) in order to give him/her a feeling of success or accomplishment.

29. Help the student identify how he/she wishes things were in the environment and work with the student toward these goals.

70 Is tired, listless, apathetic, unmotivated, not interested in school

1. Investigate the student's nutrition and amount of rest he/she is getting outside of school.

2. Reinforce the student for showing an interest and participating in school activities: (a) give the student a tangible reward (e.g., classroom privileges, line leading, passing out materials, five minutes free time, etc.) or (b) give the student an intangible reward (e.g., praise, handshake, smile, etc.).

3. Speak with the student to explain: (a) what he/she is doing wrong (e.g., failing to show an interest and participate in school activities) and (b) what he/she should be doing (e.g., showing an interest and participating in school activities).

4. Establish classroom rules (e.g., work on-task, work quietly, remain in your seat, finish task, meet task expectations). Reiterate rules often and reinforce students for following rules.

5. Reinforce those students in the classroom who show an interest and participate in school activities.

6. Reinforce the student for showing an interest and participating in school activities based on the length of time he/she can be successful. Gradually increase the length of time required for reinforcement as the student demonstrates success.

7. Write a contract with the student specifying what behavior is expected (e.g., showing an interest and participating in school activities) and what reinforcement will be made available when the terms of the contract have been met.

8. Communicate with parents (e.g., notes home, phone calls, etc.) in order to share information concerning the student's progress and so that they may reinforce the student at home for showing an interest and participating in school activities.

9. Communicate with parents, agencies, or appropriate parties in order to inform them of the problem, determine the cause of the problem, and consider possible solutions to the problem.

10. Evaluate the appropriateness of the task to determine: (a) if the task is too easy, (b) if the task is too difficult, and (c) if the length of time scheduled to complete the task is appropriate.

11. Call on the student when he/she can answer successfully.

12. Avoid competition. Failure may cause the student to lose interest or not participate in school activities.

13. Allow the student more decision-making opportunities relative to class activities and assignments.

14. Present tasks in the most attractive and interesting manner possible.

15. Give the student responsibilities in the classroom (e.g., teacher assistant, peer tutor, group leader, etc.).

16. Provide a full schedule of daily events to keep the student actively involved. (See Appendix for Schedule of Daily Events.)

17. Provide the student with as many academic and social successes as possible.

18. Evaluate the appropriateness of the task in relation to the student's ability to perform the task successfully.

19. Determine the student's preferred activities, interests, etc., and incorporate them into his/her daily schedule, program, etc., at various points throughout the day.

20. Provide the student with "real-life" experiences from the environment. Have individuals from the work force (e.g., mechanic, draftsman, secretary, etc.) visit the class to relate the importance of school to work experiences that involve math, reading, writing, etc.

21. Show an interest in the student (e.g., acknowledge the student, ask the student's opinion, spend time working one-on-one with the student, etc.).

22. Investigate the possibility of the student being involved in the use of drugs or alcohol.

71 Is overly critical of self in school-related performance, abilities, personal appearance, etc.

1. Explain to the student that he/she should be happy with his/her own best effort rather than perfection.

2. Reinforce the student for accepting errors that he/she makes.

3. Speak with the student to explain: (a) what he/she is doing wrong (e.g., being overly critical of himself/herself) and (b) what he/she should be doing (e.g., being more constructive in self-criticism when evaluating himself/herself).

4. Reward others for accepting errors they make.

5. Write a contract with the student specifying what behavior is expected (e.g., accepting his/her own best effort) and what reinforcement will be made available when the terms of the contract have been met.

6. Evaluate the appropriateness of the task to determine: (a) if the task is too easy, (b) if the task is too difficult, and (c) if the length of time scheduled for the task is appropriate.

7. Reinforce the student for improvement rather than expecting excellence.

8. Recognize the student often and in various settings (e.g., hallways, cafeteria, etc.).

9. Provide the student with positive feedback which indicates he/she is successful, competent, important, valuable, etc.

10. Provide the student with success-oriented tasks. The expectation is that success will result in more positive attitudes and perceptions toward self and environment.

11. Provide the student with as many social and academic successes as possible.

12. Make the necessary adjustments in the environment to prevent the student from experiencing stress, frustration, etc.

13. Assign a peer to help the student with class assignments, homework, etc.

14. Emphasize individual differences and that everyone has strengths and weaknesses.

15. Reduce emphasis on competition and perfection. Repeated failure may result in unwarranted self-blame or self-criticism.

16. Encourage the student to refrain from comparing his/her performance to other students' performance and emphasize attention to personal improvement (e.g., maintain records of own progress rather than comparing work to others').

17. Provide the student with evidence of his/her ability in order that he/she might better understand that self-blame/criticism is unwarranted.

18. Have the student regularly record his/her own progress in order to have tangible evidence of success.

19. Deliver praise and constructive criticism consistently to all students.

20. Make cleaning up accidents a group responsibility in order to convey the idea that we all make mistakes and accidents are common to all of us.

21. Call on the student when he/she will most likely be able to answer correctly.

22. Encourage the student to act as a peer tutor in order that he/she may recognize his/her own strengths and abilities.

23. Reduce activities which might threaten the student (e.g., announcing test score ranges or test scores aloud, making students read aloud in class, emphasizing the success of a particular student or students, etc.).

24. Help the student learn those skills necessary to improve his/her personal appearance and hygiene.

25. Make certain that your comments take the form of constructive criticism rather than criticism that can be perceived as personal, threatening, etc. (e.g., instead of saying, "You always make that same mistake," say, "A better way to do that might be . . .").

26. Deliver a predetermined signal when the student begins to be overly critical of self.

27. Assess the appropriateness of the social situation and place the student in the group in which he/she would be most successful.

28. Pair the student with a younger or less capable peer in order to enhance his/her feelings of success or accomplishment.

29. Deliver praise and recognition privately in order that the student is not aware of the performance of others.

30. Encourage all students to be complimentary of each other's performance.

A Reminder: Make certain that the self-blame or self-criticism is in fact unwarranted.

72 Frowns, scowls, looks unhappy during typical classroom situations

1. Share concerns with administration and seek referral to an agency for investigation of abuse or neglect.

2. Communicate your concern to the student.

3. Reinforce the student for engaging in appropriate behavior: (a) give the student a tangible reward (e.g., classroom privileges, line leading, passing out materials, five minutes free time, etc.) or (b) give the student an intangible reward (e.g., praise, handshake, smile, etc.).

4. Provide the student with success-oriented tasks (i.e., the expectation is that success will result in more positive attitudes and perceptions toward self and environment).

5. Assign a peer to engage in recreational activities with the student in order to develop a friendship.

6. Provide the student with positive feedback that indicates that he/she is successful, competent, important, valuable, etc.

7. Give the student additional responsibilities (e.g., chores, errands, etc.) to give him/her a feeling of success or accomplishment.

8. Identify individuals the student may contact with his/her concerns or problems (e.g., guidance counselor, school nurse, social worker, school psychologist, etc.).

9. Create the most positive environment possible.

10. Seek the student's input in planning the curriculum and extracurricular activities, classes, etc. (i.e., attempt to include student preferences and favored activities).

11. Follow less desirable activities with more desirable activities throughout the day in order to maintain interest and variety.

12. Facilitate the development of friendships with peers (e.g., assign activities for the student involving peers, give the student and a peer joint responsibilities, etc.).

13. Reduce the emphasis on competition. Repeated failure will most likely contribute to the student's unhappiness.

14. Teach the student to be satisfied with his/her own best effort rather than insisting on perfection (e.g., reduce the emphasis on competition, help the student realize that success is individually defined).

15. De-emphasize arbitrary levels of success (i.e., rather than absolute excellence, progress of any amount should be considered a measure of success).

16. Respect the student's right to privacy when appropriate.

17. Take the time to listen so that the student realizes that your concern/interest is genuine.

18. Maintain consistency in interactions (e.g., do not provide extra attention when the student is demonstrating facial expressions of displeasure).

19. Ask the student why he/she frowns, scowls, looks unhappy during typical classroom situations. The student may have the most accurate perception.

20. Communicate with parents, agencies, or appropriate parties in order to inform them of the problem, determine the cause of the problem, and consider possible solutions to the problem.

73 Is pessimistic

1. Reinforce the student for being more positive in reacting to situations (e.g., attempting a task, making a positive comment about an activity, etc.): (a) give the student a tangible reward (e.g., classroom privileges, line leading, passing out materials, five minutes free time, etc.) or (b) give the student an intangible reward (e.g., praise, handshake, smile, etc.).

2. Speak to the student to explain: (a) what he/she is doing wrong (e.g., complaining, not taking part, reacting negatively, etc.) and (b) what he/she should be doing (e.g., taking part, being enthusiastic, etc.).

3. Establish classroom rules (e.g., work on-task, work quietly, remain in your seat, finish task, meet task expectations). Reiterate rules often and reinforce students for following rules.

4. Reinforce those students in the classroom who are positive in reacting to situations.

5. Reinforce the student for being more positive based on the length of time he/she can be successful. Gradually increase the length of time required for reinforcement as the student demonstrates success.

6. Write a contract with the student specifying what behavior is expected (e.g., making positive comments) and what reinforcement will be made available when the terms of the contract have been met.

7. Communicate with parents (e.g., notes home, phone calls, etc.) in order to share information concerning the student's progress and so that they may reinforce the student at home for being more positive at school.

8. Communicate with parents, agencies, or appropriate parties in order to inform them of the problem, determine the cause of the problem, and consider possible solutions to the problem.

9. Evaluate the appropriateness of the task to determine: (a) if the task is too easy, (b) if the task is too difficult, and (c) if the length of time scheduled to complete the task is appropriate.

10. Identify a peer to act as a model for the student to imitate positive reactions to situations.

11. Have the student question any directions, explanations, instructions he/she does not understand.

12. Remove the student from the group or activity until he/she can be more positive.

13. Provide the student with positive feedback which indicates he/she is successful, competent, important, respected, etc.

14. Modify the environment to reduce situations which cause the student to be pessimistic (e.g., determine those activities the student dislikes and avoid forcing the student to engage in those activities).

15. Encourage the student to participate in those activities in which he/she is successful.

16. Provide the student with many social and academic successes.

17. Identify individuals the student may contact concerning his/her unhappiness (e.g., guidance counselor, school nurse, social worker, school psychologist, etc.).

18. Encourage and help the student make friends (e.g., pair the student with a peer; when that relationship is successful, introduce other peers).

19. Explain to the student that feelings of pessimism are natural but public display of that emotion should be limited.

20. Make the student aware of natural consequences that occur due to his/her displays of pessimism (e.g., others prefer not to interact with him/her, he/she will not be chosen by peers to join in activities, etc.).

21. Provide the student with as many positive interactions as possible (e.g., recognize the student, greet the student, compliment his/her attire, etc.).

22. Require the student to make at least one positive comment about himself/herself on a daily basis. Gradually increase the number of positive comments required as the student demonstrates success.

23. Encourage and assist the student in joining extracurricular activities, clubs, etc.

24. Give the student additional responsibilities (e.g., chores, errands, etc.) to give him/her a feeling of success or accomplishment.

25. Help the student identify how he/she wishes things were in the environment and work with the student toward those goals.

26. Take time to talk with the student in order that he/she realizes your interest in him/her is genuine.

27. Conduct a reinforcer survey with the student in order to determine his/her reinforcer preferences. (See Appendix for Reinforcer Survey.)

28. Communicate with parents in order to determine what the student finds reinforcing at home.

29. Help the student to be satisfied with his/her best effort rather than insisting on perfection.

30. Identify the words or phrases the student uses to indicate his/her pessimism. Help the student recognize and in turn limit the statements.

31. Give the student a predetermined signal when he/she begins to be pessimistic.

74 Indicates concern regarding problems or situations in the home or is unable to deal with classroom requirements because of out-of school situations

1. Discuss concerns with other professionals to determine if further investigation is warranted (e.g., abuse or neglect).

2. Record or chart the number of times the student expresses concerns or worries about school or home to make the student aware of the frequency of his/her behavior.

3. Evaluate the appropriateness of the task to determine if: (a) the task is too easy, (b) the task is too difficult, and (c) the length of time scheduled for the task is appropriate.

4. Take the time to listen so that the student realizes that your concern is genuine.

5. Explain that the concerns or worries, while legitimate, are not unusual for students (e.g., everyone worries about tests, grades, etc.).

6. Identify persons the student may contact with his/her worries or concerns (e.g., guidance counselor, school nurse, social worker, school psychologist, etc.).

7. Discuss ways in which to practice self-improvement.

8. Provide the student with opportunities for social and academic success.

9. Separate the student from a peer who may be encouraging or stimulating the inappropriate behavior.

10. Provide praise and recognition as often as possible.

11. Encourage participation in school and extracurricular activities.

12. Reduce the emphasis on competition. Repeated failure may heighten anxiety about performance.

13. Provide opportunities for tutoring from peers or teacher.

14. Provide parents with necessary information to help the student with homework and study activities at home.

15. Try various groupings in order to determine the situation in which the student is most successful.

16. Make the necessary adjustments in the environment to prevent the student from experiencing stress, frustration, anxiety, etc.

17. Structure the environment in such a way that time does not permit opportunities for the student to dwell on concerns or worries.

18. Have peers invite the student to participate in extracurricular activities.

19. Demonstrate respect for the student's opinions, responses, suggestions, etc.

20. Provide the student with alternative approaches to testing (e.g., test the student orally, make tests shorter, allow the student to respond orally, allow the student to take the test in the resource room, etc.).

21. Assign a peer to sit/work directly with the student.

22. Call attention to the student's accomplishments (e.g., publicly or privately depending on which is more appropriate).

23. Avoid discussion of topics sensitive to the student (e.g., divorce, death, unemployment, alcoholism, etc.).

24. Provide the student with opportunities for special project responsibilities, leadership, etc.

25. Provide as many enjoyable and interesting activities as possible.

A Reminder: Do not "force" the student to participate in any activity.

75 Demonstrates self-destructive behavior

1. Reinforce the student for engaging in appropriate behavior: (a) give the student a tangible reward (e.g., classroom privileges, line leading, passing out materials, five minutes free time, etc.) or (b) give the student an intangible reward (e.g., praise, handshake, smile, etc.).

2. Speak with the student to explain: (a) what he/she is doing wrong (e.g., hurting self) and (b) what he/she should be doing (e.g., talking about the situation, self-controlling, problem-solving, etc.).

3. Establish classroom rules (e.g., work on-task, work quietly, remain in your seat, finish task, meet task expectations). Reiterate rules often and reinforce students for following rules.

4. Reinforce those students in the classroom who engage in appropriate behaviors.

5. Reinforce the student for demonstrating appropriate behavior based on the length of time he/she can be successful. Gradually increase the amount of time required for reinforcement as the student demonstrates success.

6. Remove the student from the group or activity until he/she can demonstrate appropriate behavior and self-control.

7. Write a contract with the student specifying what behavior is expected (e.g., not engaging in self-destructive behavior) and what reinforcement will be made available when the terms of the contract have been met.

8. Communicate with the parents (e.g., notes home, phone calls, etc.) in order to share information concerning the student's progress and so that they may reinforce the student at home for appropriate behavior at school.

9. Evaluate the appropriateness of the task to determine if: (a) the task is too easy, (b) the task is too difficult, and (c) the length of time scheduled for the task is appropriate.

10. Prevent frustrating or anxiety-producing situations from occurring (e.g., give the student tasks on his/her ability level, give the student the number of tasks that he/she can tolerate in one sitting, stop social interactions which stimulate the student to become self-destructive, etc.).

11. Interact frequently with the student to prevent self-destructive behavior by meeting the student's needs as they occur.

12. Maintain visibility to and from the student. The teacher should be able to see the student and the student should be able to see the teacher, making eye contact possible at all times.

13. Facilitate on-task behavior by providing a full schedule of daily events. Prevent lag time from occurring when the student would be free to engage in self-abusive behavior. (See Appendix for Schedule of Daily Events.)

14. Remove from the environment any object that the student may use to hurt himself/herself.

15. Provide the student with positive feedback which indicates he/she is successful, important, respected, etc.

16. Maintain a positive/calm environment (e.g., deliver positive comments, acknowledgement of successes, quiet communications, etc.).

17. Provide the student with a quiet place to work (e.g., carrel, study area).

18. Reduce the emphasis on competition. Repeated failure may result in anger and frustration which may cause the student to try to hurt himself/herself.

19. Maintain consistency in expectations in order to reduce the likelihood of the student hurting himself/herself.

20. Allow the student input relative to making decisions (e.g., changing activities, choosing activities, length of activities, etc.).

21. Provide the student with a selection of optional activities to be performed (e.g., if an activity results in self-destructive behaviors, an optional activity can be substituted).

22. Teach the student appropriate ways to deal with anxiety, frustration, and anger (e.g., move away from the stimulus, verbalize unhappiness, choose another activity, etc.).

23. Teach the student problem-solving skills: (a) identify the problem, (b) identify goals and objectives, (c) develop strategies, (d) develop a plan for action, and (e) carry out the plan.

24. Maintain consistency in daily routine.

25. Avoid discussions or prevent stimuli in the environment which remind the student of unpleasant experiences/sensitive topics (e.g., divorce, death, unemployment, alcoholism, etc.).

NOTE: Help the student accept the fact that self-improvement is more important than getting the highest grade in the class, making all A's, being the first one done with an assignment, etc., by reinforcing and grading on the basis of self-improvement.

76 Moves about unnecessarily

1. Reinforce the student for demonstrating physical self-control: (a) give the student a tangible reward (e.g., classroom privileges, line leading, passing out materials, five minutes free time, etc.) or (b) give the student an intangible reward (e.g., praise, handshake, smile, etc.).

2. Speak with the student to explain: (a) what he/she is doing wrong (e.g., moving in seat, moving about the room, running, etc.) and (b) what he/she should be doing (e.g., practicing self-control, following rules, etc.).

3. Establish classroom rules (e.g., work on-task, work quietly, remain in your seat, finish task, meet task expectations). Reiterate rules often and reinforce students for following rules.

4. Reinforce those students in the classroom who demonstrate physical self-control.

5. Reinforce the student for demonstrating appropriate behavior based on the length of time he/she can be successful. Gradually increase the length of time required for reinforcement as the student demonstrates success.

6. Remove the student from the group or activity until he/she can demonstrate appropriate behavior and self-control.

7. Write a contract with the student specifying what behavior is expected (e.g., demonstrating physical self-control) and what reinforcement will be made available when the terms of the contract have been met.

8. Communicate with the parents (e.g., notes home, phone calls, etc.) in order to share information concerning the student's progress and so that they may reinforce the student at home for demonstrating physical self-control at school.

9. Evaluate the appropriateness of the task to determine if: (a) the task is too easy, (b) the task is too difficult, and (c) the length of time scheduled for the task is appropriate.

10. Try various groupings in order to determine the situation in which the student is most comfortable.

11. Make the necessary adjustments in the environment to prevent the student from experiencing stress, frustration, anger, etc., as much as possible.

12. Interact frequently with the student to prevent excessive or unnecessary body movements.

13. Maintain visibility to and from the student. The teacher should be able to see the student and the student should be able to see the teacher, making eye contact possible at all times.

14. Facilitate on-task behavior by providing a full schedule of daily events. Prevent lag time when the student is free to engage in excessive or unnecessary body movements. (See Appendix for Schedule of Daily Events.)

15. Reduce stimuli which would contribute to unnecessary or excessive behavior.

16. Interact frequently with the student in order to maintain his/her attention to the activity (e.g., ask the student questions, ask the student's opinions, stand close to the student, seat the student near the teacher's desk, etc.).

17. Give the student additional responsibilities (e.g., chores, errands, etc.) to keep him/her actively involved and give him/her a feeling of success or accomplishment.

18. Modify or eliminate situations at school which cause the student to experience stress or frustration.

19. Maintain supervision at all times and in all parts of the school environment.

20. Prevent the student from becoming overly stimulated by an activity (i.e., monitor or supervise student behavior to limit overexcitement in physical activities, games, parties, etc.).

21. Provide the student with a predetermined signal when he/she exhibits inappropriate behavior.

22. Make certain that reinforcement is not inadvertently given for inappropriate behavior (e.g., attending to the student only when he/she engages in excessive/unnecessary body movements).

23. Separate the student from the peer who stimulates the inappropriate behavior.

24. Provide the student with the most attractive and interesting activities possible.

25. Provide the student with a calm, quiet environment in which to work.

26. Provide the student with a quiet place in the environment where he/she may go when he/she becomes upset. This is not meant as punishment, but as a means of helping the student be able to function more successfully in his/her environment.

27. Provide the student frequent opportunities to participate, take a turn, etc., in order to keep him/her involved in the activity.

28. Avoid discussion of topics sensitive to the student (e.g., divorce, death, unemployment, alcoholism, etc.).

29. Identify a peer to act as a model for the student to imitate staying in his/her seat.

30. Have the student question any directions, explanations, instructions he/she does not understand.

31. Schedule short activities for the student to perform while seated. Gradually increase the length of the activities as the student demonstrates success at staying in his/her seat.

32. Give the student frequent opportunities to leave his/her seat for appropriate reasons (e.g., getting materials, running errands, assisting the teacher, etc.).

33. Seat the student near the teacher.

34. Make certain the student has all necessary materials at his/her desk in order to reduce the need to leave his/her seat.

35. Have the student chart the length of time he/she is able to remain in his/her seat.

36. Work the first few problems of an assignment with the student in order that he/she will know what is expected.

77 Speakes in an unnatural voice

1. Reinforce the student for speaking in a natural voice: (a) give the student a tangible reward (e.g., classroom privileges, line leading, passing out materials, five minutes free time, etc.) or (b) give the student an intangible reward (e.g., praise, handshake, smile, etc.).

2. Speak to the student to explain: (a) what he/she is doing wrong (e.g., using an unnatural voice) and (b) what he/she should be doing (e.g., using a natural voice).

3. Reinforce those students in the classroom who use a natural voice when speaking.

4. Reinforce the student for speaking in a natural voice based on the length of time he/she can be successful. Gradually increase the length of time required for reinforcement as the student demonstrates success.

5. Write a contract with the student specifying what behavior is expected (e.g., using a natural voice) and what reinforcement will be made available when the terms of the contract have been met.

6. Communicate with parents (e.g., notes home, phone calls, etc.) in order to share information concerning the student's progress and so that they may reinforce the student at home for using a natural voice at school.

7. Communicate with parents, agencies, or appropriate parties in order to inform them of the problem, determine the cause of the problem, and solutions to the problem.

8. Evaluate the appropriateness of the task to determine: (a) if the task is too easy, (b) if the task is too difficult, and (c) if the length of time scheduled to complete the task is appropriate.

9. Identify a peer to act as a model for the student to imitate the use of a natural voice when speaking.

10. Give the student a predetermined signal when he/she begins to use an unnatural voice.

11. Avoid topics, situations, etc., which cause the student to speak in an unnatural voice (e.g., death, divorce, unemployment, alcoholism, etc.).

12. Require the student to use a natural voice at all times in the classroom.

13. Make certain that all adults (e.g., school and home) require the student to speak in a natural voice.

14. Place the student in situations in which he/she is comfortable and most likely to use a natural voice.

15. Make certain that the student's unnatural voice is not inadvertently reinforced by overattending to it (i.e., the student may speak in an unnatural voice because of the constant attention given to him/her).

16. Ignore the student's unnatural voice if it occurs infrequently or only in stimulating situations.

78 Speaks incoherently

1. Reinforce the student for using complete statements or thoughts when speaking: (a) give the student a tangible reward (e.g., classroom privileges, line leading, passing out materials, five minutes free time, etc.) or (b) give the student an intangible reward (e.g., praise, handshake, smile, etc.).

2. Reinforce those students in the classroom who use complete statements or thoughts when speaking.

3. Write a contract with the student specifying what behavior is expected (e.g., using complete statements or thoughts when speaking) and what reinforcement will be made available when the terms of the contract have been met.

4. Allow the student to speak without being interrupted or hurried.

5. Tape record a spontaneous monologue given by the student. Transcribe his/her speech from the tape and have the student listen to what he/she said. Have the student correct errors and practice speaking in more complete statements or thoughts.

6. Have the student keep a list of times and/or situations in which he/she is nervous, anxious, etc., and has more trouble with speech than usual. Help the student identify ways to feel more successful with those situations.

7. Demonstrate acceptable and unacceptable speech, using complete/incomplete statements and thoughts and have the student critique each example.

8. When the student has difficulty during a conversation, remind him/her that this occasionally happens to everyone and he/she should not become upset.

9. When the student fails to use complete thoughts (e.g., says, "Ball," and points) elaborate on what was said, (e.g., "So you want to play with the ball?"). This provides a model for more complete statements and thoughts.

10. Have the student role-play various situations in which good speech is important (e.g., during a job interview).

11. Make a list of what attributes are likely to help a person become a good speaker (e.g., takes his/her time, thinks of what to say before starting, etc.).

12. Reduce the emphasis on competition. Competitive activities may cause the student to hurry and fail to speak in complete statements or thoughts.

13. Break down the qualities a good speaker possesses (e.g., rate, diction, volume, vocabulary, etc.) and have the student evaluate himself/herself on each characteristic. Set a goal for improvement in only one or two areas at a time.

14. Have the student identify who he/she thinks is a good speaker and why.

15. Have a peer act as a model for speaking in complete statements or thoughts. Assign the students to work together, perform assignments together, etc.

16. Make a list of the most common incomplete statements or thoughts the student uses. Spend time with the student practicing how to make these statements or thoughts complete.

17. Verbally correct the student when he/she does not use complete sentences or thoughts when speaking so he/she can hear the correct version of what is being said.

18. Have the student practice descriptive statements or thoughts he/she can use when speaking.

19. Be certain to act as a model for the student to imitate speaking in complete statements or thoughts (e.g., speak clearly, slowly, concisely, and in complete sentences, statements, and thoughts).

20. Prepare simple oral reading passages in written form in which phrases are separated by large spaces (indicating "pause"). Have the student practice reading the passages aloud.

21. Have the student practice techniques for relaxing (e.g., deep breathing, tensing and relaxing muscles, etc.) which he/she can employ when he/she starts to become dysfluent.

22. If the student is speaking too rapidly, remind him/her to slow down and take his/her time. Be sure to give him/her undivided attention so he/she will not feel a need to hurry or compete with others for attention.

23. Do not require the student to speak in front of other students if he/she is uncomfortable doing so. Have the student speak to the teacher or another student privately if he/she would be more comfortable.

24. Have the student read simple passages and tape record them. Then have him/her listen and underline words or phrases that were omitted, added, substituted, or rearranged.

79 Engages in nervous habits

1. Reinforce the student for demonstrating appropriate behavior: (a) give the student a tangible reward (e.g., classroom privileges, line leading, passing out materials, five minutes free time, etc.) or (b) give the student an intangible reward (e.g., praise, handshake, smile, etc.).

2. Speak with the student to explain: (a) what he/she is doing wrong (e.g., chewing on pencil, nail biting, twirling objects, etc.) and (b) what he/she should be doing (e.g., practicing self-control, working on-task, performing responsibilities, etc.).

3. Establish classroom rules (e.g., work on-task, work quietly, remain in your seat, finish task, meet task expectations). Reiterate rules often and reinforce students for following rules.

4. Reinforce those students in the classroom who demonstrate appropriate behavior.

5. Reinforce the student for demonstrating appropriate behavior (academic or social) based on the length of time he/she can be successful. Gradually increase the length of time required for reinforcement as the student demonstrates success.

6. Remove the student from the group or activity when he/she engages in nervous habits.

7. Write a contract with the student specifying what behavior is expected (e.g., demonstrating appropriate behavior) and what reinforcement will be made available when the terms of the contract have been met.

8. Communicate with the parents (e.g., notes home, phone calls, etc.) in order to share information concerning the student's progress and so that they may reinforce the student at home for demonstrating appropriate behavior at school.

9. Evaluate the appropriateness of the task to determine if: (a) the task is too easy, (b) the task is too difficult, and (c) the length of time scheduled for the task is appropriate.

10. Provide the student with a predetermined signal when he/she engages in nervous habits.

11. Reduce situations which may contribute to nervous behavior (e.g., testing situations, timed activities, competition, etc.).

12. Prevent the student from becoming overly stimulated by an activity.

13. Try various groupings in order to determine the situation in which the student is most comfortable.

14. Provide the student with as many social and academic successes as possible.

15. Make the necessary adjustments in the environment to prevent the student from experiencing stress, frustration, anger, etc.

16. Assign a peer tutor to work directly with the student in order to prevent stress, frustration, anxiety, etc.

17. Interact frequently with the student in order to maintain his/her involvement in class assignments.

18. Allow the student additional time in which to complete class assignments or homework.

19. Interact frequently with the student to reduce nervous behavior.

20. Remove from the environment any object which may be used by the student to engage in nervous habits (e.g., pencils, pens, rubberbands, paperclips, etc.).

21. Reduce the emphasis on competition and perfection.

22. Reduce stimuli which may cause the student to engage in nervous habits (e.g., noise, movement, etc.).

23. Prevent situations in which peers contribute to the student's nervous behaviors.

24. Provide the student with another activity designed to result in productive behavior (e.g., coloring, cutting, using a calculator, working with a peer, etc.).

25. Structure the environment in order that time does not allow the student the opportunity to engage in nervous habits.

26. Encourage the student to practice self-control activities designed to allow him/her to gain composure before continuing an activity (e.g., placing hands on desk, sitting with feet on the floor, making eye contact with the instructor, etc.).

27. Provide the student with a high-interest activity which he/she prefers.

28. Provide a calm/pleasant atmosphere.

29. Avoid discussion of topics that are sensitive to the student (e.g., divorce, death, unemployment, alcoholism, etc.).

80 Throws temper tantrums

1. Reinforce the student for dealing with unhappiness in an appropriate manner (e.g., verbally stating his/her unhappiness, problem-solving, etc.): (a) give the student a tangible reward (e.g., classroom privileges, line leading, passing out materials, five minutes free time, etc.) or (b) give the student an intangible reward (e.g., praise, handshake, smile, etc.).

2. Speak with the student to explain: (a) that you recognize that he/she is unhappy and (b) appropriate ways to deal with unhappiness.

3. Establish classroom rules (e.g., work on-task, work quietly, remain in your seat, finish task, meet task expectations). Reiterate rules often and reinforce students for following rules.

4. Reinforce those students in the classroom who deal with unhappiness in an appropriate manner.

5. Reinforce the student for dealing with unhappiness in an appropriate manner based on the number of times he/she can be successful. Gradually increase the amount of time required for reinforcement as the student demonstrates success.

6. Remove the student from the group or activity until he/she can demonstrate appropriate behavior and self-control.

7. Write a contract with the student specifying what behavior is expected (e.g., dealing with unhappiness in an appropriate manner) and what reinforcement will be made available when the terms of the contract have been met.

8. Communicate with parents (e.g., notes home, phone calls, etc.) in order to share information concerning the student's progress and so that they may reinforce the student at home for dealing with unhappiness in an appropriate manner at school.

9. Evaluate the appropriateness of the task to determine: (a) if the task is too easy, (b) if the task is too difficult, and (c) if the length of time scheduled for the task is appropriate.

10. Communicate with parents, agencies, or appropriate parties in order to inform them of the problem, determine the cause of the problem, and consider possible solutions to the problem.

11. Assess the situations in which the student throws tantrums. Based on these observations, determine ways to prevent situations from stimulating the student to throw tantrums.

12. Try various groupings in order to determine the situation in which the student is most comfortable.

13. Provide the student with many social and academic successes.

14. Take the time to talk with the student in order that he/she realizes that your interest in him/her is genuine.

15. Teach/demonstrate methods for dealing with problems early in order to prevent problems from becoming overwhelming.

16. Encourage and help the student to make friends (e.g., pair the student with a peer and when that relationship is successful introduce other peers).

17. Explain to the student that feelings of unhappiness are natural, but there is an appropriate length of time for public display of that emotion.

18. When natural consequences occur as a result of the student's tantrums, point them out to him/her (e.g., peers prefer not to interact with him/her, property is damaged or destroyed resulting in loss of use or costly replacement, etc.).

19. Provide the student with as many positive interactions as possible (e.g., recognize the student, greet the student, compliment his/her attire, etc.).

20. Provide the student with preferred responsibilities throughout the school environment.

21. Make certain that reinforcement is not inadvertently given for inappropriate behavior (e.g., attending to the student only when he/she throws tantrums).

22. Make certain that consequences for both appropriate and inappropriate behavior are consistent.

23. Encourage and assist the student in joining extracurricular activities, clubs, etc.

24. Move the student away from the peer(s) who may be causing his/her unhappiness.

25. Discourage the student from engaging in those activities which cause him/her unhappiness.

26. Provide the student with positive feedback which indicates he/she is successful, competent, important, respected, etc.

27. Encourage the student to use problem-solving skills: (a) identify the problem, (b) identify goals and objectives, (c) develop strategies, (d) develop a plan for action, and (e) carry out the plan.

28. Identify individuals the student may contact concerning his/her unhappiness (e.g., guidance counselor, school nurse, social worker, school psychologist, etc.).

29. Give the student additional responsibilities (e.g., chores, errands, etc.) to give him/her a feeling of success or accomplishment.

30. Structure the environment so that the student does not have time to dwell on real or imagined problems.

31. Help the student identify how he/she wishes things were in the environment and work with the student toward those goals.

32. Teach the student alternative ways to deal with demands, challenges, and pressures of the school-age experience (e.g., deal with problems when they arise, practice self-control at all times, share problems or concerns with others, etc.).

33. Teach the student alternative ways to communicate his/her unhappiness (e.g., written, spoken, etc.).

34. Avoid topics, situations, etc., which remind the student of unpleasant experiences or problems (e.g., divorce, death, unemployment, alcoholism, etc.).

35. Follow less desirable activities with more desirable activities.

36. Provide the student with alternative activities to perform in case some activities prove upsetting.

37. Give the student some decision-making power (e.g., seating assignment, order of tasks, daily schedule, etc.).

38. Reduce the emphasis on competition. Repeated failure may cause the student to throw a tantrum.

81 Reacts physically in response to excitement, disappointment, surprise, happiness, fear, etc.

1. Reinforce the student for demonstrating physical self-control: (a) give the student a tangible reward (e.g., classroom privileges, line leading, passing out materials, five minutes free time, etc.) or (b) give the student an intangible reward (e.g., praise, handshake, smile, etc.).

2. Speak with the student to explain: (a) what he/she is doing wrong (e.g., shaking, flapping hands, etc.) and (b) what he/she should be doing (e.g., practicing self-control).

3. Establish classroom rules (e.g., work on-task, work quietly, remain in your seat, finish task, meet task expectations). Reiterate rules often and reinforce students for following rules.

4. Reinforce those students in the classroom who demonstrate physical self-control.

5. Reinforce the student for demonstrating physical self-control based on the length of time he/she can be successful. Gradually increase the amount of time required for reinforcement as the student demonstrates success.

6. Write a contract with the student specifying what behavior is expected (e.g., demonstrating physical self-control) and what reinforcement will be made available when the terms of the contract have been met.

7. Remove the student from the group or activity until he/she can demonstrate appropriate behavior and self-control.

8. Communicate with the parents (e.g., notes home, phone calls, etc.) in order to share information concerning the student's progress and so that they may reinforce the student at home for demonstrating physical self-control at school.

9. Evaluate the appropriateness of the task to determine: (a) if the task is too easy, (b) if the task is too difficult, and (c) if the length of time scheduled for the task is appropriate.

10. Try various groupings in order to determine the situation in which the student is most comfortable.

11. Make the necessary adjustments in the environment to prevent the student from experiencing stress, frustration, anger, etc., as much as possible.

12. Maintain visibility to and from the student. The teacher should be able to see the student and the student should be able to see the teacher, making eye contact possible at all times.

13. Facilitate on-task behavior by providing a full schedule of activities. Prevent lag time from occurring when the student would be more likely to engage in involuntary physical behavior.

14. Seat the student close to the teacher.

15. Reduce stimuli that contributes to unnecessary or excessive behavior.

16. Interact frequently with the student in order to direct his/her attention to the activity (e.g., ask the student questions, ask the student's opinions, stand close to the student, seat the student near the teacher's desk, etc.).

17. Maintain supervision at all times and in all parts of the school environment.

18. Prevent the student from becoming overly stimulated by an activity (e.g., monitor or supervise student behavior to limit overexcitement in physical activities, games, parties, etc.).

19. Expose the student to increased stimuli in the environment on a gradual basis after success has been demonstrated.

20. Teach the student appropriate ways to react to personal or school experiences (e.g., calling attention to the problem, practicing problem-solving, moving away from the situation if it is threatening, etc.).

21. Provide the student with as many social and academic successes as possible.

22. Present the task in the most attractive and interesting manner possible.

23. Identify individuals the student may contact with his/her worries or concerns (e.g., guidance counselor, school nurse, social worker, school psychologist, etc.).

24. Prevent frustrating or anxiety producing situations from occurring (e.g., give the student tasks only on his/her ability level, give the student only the number of tasks that he/she can tolerate in one sitting, reduce social interactions which stimulate the student to demonstrate involuntary physical reactions, etc.).

25. Be mobile in order to be frequently near the student.

26. Structure the environment in such a way so that the student does not have time to dwell on problems that are either real or imagined.

27. Teach the student problem-solving skills: (a) identify the problem, (b) identify goals and objectives, (c) develop strategies, (d) develop a plan for action, and (e) carry out the plan.

28. Provide an environment which is calm, consistent, and structured.

29. Provide the student with a predetermined signal if he/she begins to exhibit the inappropriate behavior.

30. Make certain that positive reinforcement is not inadvertently given for inappropriate behavior (e.g., responding to the student when he/she makes errors, responding to the student when he/she feigns a need for help, etc.).

31. Encourage the student to practice self-control activities designed to allow him/her to compose himself/herself before continuing an activity (e.g., placing hands on desk, sitting with feet flat on the floor, making eye contact with the instructor, etc.).

32. Provide the student with a quiet place to work when involuntary physical reactions occur. This is not meant as punishment, but as a means of helping the student be more successful in his/her environment.

82 Becomes pale, may throw up, or passes out when anxious or frightened

1. Determine that the physical symptom is not the result of a medical problem, neglect, abuse, or drug use.

2. Discuss concerns with other professionals to determine if further investigation is warranted.

3. Take the time to listen so that the student realizes your concern and interest in him/her is genuine.

4. Identify individuals the student may contact if his/her symptoms persist (e.g., guidance counselor, school nurse, social worker, school psychologist, parents, etc.).

5. Provide the student with as many social and academic successes as possible.

6. Prevent frustrating or anxiety producing situations from occurring (e.g., give the student tasks only on his/her ability level, give the student only those number of tasks which he/she can tolerate in one sitting, reduce social interactions which stimulate the student to become angry or upset, etc.).

7. Provide the student with success-oriented tasks (the expectation is that success will result in more positive attitudes and perceptions toward self and environment).

8. Provide the student with positive feedback which indicates that he/she is successful, competent, important, valuable, etc.

9. Teach the student problem-solving skills: (a) identify the problem, (b) identify goals and objectives, (c) develop strategies, (d) develop a plan for action, and (e) carry out the plan.

10. Determine which activities the student most enjoys and include those activities as much as possible in the daily routine.

11. Provide the student with opportunities to rest if necessary.

12. Have the parents reinforce the student at home for a balanced program of nutrition, rest, and exercise.

13. Reinforce the student for eating a nutritional lunch at school.

14. Arrange alternative lunches for the student at school (e.g., bring lunch from home, eat off campus, suggest an additional entree from the cafeteria, etc.).

15. Reduce the emphasis on competition. High levels of competition or repeated failure may result in physical symptoms such as paleness, throwing up, etc.

16. Emphasize individual success or progress rather than comparing performance to other students.

17. Communicate with the parents (e.g., notes home, phone calls, etc.) in order to share information concerning the student's progress and so that they may reinforce the student at home for dealing with problems in appropriate ways at school.

18. Encourage the student to identify problems which result in paleness, throwing up, etc., and act on those problems to resolve their influence.

19. Encourage the student to take responsibility for his/her assignments and obligations in an ongoing fashion rather than waiting until the night before or the day the assignment is due.

20. Help the student recognize problems that are within his/her ability to deal with and not to worry needlessly about situations for which he/she has no control.

21. Explain, if appropriate, that the concerns or worries, while legitimate, are not unusual for students (e.g., everyone worries about tests, grades, etc.).

22. Offer to provide extra academic help for the student when he/she experiences a problem that interferes with his/her academic performance.

83 Demonstrates phobic-type reactions

1. Reinforce the student for taking part in activities: (a) give the student a tangible reward (e.g., classroom privileges, line leading, passing out materials, five minutes free time, etc.) or (b) give the student an intangible reward (e.g., praise, handshake, smile, etc.).

2. Speak to the student to explain: (a) what he/she is doing wrong (e.g., avoiding activities) and (b) what he/she should be doing (e.g., taking part in activities).

3. Reinforce those students in the classroom who take part in activities.

4. Reinforce the student for taking part in activities based on the length of time he/she can do so comfortably. Gradually increase the number of times required for reinforcement as the student demonstrates success.

5. Write a contract with the student specifying what behavior is expected (e.g., changing clothing for physical education) and what reinforcement will be made available when the terms of the contract have been met.

6. Communicate with parents (e.g., notes home, phone calls, etc.) in order to share information concerning the student's progress and so that they may reinforce the student at home for taking part in activities at school.

7. Identify a peer to act as a model for the student to imitate taking part in activities.

8. Have the student question any directions, explanations, instructions he/she does not understand.

9. Evaluate the appropriateness of the expectations for taking part in activities based on the student's ability to perform the task.

10. If necessary, provide the student with a private place in which to change clothing for physical education.

11. Make certain the student has adequate time in which to perform activities.

12. To the extent necessary, provide assistance to the student for changing his/her clothing for physical education.

13. Have the student engage in activities which require minimal participation. Gradually increase the student's participation as he/she becomes more comfortable.

14. Make certain that the physical education clothing the student is expected to wear is appropriate.

15. If the student is reluctant to change clothing for physical education in the presence of others, allow the student to change clothing in private. Gradually increase the number of peers in whose presence the student changes clothing as he/she becomes more comfortable.

16. Be certain the student makes appropriate use of the time provided for activities.

17. If necessary, provide additional time for the student to change clothing for physical education. Gradually reduce the additional time provided as the student demonstrates success.

18. Make certain the student has the necessary clothing for physical education.

19. Prevent peers from making the student uncomfortable when he/she takes part in activities (i.e., prevent other students from making fun, teasing, etc.).

20. When requiring the student to engage in an activity in which he/she is uncomfortable, pair the student with a peer/friend in order to reduce his/her discomfort.

21. Evaluate the necessity of requiring the student to participate in activities in which he/she is uncomfortable.

22. Provide a pleasant/calm atmosphere.

23. Provide the student with alternatives to activities which make him/her uncomfortable (e.g., allow the student to write a poem instead of reciting it in front of a group).

24. Allow the student to be an observer of activities without requiring him/her to be an active participant.

25. Allow the student to perform functions or activities which require little participation (e.g., scorekeeper, note taker, etc.).

26. Ask the student to identify under what circumstances he/she would be willing to participate in activities (i.e., the student may be able to suggest acceptable conditions under which he/she would be comfortable participating in activities).

27. Provide a schedule whereby the student gradually increases the length of time spent at school each day, in the classroom, in a particular class or activity, etc.

28. Communicate with parents, agencies, or appropriate parties in order to inform them of the problem, determine the cause of the problem, and consider possible solutions to the problem.

29. If the student is extremely uncomfortable at school, allow a parent, relative, or friend to stay with the student all day if necessary. Gradually reduce the length of time the person remains with the student as the student becomes more comfortable.

A Reminder: Do not "force" the student to participate in any activity which makes him/her uncomfortable.

84 Does not follow the rules of the classroom

1. Reinforce the student for following the rules of the classroom: (a) give the student a tangible reward (e.g., classroom privileges, line leading, passing out materials, five minutes free time, etc.) or (b) give the student an intangible reward (e.g., praise, handshake, smile, etc.).

2. Speak with the student to explain: (a) what he/she is doing wrong (e.g., failing to follow classroom rules) and (b) what he/she should be doing (e.g., following the rules of the classroom).

3. Establish classroom rules (e.g., work on-task, work quietly, remain in your seat, finish task, meet task expectations). Reiterate rules often and reinforce students for following rules.

4. Reinforce those students who follow the rules of the classroom.

5. Reinforce the student for following the rules of the classroom based on the length of time he/she can be successful. Gradually increase the length of time required for reinforcement as the student demonstrates success.

6. Remove the student from the group or activity until he/she can demonstrate acceptable behavior and self-control.

7. Write a contract with the student specifying what behavior is expected (e.g., following classroom rules) and what reinforcement will be made available when the terms of the contract have been met.

8. Communicate with parents (e.g., notes home, phone calls, etc.) in order to share information concerning the student's progress and so that they may reinforce the student at home for following the rules of the classroom.

9. Evaluate the appropriateness of the assigned task to determine: (a) if the task is too easy, (b) if the task is too difficult, and (c) if the length of time scheduled for the task is appropriate.

10. Structure the environment in such a way that the student remains active and involved while demonstrating acceptable behavior.

11. Maintain visibility to and from the student. The teacher should be able to see the student and the student should be able to see the teacher, making eye contact possible at all times.

12. Give the student preferred responsibilities.

13. Present tasks in the most interesting and attractive manner possible.

14. Maintain maximum supervision of the student, gradually decreasing supervision over time.

15. Have the student maintain a chart representing the amount of time spent following classroom rules, with reinforcement for increasing acceptable behavior.

16. Practice mobility to be frequently near the student.

17. Provide the student with many social and academic successes.

18. Provide the student with positive feedback that indicates he/she is successful.

19. Post rules in various places, including the student's desk.

20. Make certain the student receives the information necessary to perform activities (e.g., written information, verbal directions, reminders, etc.).

21. Teach the student direction-following skills.

22. Maintain a positive and professional relationship with the student (e.g., an adversary relationship is likely to result in failure to follow directions).

23. Be a consistent authority figure (e.g., be consistent in relationship with students).

24. Provide the student with optional courses of action in order to prevent total refusal to obey teacher directives.

25. Intervene early to prevent the student's behavior from leading to contagion for other students.

26. Have the student question any directions, explanations, instructions he/she does not understand.

27. Require the student to verbalize the classroom rules at designated times throughout the day (e.g., before school, recess, lunch, at the end of the day, etc.).

28. Deliver directions in a step-by-step sequence.

29. Have a peer act as a model for following the rules of the classroom.

30. Interact with the student frequently to determine if directives are being followed.

31. Maintain consistency in rules, routine, and general expectations of conduct and procedure.

32. Provide the student with a list of rules and/or behavior expectations.

33. Help the student identify specific rules he/she has difficulty following and make these areas goals for behavior improvement.

34. Separate the student from the peer(s) who stimulates his/her inappropriate behavior.

35. Make certain that rules and behavior expectations are consistent throughout the school and classrooms.

85 Does not wait appropriately for an instructor to arrive

1. Reinforce the student for waiting appropriately for an instructor to arrive: (a) give the student a tangible reward (e.g., classroom privileges, line leading, passing out materials, five minutes free time, etc.) or (b) give the student an intangible reward (e.g., praise, handshake, smile, etc.).

2. Speak to the student to explain: (a) what he/she is doing wrong (e.g., leaving seat, talking, making noises, etc.) and (b) what he/she should be doing (e.g., sitting in seat or assigned area, remaining quiet, etc.).

3. Establish classroom rules (e.g., stay in seat or assigned area, remain quiet, work on assigned task). Reiterate rules often and reinforce students for following rules.

4. Reinforce those students in the classroom who stay in their seat or assigned area, remain quiet, and work on assigned tasks.

5. Reinforce the student for waiting appropriately for an instructor to arrive based on the length of time he/she can be successful. Gradually increase the length of time required for reinforcement as the student demonstrates success.

6. Write a contract with the student specifying what behavior is expected (e.g., stay in seat or assigned area, remain quiet, and work on assigned task) and what reinforcement will be made available when the terms of the contract have been met.

7. Communicate with parents (e.g., notes home, phone calls, etc.) in order to share information concerning the student's progress and so that they may reinforce the student at home for waiting appropriately for an instructor to arrive at school.

8. Identify a peer to act as a model for the student to imitate appropriate behavior (e.g., staying in seat or assigned area, remaining quiet, working on an assigned task, etc.) when an instructor is detained.

9. Have the student question any directions, explanations, instructions he/she does not understand.

10. Assign a peer to act as a model for the student or to supervise the student when an instructor is detained.

11. Provide a list of possible activities for the students to engage in when an instructor is detained (e.g., color, write a letter to a friend, work on assigned tasks, organize work area, look at a magazine, etc.).

86 Does not wait appropriately for assistance or attention from an instructor

1. Reinforce the student for waiting appropriately for assistance or attention from an instructor: (a) give the student a tangible reward (e.g., classroom privileges, line leading, passing out materials, five minutes free time, etc.) or (b) give the student an intangible reward (e.g., praise, handshake, smile, etc.).

2. Speak to the student to explain: (a) what he/she is doing wrong (e.g., leaving his/her seat, talking to other students, etc.) and (b) what he/she should be doing (e.g., remaining quietly seated or in an assigned area).

3. Establish classroom rules (e.g., remain quietly seated or in an assigned area). Reiterate rules often and reinforce students for following rules.

4. Reinforce those students in the classroom who remain quietly seated in an assigned area.

5. Reinforce the student for waiting appropriately for assistance or attention from an instructor based on the length of time he/she can be successful. Gradually increase the length of time required for reinforcement as the student demonstrates success.

6. Write a contract with the student specifying what behavior is expected (e.g., remaining quietly seated or in an assigned area) and what reinforcement will be made available when the terms of the contract have been met.

7. Communicate with parents (e.g., notes home, phone calls, etc.) in order to share information concerning the student's progress and so that they may reinforce the student at home for waiting appropriately for assistance or attention from an instructor at school.

8. Evaluate the appropriateness of the task to determine: (a) if the task is too easy, (b) if the task is too difficult, and (c) if the length of time scheduled to complete the task is appropriate.

9. Identify a peer to act as a model for the student to imitate appropriate behavior (e.g., remaining quietly seated or in an assigned area) when waiting for assistance or attention from an instructor.

10. Have the student question any directions, explanations, instructions he/she does not understand.

11. Tell the student that you will assist him/her as soon as possible (e.g., "Stephen, I'll be with you shortly.") in order to increase the probability that the student will wait appropriately for assistance.

12. Identify a peer from whom the student may seek assistance.

13. Attempt to provide assistance immediately. Gradually increase the length of time the student must wait for assistance when you are helping another student, instructing a small group activity, etc.

14. Encourage the student to go on to the next problem, go on to another part of the assignment, begin a new assignment, etc., when waiting for assistance or attention from an instructor.

15. Establish alternative activities for the student to perform when waiting for assistance or attention from an instructor (e.g., check work already completed, color, look at a magazine, organize work area, begin another task, etc.).

16. Position yourself in order that visibility to and from the student may be maintained until assistance can be provided.

17. Maintain verbal communication with the student until assistance can be provided (e.g., "Thank you for waiting quietly. I'll be there shortly.").

87 Demonstrates inappropriate behavior in the presence of a substitute teacher

1. Reinforce the student for demonstrating appropriate behavior in the presence of a substitute teacher: (a) give the student a tangible reward (e.g., classroom privileges, line leading, passing out materials, five minutes free time, etc.) or (b) give the student an intangible reward (e.g., praise, handshake, smile, etc.).

2. Speak to the student to explain: (a) what he/she is doing wrong (e.g., not following the substitute teacher's directions, not following classroom rules, etc.) and (b) what he/she should be doing (e.g., following the substitute teacher's directions, following classroom rules, etc.).

3. Establish classroom rules (e.g., work on-task, work quietly, remain in your seat, finish task, meet task expectations). Reiterate rules often and reinforce students for following rules.

4. Reinforce those students in the classroom who demonstrate appropriate behavior in the presence of a substitute teacher.

5. Write a contract with the student specifying what behavior is expected (e.g., following the substitute teacher's directions) and what reinforcement will be made available when the terms of the contract have been met.

6. Communicate with parents (e.g., notes home, phone calls, etc.) in order to share information concerning the student's progress and so that they may reinforce the student at home for demonstrating appropriate behavior in the presence of a substitute teacher.

7. Evaluate the appropriateness of the task to determine: (a) if the task is too easy, (b) if the task is too difficult, and (c) if the length of time scheduled to complete the task is appropriate.

8. Have the student question any directions, explanations, instructions he/she does not understand.

9. Prepare a substitute teacher information packet that includes all information pertaining to the classroom (e.g., student roster, class schedule, class rules, behavior management techniques, class helpers, etc.).

10. Make certain that the student understands that classroom rules and behavioral consequences are in effect when a substitute teacher is in the classroom.

11. Inform the substitute teacher of all privileges the students have both in and outside of the classroom.

12. Indicate various activities that the student can engage in when he/she has completed his/her work for the day.

13. Indicate the name of several teachers and where they can be found in case the substitute teacher should need their assistance.

14. Inform the substitute teacher of the classroom rules and consequences if the rules are not followed by the student.

15. Express the need for the substitute teacher to maintain consistency of discipline while both in and outside of the classroom.

16. Indicate where all needed materials are located in order to maintain structure in the classroom.

17. Have the student work on practice work (e.g., work that has already been taught to the student and that he/she knows how to do) in order to reduce frustration and feelings of failure.

18. Set aside 10 minutes at the beginning of the day for the substitute teacher to develop rapport with the students (e.g., introduce himself/herself to the class, learn the students' names, talk about things the students enjoy doing, etc.).

19. Schedule a fun educational activity (e.g., computer games) during the day in order to provide incentive for the student to stay on-task and behave appropriately.

20. Assign a "special job" for the student to perform when there is a substitute teacher in the classroom (e.g., substitute teacher's assistant, line leader, class monitor, etc.). Inform the substitute teacher of this "special job."

21. Indicate to the student that the substitute teacher is in charge of the classroom at all times.

22. Have the substitute teacher present instructions/directions in a variety of ways (e.g., orally, written, etc.).

23. Make an attempt to use a substitute teacher who has skills necessary to deal with problem behavior and special needs students.

24. Make certain that the substitute teacher is familiar with the behavioral support system used in the classroom (e.g., rules, point system, reinforcers, etc.).

25. If possible, communicate directly with the substitute teacher in order to share information which will contribute to the student's success.

26. Identify a student(s) to act as an assistant to the substitute teacher during the day's activities (e.g., the student(s) provides accurate information about the schedule of activities, behavioral support system, etc.).

27. Provide the substitute teacher with detailed information on the activities and assignments.

28. Assign the student specific activities to perform on any day when a substitute teacher may be responsible for the classroom (e.g., assistant to the substitute teacher, "errand runner," line leading, class monitor, etc.).

29. Make certain the substitute teacher follows all procedures indicated by the classroom teacher (e.g., academic activities, behavioral support system, etc.).

30. Have the substitute teacher provide a written review of the day as feedback for the classroom teacher (e.g., activities completed, student behavior, absences, incidents concerning individual students, etc.).

31. Have special or unique responsibilities performed by other personnel in the building (e.g., administering medication, feeding, toileting, etc.).

32. Have the student self-record his/her own behavior when a substitute teacher is in the classroom.

33. Assign a peer to work with the student to act as a model for appropriate behavior and provide information necessary for success.

34. If an aide works in the classroom, have the aide monitor the student's behavior, provide reinforcement, deliver instructions, etc.

35. If there is an aide in the classroom, have the aide work with the student on a one-to-one basis throughout the day.

36. Provide the student with an individualized schedule of daily events. The schedule should be attached to the student's desk or carried with him/her at all times.

37. Instruct the substitute teacher to interact with the student frequently in order to provide reinforcement, deliver instructions, provide encouragement, etc.

38. Have the substitute teacher maintain visibility to and from the student. The substitute teacher should be able to see the student and the student should be able to see the substitute teacher, making eye contact possible at all times.

39. Provide the student with as many high-interest activities as possible.

40. Provide a quiet place for the student to work.

41. Make the student aware of the natural consequences concerning inappropriate behavior in the presence of a substitute teacher (e.g., removal from the classroom, loss of privileges, etc.).

42. Have a peer deliver instructions to the student.

43. Begin the day or class with an activity which is of high interest to the student.

44. Present activities in the most attractive and interesting manner possible.

45. Do not schedule highly stimulating activities when a substitute teacher is in the classroom.

46. Structure the environment in order to reduce the opportunity for inappropriate behavior (e.g., reduce periods of inactivity by having the student actively involved at all times).

47. Provide the substitute teacher with a seating chart and indicate the student(s) who needs additional supervision.

48. Indicate for the substitute teacher those peers who might be likely to stimulate the student's inappropriate behavior (it may be necessary to keep the students separated).

49. Have the substitute teacher check the student's completed assignments in order to make certain that work is not carelessly performed.

50. Write a contract with the student or entire class for reinforcement based on appropriate behavior when a substitute teacher is present.

51. Have the substitute teacher maintain mobility in order to be frequently near the student.

52. Make certain the student receives the necessary information to perform activities (e.g., written information, verbal directions, reminders, etc.).

53. Make certain the substitute teacher is consistent with the program established by the classroom teacher (e.g., schedule, delivering instructions, task requirements, reinforcement, negative consequences, etc.).

54. Provide the student with a clearly identified list of consequences for inappropriate behavior in the presence of a substitute teacher.

55. Have the substitute teacher help the student begin assignments, check his/her work, provide immediate feedback, etc.

56. Have the student maintain a record of his/her academic performance while the substitute teacher is in the classroom.

57. Inform the students in advance when it will be necessary for a substitute teacher to be in the classroom and establish expectations for behavior and academic performance.

58. Provide the substitute teacher with instructions for action to be taken if the student becomes abusive or threatening.

88 Does not demonstrate appropriate use of school-related materials

1. Reinforce the student for demonstrating appropriate use of school-related materials: (a) give the student a tangible reward (e.g., classroom privileges, line leading, passing out materials, five minutes free time, etc.) or (b) give the student an intangible reward (e.g., praise, handshake, smile, etc.).

2. Speak to the student to explain: (a) what he/she is doing wrong (e.g., failing to use school-related materials appropriately) and (b) what he/she should be doing (e.g., using school-related materials as directed).

3. Establish classroom rules (e.g., work on-task, work quietly, remain in your seat, finish task, meet task expectations). Reiterate rules often and reinforce students for following rules.

4. Reinforce those students in the classroom who use school-related materials appropriately.

5. Reinforce the student for using school-related materials appropriately based on the length of time he/she can be successful. Gradually increase the length of time required for reinforcement as the student demonstrates success.

6. Write a contract with the student specifying what behavior is expected (e.g., appropriate use of school-related materials) and what reinforcement will be made available when the terms of the contract have been met.

7. Communicate with parents (e.g., notes home, phone calls, etc.) in order to share information concerning the student's progress and so that they may reinforce the student at home for using school-related materials appropriately at school.

8. Evaluate the appropriateness of the task to determine: (a) if the task is too easy, (b) if the task is too difficult, and (c) if the length of time scheduled to complete the task is appropriate.

9. Identify a peer to act as a model for the student to imitate appropriate use of school-related materials.

10. Have the student question any directions, explanations, instructions he/she does not understand.

11. Provide time at the beginning of each day to help the student organize his/her school-related materials.

12. Provide time at various points throughout the day to help the student organize his/her school-related materials (e.g., before school, recess, lunch, end of the day, etc.).

13. Provide the student with adequate work space (e.g., a larger desk or table at which to work).

14. Provide storage space for school-related materials the student is not using at any particular time.

15. Reduce distracting stimuli (e.g., place the student on the front row, provide a carrel or quiet place away from distractions, etc.). This is a means of reducing distracting stimuli and not as a form of punishment.

16. Interact frequently with the student in order to prompt organizational skills and appropriate use of school-related materials.

17. Assign the student organizational responsibilities in the classroom (e.g., equipment, software materials, etc.).

18. Limit the student's use of school-related materials (e.g., provide the student with only those school-related materials necessary at any given time).

19. Act as a model for organization and appropriate use of school-related materials (e.g., putting materials away before getting others out, having a place for all materials, maintaining an organized desk area, following a schedule for the day, etc.).

20. Provide adequate transition time between activities for the student to organize himself/herself.

21. Establish a routine to be followed for organization and appropriate use of school-related materials.

22. Provide adequate time for the completion of activities.

23. Require the student to organize his/her work area at regular intervals. (It is recommended that this be done at least three times per day or more often if necessary.)

24. Supervise the student while he/she is performing school work in order to monitor quality.

25. Allow natural consequences to occur as the result of the student's inability to organize or use school-related materials appropriately (e.g., materials not maintained appropriately will be lost or not serviceable).

26. Assess the quality and clarity of directions, explanations, and instructions given to the student.

27. Assist the student in beginning each task in order to reduce impulsive behavior.

28. Provide the student with structure for all academic activities (e.g., specific directions, routine format for tasks, time units, etc.).

29. Give the student a checklist of school-related materials necessary for each activity.

30. Minimize school-related materials needed.

31. Provide an organizer for school-related materials inside the student's desk.

32. Provide the student with an organizational checklist (e.g., routine activities and steps to follow).

33. Teach the student appropriate care of school-related materials (e.g., sharpening pencils, keeping books free of marks and tears, etc.).

34. Make certain that all of the student's school-related materials are labelled with his/her name.

35. Point out to the student that loaning his/her school-related materials to other students does not reduce his/her responsibility for the materials.

36. Teach the student to conserve rather than waste school-related materials (e.g., amount of glue, paper, tape, etc., to use; putting lids, caps, and tops on materials such as markers, pens, bottles, jars, cans, etc.).

37. Teach the student appropriate ways to deal with anger and frustration rather than destroying school-related materials.

38. Teach the student to maintain school-related materials (e.g., keep materials with him/her, know where materials are at all times, secure materials in his/her locker, etc.).

39. Provide the student with an appropriate place to store/secure school-related materials (e.g., desk, locker, closet, etc.) and require him/her to store all materials when not in use.

40. Explain to the student that the failure to care for school-related materials will result in the loss of freedom to maintain materials.

41. Provide reminders (e.g., a list of school-related materials) to help the student maintain and care for school-related materials.

42. Limit the student's freedom to take school-related materials from school if he/she is unable to return such items.

43. Provide the student with verbal reminders of school-related materials needed for each activity.

44. Limit the student's opportunity to use school-related materials if he/she is unable to care for his/her own personal property.

45. Make certain that failure to have necessary school-related materials results in loss of opportunity to participate in activities or a failing grade for that day's activity.

46. Reduce the number of school-related materials for which the student is responsible. Increase the number as the student demonstrates appropriate care of materials.

47. Teach the student safety rules in the handling of school-related materials (e.g., pencils, scissors, compass; and biology, industrial arts, and home economics materials, etc.).

48. Teach the student the appropriate use of school-related materials (e.g., scissors, pencils, compass, rulers; and biology, industrial arts, and home economics materials, etc.).

49. Require that lost or damaged school-related materials be replaced by the student. If the student cannot replace the property, restitution can be made by working at school.

50. Make certain the student is not inadvertently reinforced for losing or damaging school-related materials. Provide the student with used or damaged materials, copies of the materials, etc., rather than new materials.

89 Does not demonstrate appropriate care and handling of others' property

1. Reinforce the student for demonstrating appropriate care and handling of others' property: (a) give the student a tangible reward (e.g., classroom privileges, line leading, passing out materials, five minutes free time, etc.) or (b) give the student an intangible reward (e.g., praise, handshake, smile, etc.).

2. Speak to the student to explain: (a) what he/she is doing wrong (e.g., losing property, destroying property, etc.) and (b) what he/she should be doing (e.g., putting property away, returning property, etc.).

3. Establish classroom rules (e.g., work on-task, work quietly, remain in your seat, finish task, meet task expectations). Reiterate rules often and reinforce students for following rules.

4. Reinforce those students in the classroom who demonstrate appropriate care and handling of others' property.

5. Reinforce the student for demonstrating appropriate care and handling of others' property based on the length of time he/she can be successful. Gradually increase the length of time required for reinforcement as the student demonstrates success.

6. Write a contract with the student specifying what behavior is expected (e.g., putting property away, returning property, etc.) and what reinforcement will be made available when the terms of the contract have been met.

7. Communicate with parents (e.g., notes home, phone calls, etc.) in order to share information concerning the student's progress and so that they may reinforce the student at home for demonstrating appropriate care and handling of others' property at school.

8. Evaluate the appropriateness of the task to determine: (a) if the task is too easy, (b) if the task is too difficult, and (c) if the length of time scheduled to complete the task is appropriate.

9. Identify a peer to act as a model for the student to imitate appropriate care and handling of others' property.

10. Have the student question any directions, explanations, instructions he/she does not understand.

11. Provide time at the beginning of each day to help the student organize the materials he/she will use throughout the day.

12. Provide time at various points throughout the day to help the student organize materials he/she will use throughout the day (e.g., before school, recess, lunch, end of the day, etc.).

13. Provide the student with adequate work space (e.g., a large desk or table at which to work).

14. Provide storage space for materials the student is not using at any particular time.

15. Reduce distracting stimuli (e.g., place the student on the front row, provide a carrel or quiet place away from distractions, etc.). Overstimulation may cause the student to misuse others' property.

16. Interact frequently with the student in order to prompt organizational skills and appropriate use of materials.

17. Assign the student organizational responsibilities in the classroom (e.g., equipment, software materials, etc.).

18. Limit the student's use of materials (e.g., provide the student with only those materials necessary at any given time).

19. Act as a model for organization and appropriate use of work materials (e.g., putting materials away before getting others out, having a place for all materials, maintaining an organized desk area, following a schedule for the day, etc.).

20. Provide adequate transition time between activities for the student to organize himself/herself.

21. Establish a routine to be followed for organization and appropriate use of work materials.

22. Provide adequate time for the completion of activities. Inadequate time for completion of activities may result in the student's misuse of others' property.

23. Require the student to organize his/her work area at regular intervals.

24. Allow natural consequences to occur as the result of the student's inability to appropriately care for and handle others' property (e.g., property not maintained appropriately will be lost or not serviceable).

25. Assess the quality and clarity of directions, explanations, and instructions given to the student for use in the care and handling of others' property.

26. Assist the student in beginning each task in order to reduce impulsive behavior.

27. Provide the student with structure for all academic activities (e.g., specific directions, routine format for tasks, time units, etc.).

28. Give the student a checklist of materials necessary for each activity.

29. Minimize materials needed.

30. Provide an organizer for materials inside the student's desk.

31. Provide the student with an organizational checklist (e.g., routine activities and materials needed).

32. Teach the student appropriate care and handling of others' property (e.g., sharpening pencils, keeping books free of marks and tears, etc.).

33. Make certain that all personal property is labeled with the students' names.

34. Point out to the student that borrowing personal property from others does not reduce his/her responsibility for the property.

35. Teach the student how to conserve rather than waste materials (e.g., amount of glue, paper, tape, etc., to use; putting lids, caps, and tops on materials such as markers, pens, bottles, jars, cans, etc.).

36. Teach the student appropriate ways to deal with anger and frustration rather than destroying property belonging to others (e.g., pencils, pens, workbooks, notebooks, textbooks, etc.).

37. Teach the student to maintain property belonging to others (e.g., keep property with him/her, know where property is at all times, secure property in lockers, etc.).

38. Provide the student with an appropriate place to store/secure others' property (e.g., desk, locker, closet, etc.) and require the student to store all property when not in use.

39. Teach the student that the failure to care for others' property will result in the loss of freedom to use others' property.

40. Provide reminders (e.g., a list of property or materials) to help the student maintain and care for school property.

41. Limit the student's freedom to take property from school if he/she is unable to remember to return such items.

42. Limit the student's opportunity to use others' property if he/she is unable to care for his/her own personal property.

43. Reduce the number of materials the student is responsible to care for or handle. Increase the number as the student demonstrates appropriate care of property.

44. Teach the student safety rules in the care and handling of others' property and materials (e.g., pencils, scissors, compass; biology, industrial arts, and home economics materials, etc.).

45. Require that lost or damaged property be replaced by the student. If the student cannot replace the property, restitution can be made by working at school.

46. Make certain the student is not inadvertently reinforced for losing or damaging property by providing him/her with new materials. Provide the student with used or damaged materials, copies of the materials, etc., rather than new materials.

47. Teach the student rules for the care and handling of others' property (e.g., always ask to use other's property, treat the property with care, inform the teacher if the property becomes damaged, return the property in the same or better condition than when it was borrowed, etc.).

48. Do not permit peers to allow the student to use their property if he/she is not able to care for it properly.

49. Remove others' property from the student if he/she is unable to appropriately care for and handle the property.

50. Maintain mobility throughout the classroom in order to supervise the student's care and handling of other's property.

51. Permit the student to use only the amount of property that he/she can care for and handle appropriately. Gradually increase the amount of property as the student demonstrates success.

90 Does not raise hand when appropriate

1. Reinforce the student for raising his/her hand when appropriate: (a) give the student a tangible reward (e.g., classroom privileges, line leading, passing out materials, five minutes free time, etc.) or (b) give the student an intangible reward (e.g., praise, handshake, smile, etc.).

2. Speak to the student to explain: (a) what he/she is doing wrong (e.g., talking out, engaging in a behavior without raising his/her hand to get permission, etc.) and (b) what he/she should be doing (e.g., raising his/her hand for permission to speak, move about the room, etc.).

3. Establish classroom rules (e.g., work on-task, work quietly, remain in your seat, raise hand, finish task, meet task expectations). Reiterate rules often and reinforce students for following rules.

4. Reinforce those students in the classroom who raise their hand when appropriate.

5. Reinforce the student for raising his/her hand when appropriate based on the number of times he/she can be successful. Gradually increase the number of times required for reinforcement as the student demonstrates success.

6. Write a contract with the student specifying what behavior is expected (e.g., raising his/her hand for teacher assistance) and what reinforcement will be made available when the terms of the contract have been met.

7. Communicate with parents (e.g., notes home, phone calls, etc.) in order to share information concerning the student's progress and so that they may reinforce the student at home for raising his/her hand when appropriate at school.

8. Identify a peer to act as a model for the student to imitate raising his/her hand when appropriate.

9. Have the student question any directions, explanations, instructions he/she does not understand by raising his/her hand.

10. Evaluate the appropriateness of requiring the student to raise his/her hand. The student may not be capable or developmentally ready for hand raising. Have the student use other appropriate means of gaining attention.

11. Establish rules specifically for hand raising (e.g., raise hand for permission to talk, leave seat, etc.).

12. Allow natural consequences to occur as a result of the student raising or failing to raise his/her hand (e.g., students who raise their hand will have their needs met, those students who fail to raise their hand will not have their needs met until they raise their hand, etc.).

13. Provide the student with verbal reminders to raise his/her hand (e.g., at the beginning of the day, beginning of the activity, when he/she forgets, etc.).

14. Have a peer model appropriate hand raising for new students, students who do not raise their hand, etc.

15. Post hand raising rules in the classroom.

16. Make certain that the student is not inadvertently reinforced for failing to raise his/her hand. The student may be getting the teacher's attention by talking out.

17. Acknowledge the student immediately upon raising his/her hand (e.g., let the student know you see his/her hand, call upon the student, go to the student, etc.).

18. Be certain to let the student know that you will be with him/her as soon as possible when it is necessary to be detained (e.g., working with another student, speaking with another teacher, instructing a small group, etc.).

19. Do not grant the student's request until he/she raises his/her hand.

20. Make certain that hand raising expectations are consistently applied.

21. Provide the student with alternative appropriate attention-seeking methods (e.g., display "help" sign on desk).

22. Maintain mobility throughout the classroom in order to "catch" the student displaying appropriate attention-seeking behavior (e.g., hand raising).

91 Does not take notes during class when necessary

1. Reinforce the student for taking notes during class when necessary: (a) give the student a tangible reward (e.g., classroom privileges, line leading, passing out materials, five minutes free time, etc.) or (b) give the student an intangible reward (e.g., praise, handshake, smile, etc.).

2. Speak to the student to explain: (a) what he/she is doing wrong (e.g., failing to take notes) and (b) what he/she should be doing (e.g., taking notes).

3. Establish classroom rules (e.g., take notes when necessary, work on-task, work quietly, remain in your seat, finish task, meet task expectations). Reiterate rules often and reinforce students for following rules.

4. Reinforce those students in the classroom who take notes during class when necessary.

5. Reinforce the student for taking notes during class when necessary based on the length of time he/she can be successful. Gradually increase the length of time required for reinforcement as the student demonstrates success.

6. Write a contract with the student specifying what behavior is expected (e.g., taking notes) and what reinforcement will be made available when the terms of the contract have been met.

7. Communicate with parents (e.g., notes home, phone calls, etc.) in order to share information concerning the student's progress and so that they may reinforce the student at home for taking notes during class when necessary.

8. Evaluate the appropriateness of note-taking to determine: (a) if the task is too easy, (b) if the task is too difficult, and (c) if the length of time scheduled to complete the task is appropriate.

9. Identify a peer to act as a model for the student to imitate appropriate note-taking during class when necessary.

10. Have the student question any directions, explanations, instructions he/she does not understand.

11. Teach the student note-taking skills (e.g., copy main ideas from the board, identify main ideas from lectures, condense statements into a few key words, etc.).

12. Provide a standard format for direction or explanation note-taking (e.g., have paper and pencil or pen ready, listen for the steps in directions or explanations, write a shortened form of directions or explanations, ask to have any steps repeated when necessary, etc.).

13. Provide a standard format for lecture note-taking (e.g., have paper and pencil or pen ready, listen for main ideas of important information, write a shortened form of main ideas or important information, ask to have any main ideas or important information repeated when necessary, etc.).

14. While delivering instructions, directions, lectures, etc., point out to the student that information should be written in the form of notes.

15. Have the student practice legible manuscript or cursive handwriting during simulated and actual note-taking activities.

16. Have the student keep his/her notes organized in a folder for each subject or activity.

17. Check the student's notes before he/she begins an assignment in order to determine if they are correct and adequate for the assignment.

18. Provide the student with an outline or questions to be completed during teacher delivery of instructions, directions, lectures, etc.

19. Provide the student with samples of notes taken from actual instructions, directions, lectures, etc., given in the classroom in order that he/she may learn what information is necessary for note-taking.

20. Make certain the student is in the best location in the classroom to receive information for note-taking (e.g., near the board, teacher, or other source of information).

21. Make certain you can easily provide supervision of the student's note-taking.

22. Make certain to maintain visibility to and from the student when delivering instructions, directions, lectures, etc., in order to enhance the likelihood of successful note-taking.

23. Make certain that instructions, directions, lectures, etc., are presented clearly and loudly enough for the student to hear.

24. Match the rate of delivery of instructions, directions, lectures, etc., to the student's ability to take notes.

25. Provide the student with both verbal and written instructions.

26. Provide instructions, directions, lectures, etc., in sequential steps in order to enhance student note-taking.

27. Provide delivery of information in short segments for the student to take notes. Gradually increase the length of delivery as the student experiences success in note-taking.

28. Make certain that the vocabulary used in delivering instructions, directions, lectures, etc., is appropriate for the student's ability level.

29. Place the student next to a peer in order that the student can copy notes taken by the peer.

30. Make certain the student has all necessary materials for note-taking (e.g., paper, pencil, pen, etc.).

31. Make certain the student uses any necessary aids in order to facilitate note-taking (e.g., eyeglasses, hearing aid, etc.).

32. Make certain the student has adequate surface space on which to write when taking notes (e.g., uncluttered desk top).

33. Reduce distracting stimuli that would interfere with the student's note-taking (e.g., other students talking, outdoor activities, movement in the classroom, hallway noise, etc.).

34. Present the information in the most interesting manner possible.

35. As an alternative to note-taking have the student tape record instructions, directions, lectures, etc.

36. Summarize the main points of instructions, directions, lectures, etc., for the student.

92 Does not resolve conflict situations appropriately

1. Reinforce the student for demonstrating the ability to appropriately solve problems in conflict situations: (a) give the student a tangible reward (e.g., classroom privileges, line leading, passing out materials, five minutes free time, etc.) or (b) give the student an intangible reward (e.g., praise, handshake, smile, etc.).

2. Speak to the student to explain: (a) what he/she is doing wrong (e.g., fighting, name calling, etc.) and (b) what he/she should be doing (e.g., withdrawing from conflict situations, compromising, etc.).

3. Reinforce those students in the classroom who demonstrate the ability to appropriately solve problems in conflict situations.

4. Reinforce the student for demonstrating the ability to appropriately solve problems in conflict situations based on the number of times he/she can be successful. Gradually increase the number of times required for reinforcement as the student demonstrates success.

5. Write a contract with the student specifying what behavior is expected (e.g., withdrawing from conflict situations) and what reinforcement will be made available when the terms of the contract have been met.

6. Communicate with parents (e.g., notes home, phone calls, etc.) in order to share information concerning the student's progress and so that they may reinforce the student at home for demonstrating the ability to appropriately solve problems in conflict situations at school.

7. Identify a peer to act as a model for the student to imitate the ability to appropriately solve problems in conflict situations.

8. Have the student question any directions, explanations, instructions he/she does not understand.

9. Evaluate the student's problem-solving ability and limit his/her exposure to conflict situations to a level he/she can deal with appropriately.

10. Teach the student a variety of ways to solve problems in conflict situations (e.g., withdrawing, reasoning, calling upon an arbitrator, apologizing, compromising, allowing others the benefit of the doubt, etc.).

11. Model for the student a variety of ways to solve problems in conflict situations (e.g., withdrawing, reasoning, apologizing, compromising, etc.).

12. Provide the student with hypothetical conflict situations and require him/her to suggest appropriate solutions to the situation.

13. Have the student role-play ways to solve problems in conflict situations with peers and adults (e.g., withdrawing, reasoning, calling upon an arbitrator, apologizing, compromising, allowing others the benefit of the doubt, etc.).

14. Make certain the student understands that natural consequences may occur if he/she reacts inappropriately in conflict situations (e.g., peers will not want to interact, teachers will have to intervene, etc.).

15. Teach the student to solve problems in conflict situations before the situation becomes too difficult for him/her to solve.

16. Teach the student to avoid becoming involved in conflict situations (e.g., move away from the situation, change his/her behavior, etc.).

17. Explain to the student that it is natural for conflict situations to occur. What is important is how he/she reacts to the situation.

18. Identify typical conflict situations for the student and discuss appropriate solutions to specific situations (e.g., peers taking things from him/her, peers hitting or grabbing, peers not following rules, etc.).

19. When the student has responded inappropriately to a conflict situation, take time to explore with him/her appropriate solutions which may have been used in dealing with the problem.

20. Maintain mobility throughout the classroom in order to supervise student interactions and intervene in conflict situations in which the student(s) is unable to successfully resolve the problem.

93 Does not make appropriate use of free time

1. Reinforce the student for making appropriate use of free time: (a) give the student a tangible reward (e.g., classroom privileges, line leading, passing out materials, five minutes free time, etc.) or (b) give the student an intangible reward (e.g., praise, handshake, smile, etc.).

2. Speak to the student to explain: (a) what he/she is doing wrong (e.g., talking loudly, out of seat, etc.) and (b) what he/she should be doing (e.g., talking quietly, sitting quietly, etc.).

3. Establish free time rules (e.g., find an activity, work or spend the time quietly, remain in assigned areas, put materials away when free time is over). Reiterate rules often and reinforce student for following rules.

4. Reinforce those students in the classroom who make appropriate use of free time.

5. Reinforce the student for making appropriate use of free time based on the length of time he/she can be successful. Gradually increase the length of time required for reinforcement as the student demonstrates success.

6. Write a contract with the student specifying what behavior is expected (e.g., talking quietly, sitting quietly, studying, etc.) and what reinforcement will be made available when the terms of the contract have been met.

7. Communicate with parents (e.g., notes home, phone calls, etc.) in order to share information concerning the student's progress and so that they may reinforce the student at home for making appropriate use of free time at school.

8. Identify a peer to act as a model for the student to imitate appropriate use of free time.

9. Have the student question any directions, explanations, instructions he/she does not understand.

10. Evaluate the appropriateness of free time in order to determine whether or not the student can be successful with the activity and the length of time scheduled.

11. Encourage the student's peers to include him/her in free time activities.

12. Encourage the student to assist younger peers in free time activities.

13. Develop, with the student, a list of high-interest free time activities that require various amounts of time to perform.

14. Place free time materials (e.g., paper, pencil, glue, crayons, games, etc.) in a location where the student can obtain them on his/her own.

15. Establish centers of high-interest activities at appropriate levels of difficulty for the student's use at free time.

16. Provide a quiet, reasonably private area to do nothing for free time.

17. Separate the student from the peer(s) who stimulates his/her inappropriate use of free time.

18. Encourage the student to plan his/her use of free time in advance.

19. Provide sign-up sheets for free time activities.

20. Give the student an individual schedule to follow in order that when an activity is finished he/she knows what to do next.

21. Assign a peer for the student to interact with during free time.

22. Identify a specified activity for the student to engage in during free time.

23. Have the student act as a peer tutor during free time.

24. Have the student act as a teacher assistant during free time.

25. Allow the student to go to other classrooms for specified activities during free time (e.g., typing, home economics, industrial arts, etc.).

26. Have the student begin an ongoing project to work on during free time which will in turn be a regular free time activity.

27. Make certain that free time is contingent upon academic productivity and accuracy (e.g., the student must finish three activities with 80% accuracy before having free time).

28. Provide high-interest free time activities for completion of assignments (e.g., listening to music, reading, socializing, going to another part of the building, etc.).

29. Provide the student with a list of quiet activities to engage in when he/she finishes assignments early.

30. Find educationally related free time activities for the student to perform (e.g., flash card activities with peers, math, reading, or spelling board games, etc.).

31. Engage in free time activities with the student in order to model appropriate use of free time.

32. Make certain that the free time activity is not so overstimulating as to cause the student to demonstrate inappropriate behavior.

33. Make certain the student is able to successfully engage in the free time activity (e.g., the student understands the rules, the student is familiar with the activity, the student will be compatible with other students engaged in the activity, etc.).

34. Provide supervision of free time activities in order to monitor the student's appropriate use of free time.

35. Make certain the student is aware of the length of free time available when beginning the free time activity.

36. Make certain the student understands that failing to make appropriate use of free time may result in termination of free time and/or loss of future free time.

37. Make certain the student understands that failure to conclude free time activities and return to assignments may result in loss of opportunity to earn free time.

38. Provide the student with frequent short-term free time activities in order that he/she can learn to finish free time projects at another time and be willing to go back to assignments.

94 Fails to work appropriately with peers in a tutoring situation

1. Reinforce the student for working appropriately with peers in a tutoring situation: (a) give the student a tangible reward (e.g., classroom privileges, line leading, passing out materials, five minutes free time, etc.) or (b) give the student an intangible reward (e.g., praise, handshake, smile, etc.).

2. Speak to the student to explain: (a) what he/she is doing wrong (e.g., not attending to the tutor, arguing with peers, etc.) and (b) what he/she should be doing (e.g., attending to the tutor, doing his/her own work, etc.).

3. Establish tutoring rules (e.g., work on-task, work quietly, remain in your seat, finish task, meet task expectations). Reiterate rules often and reinforce students for following rules.

4. Reinforce those students in the classroom who work appropriately with peers in a tutoring situation.

5. Reinforce the student for working appropriately with peers in a tutoring situation based on the length of time he/she can be successful. Gradually increase the length of time required for reinforcement as the student demonstrates success.

6. Write a contract with the student specifying what behavior is expected (e.g., attending to the tutor, taking turns, sharing materials, etc.) and what reinforcement will be made available when the terms of the contract have been met.

7. Communicate with parents (e.g., notes home, phone calls, etc.) in order to share information concerning the student's progress and so that they may reinforce the student at home for working appropriately with peers in a tutoring situation at school.

8. Evaluate the appropriateness of the tutoring situation in order to determine: (a) if the task is too easy, (b) if the task is too difficult, and (c) if the length of time scheduled to complete the task is appropriate.

9. Identify a peer to act as a model for the student to imitate working appropriately with peers in a tutoring situation.

10. Have the student question any directions, explanations, instructions he/she does not understand.

11. Make certain that the student and peer tutor are compatible (e.g., the student accepts his/her role in the tutoring situation, the student and peer tutor are accepting of one another, the peer tutor has skills and knowledge to share, etc.).

12. Be certain that the opportunity to work with a peer tutor is contingent upon appropriate behavior prior to and during the tutoring situation.

13. Make certain that the students being tutored in a tutoring situation are on the same ability level.

14. Teach the student appropriate behavior for peer tutoring situations (e.g., follow directions, work quietly, take turns, share materials, etc.).

15. Supervise tutoring situations closely in order to make certain that the student's behavior is appropriate, the task is appropriate, he/she is learning from the situation, etc.

16. Make certain the tutoring activity involves practice, drill, or repetition of information or skills previously presented.

17. Determine the peer(s) the student would most prefer to interact with in tutoring situations and attempt to group these students together for peer tutoring.

18. Assign an outgoing, nonthreatening peer to act as a peer tutor.

19. Structure the environment so that the student has many opportunities for success in the tutoring situation.

20. Assign the student to tutoring situations in which he/she is likely to interact successfully with other peers being tutored.

21. Conduct a sociometric activity with the class in order to determine the peer(s) who would most prefer to interact with the student in tutoring situations.

22. Make certain the student demonstrates appropriate behavior in tutoring situations prior to pairing him/her with a peer.

23. Make certain that the student understands that interacting with a peer(s) in tutoring situations is contingent upon appropriate behavior.

24. Supervise tutoring situations closely in order that the peer(s) with whom the student works does not stimulate inappropriate behavior.

25. Make certain that the tutoring situation is not so overstimulating as to make successful interactions with another peer(s) difficult.

26. Reduce the emphasis on competition. Fear of failure may stimulate inappropriate behavior in tutoring situations.

27. Teach the student problem-solving skills in order that he/she may better deal with problems that may occur in interactions with another peer(s) in tutoring situations (e.g., talking, walking away, calling upon an arbitrator, compromising, etc.).

28. Find a peer with whom the student is most likely to be able to successfully interact in tutoring situations (e.g., a student with similar interests, background, ability, behavior patterns, etc.).

29. Structure the activities of the tutoring situation according to the needs/abilities of the student (e.g., establish rules, limit the stimulation of the activity, limit the length of the activity, consider the time of day, etc.).

30. Limit opportunities for interaction in tutoring situations on those occasions in which the student is not likely to be successful (e.g., the student has experienced academic or social failure prior to the scheduled tutoring activity).

31. Select nonacademic activities designed to enhance appropriate interaction of the student and a peer(s) (e.g., board games, model building, coloring, etc.).

32. Through interviews with other students and observations, determine those characteristics of the student which interfere with successful interactions during tutoring situations in order to determine skills or behaviors the student needs to develop for successful interactions.

33. Have the student practice appropriate interactions with the teacher in tutoring situations.

34. Make certain the student is able to successfully engage in the tutoring activity (e.g., the student understands the rules, the student is familiar with the activity, the student will be compatible with the other students engaged in the free time activity, etc.).

35. Make certain the student understands that failing to interact appropriately with a peer(s) during tutoring activities may result in removal from the activity and/or loss of participation in future activities.

36. Have the student engage in the peer tutoring situation for short periods of time and gradually increase the length of time as the student demonstrates success.

37. Provide an appropriate location for the tutoring situation (e.g., quiet corner of the classroom, near the teacher's desk, etc.).

95 Does not share school materials with other students

1. Reinforce the student for sharing school materials: (a) give the student a tangible reward (e.g., classroom privileges, line leading, passing out materials, five minutes free time, etc.) or (b) give the student an intangible reward (e.g., praise, handshake, smile, etc.).

2. Speak with the student to explain: (a) what he/she is doing wrong (e.g., failing to give others the opportunity to use school materials) and (b) what he/she should be doing (e.g., sharing school materials).

3. Reinforce those students who share school materials with other students.

4. Write a contract with the student specifying what behavior is expected (e.g., sharing) and what reinforcement will be made available when the terms of the contract have been met.

5. Communicate with parents (e.g., notes home, phone calls, etc.) in order to share information concerning the student's progress and so that they may reinforce the student at home for sharing school materials at school.

6. Assess the appropriateness of the task or social situation.

7. Teach sharing by giving students an assignment which requires sharing to complete the activity (e.g., materials for making murals, bulletin boards, maps, art projects, etc.).

8. Encourage peers to share with the student.

9. Teach the student the concept of sharing by having the student borrow from others and loan things to others.

10. Have the student work directly with one peer in order to model sharing and taking turns. Gradually increase group size as the student demonstrates success.

11. Reduce competitiveness in the school environment (e.g., avoid situations where refusing to share contributes to winning, where winning or beating someone else becomes the primary objective of a game, activity, or academic exercise, etc.).

12. Create and reinforce activities in which students work together for a common goal rather than individual success or recognition. Point out that larger accomplishments are realized through group effort rather than by individual effort.

13. Put the student in charge of communal school items such as rulers, pencils, crayons, etc., in order that he/she may experience sharing.

14. Provide the student with enough materials to satisfy his/her immediate needs (e.g., one of everything). Gradually reduce the number of materials over time, requiring the student to share the available materials as he/she becomes more successful at doing so.

15. Provide special activities for the entire class to engage in at the end of the day which are contingent upon sharing school materials throughout the day.

16. Structure the classroom environment in such a way as to take advantage of natural sharing opportunities (e.g., having more group activities, allow for natural consequences when a student refuses to share, etc.).

17. Discourage students from bringing personal possessions to school which others would desire. Encourage the use of communal school property.

18. Provide enough materials, activities, etc., in order that sharing or taking turns will not always be necessary.

19. Model sharing behavior by allowing students to use your materials contingent upon the return of the items.

20. Provide the student with many opportunities to both borrow and lend materials in order to help him/her learn the concept of sharing.

21. Make certain that every student gets to use materials in order that selfishness can be reduced.

22. Point out to the student the natural rewards of sharing school materials (e.g., personal satisfaction, friendships, having people share in return, etc.).

23. Make certain that those students who are willing to share are not taken advantage of by other students.

24. Make certain that other students are sharing with the student in order that a reciprocal relationship can be expected.

25. Maintain a realistic level of expectation for sharing school materials based on the student's age level and ability to share.

26. Practice sharing by having each student work with a particular school material for an established length of time. At the end of each time period (e.g., 10 minutes) have each student pass his/her material to another student.

27. Provide the students with adequate time to complete activities requiring sharing, in order that the selfish use of school materials is not necessary for success. Students are less likely to share if sharing reduces the likelihood of finishing on time, being successful, etc.

28. Reduce the demands for the student to make verbal exchanges when sharing (i.e., shyness may inhibit sharing if the student is required to verbally communicate with others). Materials may be placed in a central location when not in use so that they may be obtained by the students.

29. Establish rules for sharing school materials (e.g., ask for materials you wish to use, exchange materials carefully, return materials when not in use, offer to share materials with others, take care of shared materials, call attention to materials that need repair). Reiterate rules often and reinforce students for following rules.

30. Do not expect the student to share all materials. Students need to "own" some materials (e.g., jewelry, clothing, etc.).

31. In group situations, provide the student with necessary materials for the activity in order that sharing problems do not disrupt the learning experience.

32. Point out to the student the natural consequences of refusing to share (e.g., students will not share in return, students will not want him/her in their group, loss of friendships, inability to successfully complete activities that require sharing, etc.).

33. Make certain that shared materials are returned to the student in order that he/she will develop a positive concept of sharing.

34. Provide the student with many experiences in which he/she shares with others and has materials returned. When the student learns that shared materials will be returned, he/she will be more likely to share in the future.

35. Make certain the student understands that if shared materials are used up, worn out, broken under normal use, etc., they will be replaced.

36. Do not make sharing mandatory until the student develops the ability to share. Sharing should not be a "must" until the student develops some degree of tolerance for sharing with others.

37. Students who cannot share with one another because of their personal dislike for each other should not be placed in the same group where sharing is required. If a student prefers not to share with one other person, it does not mean that he/she does not have the ability to share.

38. Make certain the student understands that students do not own school materials and that he/she should not be threatened to share school materials since he/she has nothing personal to lose.

96 Writes and passes notes

1. Reinforce the student for demonstrating appropriate behavior: (a) give the student a tangible reward (e.g., classroom privileges, line leading, passing out materials, five minutes free time, etc.) or (b) give the student an intangible reward (e.g., praise, handshake, smile, etc.).

2. Speak to the student to explain: (a) what he/she is doing wrong (e.g., writing and passing notes) and (b) what he/she should be doing (e.g., working quietly).

3. Establish classroom rules (e.g., work on-task, work quietly, remain in your seat, finish task, meet task expectations). Reiterate rules often and reinforce students for following rules.

4. Reinforce those students in the classroom who demonstrate appropriate behavior.

5. Reinforce the student for demonstrating appropriate behavior based on the length of time he/she can be successful. Gradually increase the length of time required for reinforcement as the student demonstrates success.

6. Write a contract with the student specifying what behavior is expected (e.g., demonstrating appropriate behavior) and what reinforcement will be made available when the terms of the contract have been met.

7. Communicate with parents (e.g., notes home, phone calls, etc.) in order to share information concerning the student's progress and so that they may reinforce the student at home for demonstrating appropriate behavior at school.

8. Identify a peer to act as a model for the student to imitate appropriate behavior.

9. Provide a full schedule of daily events. Prevent lag time from occurring when the student can engage in writing and passing notes. (See Appendix for Schedule of Daily Events.)

10. Seat the student near the teacher.

11. Maintain visibility to and from the student. The teacher should be able to see the student and the student should be able to see the teacher, making eye contact possible at all times.

12. Interact frequently with the student in order to monitor his/her behavior.

13. Remove the student from the peer(s) with whom he/she is writing and passing notes.

14. Provide students with frequent opportunities to interact with one another (e.g., before and after school, between activities, etc.).

15. Use "note writing" as a language arts activity each day.

16. Make certain the student understands the consequences of writing and passing notes.

17. Be consistent when delivering consequences to those students who write and pass notes.

97 Tattles

1. Reinforce the student for demonstrating appropriate behavior: (a) give the student a tangible reward (e.g., classroom privileges, line leading, passing out materials, five minutes free time, etc.) or (b) give the student an intangible reward (e.g., praise, handshake, smile, etc.).

2. Speak to the student to explain: (a) what he/she is doing wrong (e.g., tattling) and (b) what he/she should be doing (e.g., attending to his/her own activities).

3. Establish classroom rules (e.g., work on-task, work quietly, remain in your seat, finish task, meet task expectations). Reiterate rules often and reinforce students for following rules.

4. Reinforce those student in the classroom who demonstrate appropriate behavior.

5. Reinforce the student for demonstrating appropriate behavior based on the length of time he/she can be successful. Gradually increase the length of time required for reinforcement as the student demonstrates success.

6. Write a contract with the student specifying what behavior is expected (e.g., demonstrating appropriate behavior) and what reinforcement will be made available when the terms of the contract have been met.

7. Communicate with parents (e.g., notes home, phone calls, etc.) in order to share information concerning the student's progress and so that they may reinforce the student at home for demonstrating appropriate behavior at school.

8. Identify a peer to act as a model for the student to imitate appropriate behavior.

9. Make certain the student knows what information is appropriate to report (e.g., emergencies, injuries, fighting, etc.).

10. Make certain the student knows what information is not appropriate to report (e.g., peers whispering, not working, copying, wasting time, etc.).

11. Maintain mobility in order to prevent the student's need to tattle. If you see behavior occur, it will not be necessary for the students to call attention to it.

12. Do not inadvertently reinforce tattling by over-reacting.

13. In order to maintain objectivity, make decisions based on what you observed rather than what is reported to you.

14. Be a model for appropriate student behavior. Publicly praise and privately redirect student behavior.

15. Reduce the emphasis on competition. A highly competitive environment may increase the likelihood of tattling.

16. Explain the natural consequences of tattling to the student (e.g., peers will not want to interact with him/her, peers will retaliate, etc.).

98 Fails to find necessary locations in the building

1. Reinforce the student for demonstrating the ability to find necessary locations in the building: (a) give the student a tangible reward (e.g., classroom privileges, line leading, passing out materials, five minutes free time, etc.) or (b) give the student an intangible reward (e.g., praise, handshake, smile, etc.).

2. Speak to the student to explain: (a) what he/she is doing wrong and (b) what he/she should be doing.

3. Reinforce those students in the classroom who demonstrate the ability to find necessary locations in the building.

4. Write a contract with the student specifying what behavior is expected (e.g., going to and from the restroom in a reasonable amount of time) and what reinforcement will be available when the terms of the contract have been met.

5. Communicate with parents (e.g., notes home, phone calls, etc.) in order to share information concerning the student's progress and so that they may reinforce the student at home for finding necessary locations in the building at school.

6. Evaluate the appropriateness of the task to determine: (a) if the task is too easy, (b) if the task is too difficult, and (c) if the length of time scheduled to complete the task is appropriate.

7. Identify a peer to act as a model to demonstrate the ability to find necessary locations in the building.

8. Have the student question any directions, explanations, instructions he/she does not understand.

9. Have a peer accompany the student when he/she attempts to find locations in the building.

10. Have a peer model finding locations in the building.

11. Take the student on a personal tour of various locations in the building.

12. Limit the number of locations the student is required to find on his/her own. Gradually increase the number of locations as the student demonstrates success.

13. Develop clear, concise written directions or a map for the student to use in order to find locations in the building.

14. Color code locations in the building (e.g., boys' restroom doors painted red, girls' restroom doors painted yellow, names of locations, arrows, etc.).

15. Provide universal symbols at locations throughout the building (e.g., restroom, cafeteria, library, etc.).

16. Have the student run errands to specific locations in the building for practice in finding locations in the building.

17. Inform other personnel that the student has difficulty finding locations in the building in order that assistance and supervision may be provided.

18. Make certain the behavior demands are appropriate for the student's abilities (e.g., finding locations alone, finding locations with many other students around, etc.).

19. Teach the student to ask for directions when he/she has difficulty finding locations in the building.

20. Be consistent in applying consequences for behavior (e.g., appropriate behavior receives positive consequences while inappropriate behavior receives negative consequences).

21. Identify regular routes the student is required to use to find locations in the building.

22. Have the student carry a map of locations in the building.

23. Have the student develop his/her own directions for finding locations in the building.

24. Allow the student to move from one location to another in the building only at specified times (e.g., if he/she has difficulty finding locations in the building when other students are in the halls, allow him/her to move from one location to another when others are not present).

25. Have the student move from one location to another with a group of students until he/she develops the ability to find the locations independently.

26. Have the student identify landmarks in the building which help him/her find necessary locations in the building.

99 Does not respond appropriately to environmental cues

1. Reinforce the student for responding appropriately to environmental cues: (a) give the student a tangible reward (e.g., classroom privileges, line leading, passing out materials, five minutes free time, etc.) or (b) give the student an intangible reward (e.g., praise, handshake, smile, etc.).

2. Speak to the student to explain: (a) what he/she is doing wrong (e.g., failing to respond appropriately to bells, signs indicating restroom directions, etc.) and (b) what he/she should be doing (e.g., responding appropriately to bells, signs indicating restroom directions, etc.).

3. Reinforce those students in the classroom who respond appropriately to environmental cues.

4. Reinforce the student for responding appropriately to environmental cues based on the number of environmental cues the student can successfully follow. Gradually increase the number of environmental cues required for reinforcement as the student demonstrates success.

5. Write a contract with the student specifying what behavior is expected (e.g., responding appropriately to bells, rules, point cards, reminders, etc.) and what reinforcement will be made available when the terms of the contract have been met.

6. Communicate with parents (e.g., notes home, phone calls, etc.) in order to share information concerning the student's progress and so that they may reinforce the student at home for responding appropriately to environmental cues at school.

7. Evaluate the appropriateness of the environmental cues the student is expected to follow in order to determine: (a) if the cue is too easy, (b) if the cue is too difficult, and (c) if the length of time required to respond to the cue is appropriate.

8. Identify a peer to act as a model for the student to imitate appropriate responses to environmental cues.

9. Have the student question any environmental cues he/she does not understand.

10. Establish environmental cues that the student is expected to follow (e.g., bells, rules, point cards, reminders, etc.).

11. Provide supportive information to assist the student in responding appropriately to environmental cues (e.g., match bells ringing to the time of the day in order that the student knows that he/she should go to another class, lunch, or leave the building).

12. Provide repeated practice in responding appropriately to environmental cues.

13. Make the student responsible for identifying environmental cues for his/her peers (e.g., bells, rules, reminders, etc.).

14. Provide the student with universal environmental cues (e.g., symbols for male and female, arrows, exit signs, danger symbols, etc.).

15. Pair environmental cues with verbal explanations and immediate reinforcement for appropriate responding.

16. Prepare the student in advance of the delivery of environmental cues in order to increase successful responding.

17. Make certain the same environmental cues are used throughout all locations in and outside the building.

18. Match the environmental cues to the student's ability to respond (e.g., visual cues are used for students who cannot hear, symbols or auditory cues are used for students who cannot read, etc.).

19. Model appropriate responses to environmental cues for the student to imitate.

20. Have the student master appropriate responding to one environmental cue at a time, prioritizing environmental cues in order of importance for mastery before introducing additional cues.

21. In order to increase success in learning environmental cues, have the student observe and imitate the responses of his/her peers to environmental cues (e.g., as the student is learning to respond appropriately to doors identified as In and Out, he/she can imitate the behavior of peers who use the appropriate doors to enter and leave areas of the educational environment).

22. Reinforce the student for asking the meaning of environmental cues he/she does not understand (e.g., bells, signs, etc.).

23. Provide the student with simulation activities in the classroom in order to teach him/her successful responses to environmental cues (e.g., responses to words, symbols, directions, etc.).

24. Assign a peer to accompany the student as he/she moves throughout the educational environment to act as a tutor in teaching appropriate responses to environmental cues.

100   Does not stay in an assigned area for the specified time period

1. Reinforce the student for staying in an assigned area for the specified time period: (a) give the student a tangible reward (e.g., classroom privileges, line leading, passing out materials, five minutes free time, etc.) or (b) give the student an intangible reward (e.g., praise, handshake, smile, etc.).

2. Speak to the student to explain: (a) what he/she is doing wrong (e.g., leaving the assigned area) and (b) what he/she should be doing (e.g., staying in the assigned area for the specified time period).

3. Establish classroom rules (e.g., work on-task, work quietly, remain in assigned area, finish task, meet task expectations). Reiterate rules often and reinforce students for following rules.

4. Reinforce those students in the classroom who stay in an assigned area for the specified time period.

5. Reinforce the student for staying in an assigned area for the specified time period based on the length of time he/she can be successful. Gradually increase the length of time required for reinforcement as the student demonstrates success.

6. Write a contract with the student specifying what behavior is expected (e.g., staying in an assigned area for the specified time period) and what reinforcement will be made available when the terms of the contract have been met.

7. Communicate with parents (e.g., notes home, phone calls, etc.) in order to share information concerning the student's progress and so that they may reinforce the student at home for staying in an assigned area for the specified time period at school.

8. Evaluate the appropriateness of the task to determine: (a) if the task is too easy, (b) if the task is too difficult, and (c) if the length of time scheduled to complete the task is appropriate.

9. Identify a peer to act as a model for the student by staying in an assigned area for the specified time period.

10. Have the student question any directions, explanations, instructions he/she does not understand.

11. Evaluate the appropriateness of requiring the student to stay in an assigned area for the specified time period.

12. Establish school ground rules (e.g., remain in assigned areas, share school equipment, use appropriate language, use school property with care, etc.).

13. Have the student question any school ground rules he/she does not understand.

14. Separate the student from the peer(s) who stimulates his/her inappropriate behavior in assigned areas.

15. Have the student carry a point card with him/her at all times so that he/she can be reinforced in assigned areas in the building and on the school grounds.

16. Inform other school personnel of any behavior problems the student may have in order that supervision and assistance may be provided in assigned areas before, during, and after school.

17. Be consistent in applying consequences for behavior (i.e., appropriate behavior receives positive consequences while inappropriate behavior receives negative consequences).

18. Provide organized activities for the student to participate in before, during, and after school (e.g., board games, softball, four square, tether ball, jump rope, flash cards, etc.).

19. Identify a specified area of the school grounds to be used as a "time-out" area when the student demonstrates inappropriate behavior on the school grounds.

20. Have the student take responsibility for a younger student in assigned areas.

21. Make certain the student knows where he/she is expected to be at all times.

22. Assign a peer to remain in an assigned area for the specified time period with the student.

23. Make certain the student knows the location of all assigned areas.

24. Make certain the behavioral demands are appropriate for the student's abilities (e.g., ability to find locations of assigned areas, ability to tell time, ability to interact with peers appropriately, etc.).

25. Make certain the student is actively involved in an activity in the assigned area in order to enhance his/her ability to stay in the assigned area for the specified time period.

26. Assign the student a responsibility to perform in an assigned area in order to keep him/her actively involved (e.g., supervise others, responsible for materials, group leader, etc.).

27. Provide the student with a timer to help him/her remain in an assigned area for the specified time period.

28. Post a clock showing the times the student should enter and leave an assigned area (i.e., one clock face indicates time to enter, another clock face indicates time to leave).

29. Have the student carry a hall pass on which teachers will indicate the time of arrival and departure of assigned areas.

30. Provide the student with predetermined signals (e.g., ring a bell, turn lights on and off, etc.) to indicate when to enter and leave assigned areas.

31. Set up physical barriers or boundary markings in order to help the student remain in an assigned area.

32. Identify areas that are off limits with signs such as Danger, Keep Out, etc.

33. Provide adequate supervision in assigned areas. Gradually reduce the amount of supervision as the student demonstrates success.

34. Provide the student with many opportunities for social and academic success in assigned areas.

35. Require time spent away from an assigned area to be made up during recess, lunch, free time, etc.

36. Require the student to remain in assigned areas for short periods of time. Gradually increase the length of time as the student demonstrates success.

37. Make certain the student is able to tell time in order to increase the probability that he/she will know how long to remain in an assigned area.

38. Reduce stimuli in the assigned area which would cause the student to be unable to remain in the assigned area for the specified time period.

39. Teach the student ways to deal with stimuli or problems in assigned areas which may cause him/her to leave the area (e.g., talk to a teacher, move to a quiet place in the assigned area, avoid confrontations, etc.).

101 Runs away to avoid problems

1. Reinforce the student for dealing with problems in appropriate ways: (a) give the student a tangible reward (e.g., classroom privileges, line leading, passing out materials, five minutes free time, etc.) or (b) give the student an intangible reward (e.g., praise, handshake, smile, etc.).

2. Speak with the student to explain: (a) what he/she is doing wrong (e.g., running away from situations, out of the room, away from school, etc.) and (b) what he/she should be doing (e.g., asking for help, calling attention to the problem, practicing problem-solving skills, using self-control, etc.).

3. Establish classroom rules (e.g., work on-task, work quietly, remain in your seat, finish tasks, meet task expectations). Reiterate rules often and reinforce students for following rules.

4. Reinforce those students in the classroom who deal with problems in appropriate ways.

5. Reinforce the student for dealing with problems in appropriate ways based on the length of time he/she can be successful. Gradually increase the length of time required for reinforcement as the student demonstrates success.

6. Remove the student from the group or activity until he/she can demonstrate appropriate behavior and self-control.

7. Write a contract with the student specifying what behavior is expected (e.g., asking for help) and what reinforcement will be made available when the terms of the contract have been met.

8. Communicate with parents (e.g., notes home, phone calls, etc.) in order to share information concerning the student's progress and so that they may reinforce the student at home for dealing with problems in appropriate ways at school.

9. Evaluate the appropriateness of the task to determine: (a) if the task is too easy, (b) if the task is too difficult, and (c) if the length of time scheduled for the task is appropriate.

10. Structure the environment in order to reduce opportunities to run away from the school/classroom (e.g., change seating, increase supervision, reduce stimuli which contribute to running away, etc.).

11. Maintain supervision of the student at all times and in all parts of the school.

12. Maintain visibility to and from the student. The teacher should be able to see the student and the student should be able to see the teacher, making eye contact possible at all times.

13. Provide the student with as many academic and social successes as possible.

14. Record or chart attendance with the student.

15. Give the student a preferred responsibility to be performed at various times throughout the day.

16. Present tasks in the most attractive and interesting manner possible.

17. Interact frequently with the student in order to maintain involvement in the activity (e.g., ask the student questions, ask the student's opinion, stand close to the student, seat the student near your desk, etc.).

18. Make the necessary adjustments in the environment to prevent the student from experiencing stress, frustration, anger, etc., as much as possible.

19. Make certain all school personnel are aware of the student's tendency to run away.

20. Limit the student's independent movement in the school environment.

21. Discuss with the student ways he/she could deal with unpleasant experiences which would typically cause him/her to run away (e.g., talk to a teacher, go see a counselor, go to a quiet area in the school, etc.).

22. Identify variables in the environment which cause the student to become upset and reduce or remove those variables from the environment.

23. Do not provide the student with additional opportunities to run away by seating him/her in the hallway, sending him/her from class, etc.

24. Consider alternative forms of negative consequences if current consequences cause the student to run away. Do not use negative consequences which contribute to a worsening of the situation.

25. Intervene early to prevent the student from becoming upset enough to run away.

26. Provide the student with a quiet place as an alternative to running away. This can be a place the student elects to go as a form of self-control in place of running away.

27. Identify the student's favorite activities and provide as many of these as possible throughout the day.

102 Is under the influence of drugs or alcohol while at school

1. Reinforce the student for demonstrating appropriate behavior: (a) give the student a tangible reward (e.g., classroom privileges, line leading, passing out materials, five minutes free time, etc.) or (b) give the student an intangible reward (e.g., praise, handshake, smile, etc.).

2. Speak with the student to explain: (a) what he/she is doing wrong (e.g., using drugs or alcohol at school) and (b) what he/she should be doing (e.g., following an established code of conduct, following rules, taking care of responsibilities, etc.).

3. Establish classroom rules (e.g., work on-task, work quietly, remain in your seat, finish task, meet task expectations). Reiterate rules often and reinforce students for following rules.

4. Reinforce those students in the classroom who demonstrate appropriate behavior.

5. Reinforce the student for demonstrating appropriate behavior based on the length of time he/she can be successful. Gradually increase the length of time required for reinforcement as the student demonstrates success.

6. Remove the student from the group or activity until he/she can demonstrate appropriate behavior and self-control.

7. Write a contract with the student specifying what behavior is expected (e.g., demonstrating appropriate behavior) and what reinforcement will be made available when the terms of the contract have been met.

8. Communicate with parents (e.g., notes home, phone calls, etc.) in order to share information concerning the student's progress and so that they may reinforce the student at home for demonstrating appropriate behavior at school.

9. Communicate with parents, agencies, or appropriate parties in order to inform them of the problem, determine the cause of the problem, and consider possible solutions to the problem.

10. Provide a drug information program for the individual, the class, and the building.

11. Provide an orientation to penalties for the use of alcohol and drugs at school.

12. Involve the student in extracurricular activities as a redirection of interest.

13. Identify individuals the student may contact with his/her concerns (e.g., guidance counselor, school nurse, social worker, school psychologist, etc.).

14. Share concerns with the administration and seek referral to an agency for investigation of alcohol or drug abuse.

15. Encourage the student to become involved in athletic activities.

16. Assign the student activities which would require interactions with a respected role model (e.g., older student, high school student, college student, community leader, someone held in high esteem, etc.).

17. Provide the student with intelligent, accurate information concerning drugs and alcohol rather than sensationalized, scare tactic information.

18. Provide many opportunities for social and academic success.

19. Encourage the student to excel in a particular area of interest (e.g., provide information for him/her, provide personal and professional support, sponsor the student, etc.).

20. Provide the student with personal recognition during school hours (e.g., following up on details of earlier communications, maintain a direction for conversation, etc.).

21. Lead and direct the student. Do not lecture and make demands.

22. Maintain anecdotal records of the student's behavior to check patterns or changes in behavior.

23. When natural consequences from peers occur as the result of the use of drugs or alcohol at school (e.g., criticism, loss of friendship, etc.), bring the consequences to the attention of the student.

24. Encourage the student's parents to be positive and helpful with the student as opposed to being negative and threatening.

25. Act as a resource for parents by providing information on agencies, counseling programs, etc.

26. Teach the student to be satisfied with his/her own best effort rather than perfection. Reduce the emphasis on competition and help the student realize that success is individually defined.

27. Be willing to take the time to listen, share, and talk with the student.

28. Listen to the student and his/her problems privately.

29. Increase your own professional knowledge of laws and treatment concerning drug and alcohol use and abuse.

30. Teach the student alternative ways to deal with demands, challenges, and pressures of the school-age experience (e.g., deal with problems when they arise, practice self-control at all times, share problems or concerns with others, etc.).

31. Maintain adequate supervision at all times and in all areas of the school (e.g., hallways, bathrooms, between classes, before and after school, etc.).

103 Whines or cries in response to personal or school experiences

1. Reinforce the student for demonstrating appropriate behavior in response to unpleasant situations (e.g., failure, peer pressure, disappointment, losing in competition, etc.): (a) give the student a tangible reward (e.g., classroom privileges, line leading, passing out materials, five minutes free time, etc.) or (b) give the student an intangible reward (e.g., praise, handshake, smile, etc.).

2. Speak with the student to explain: (a) that you recognize that he/she is unhappy and (b) appropriate ways for dealing with his/her unhappiness (e.g., sharing by talking, problem-solving, etc.).

3. Establish classroom rules (e.g., work on-task, work quietly, remain in your seat, finish task, meet task expectations). Reiterate rules often and reinforce students for following rules.

4. Reinforce those students in the classroom who deal with unhappiness in an appropriate manner.

5. Reinforce the student for dealing with unhappiness in an appropriate manner based on the length of time he/she can be successful. Gradually increase the amount of time required for reinforcement as the student demonstrates success.

6. Remove the student from the group or activity until he/she can demonstrate appropriate behavior and self-control.

7. Write a contract with the student specifying what behavior is expected (e.g., dealing with unhappiness in an appropriate manner) and what reinforcement will be made available when the terms of the contract have been met.

8. Communicate with parents (e.g., notes home, phone calls, etc.) in order to share information concerning the student's progress and so that they may reinforce the student at home for dealing with unhappiness in an appropriate manner at school.

9. Evaluate the appropriateness of the task to determine: (a) if the task is too easy, (b) if the task is too difficult, and (c) if the length of time scheduled for the task is appropriate.

10. Communicate with parents, agencies, or appropriate parties in order to inform them of the problem, determine the cause of the problem, and consider possible solutions to the problem.

11. Modify the environment in order to reduce situations which cause the student to be unhappy (e.g., if the student is upset by losing in competitive activities, reduce the number of competitive activities).

12. Share concerns with the administration and seek referral to an agency for investigation of possible abuse or neglect.

13. Try various groupings in order to determine the situation in which the student is most comfortable.

14. Provide the student with many social and academic successes.

15. Take the time to talk with the student in order that he/she realizes your interest in him/her is genuine.

16. Teach/demonstrate methods for dealing with problems early in order to prevent problems from becoming overwhelming.

17. Explain to the student that feelings of unhappiness are natural, but that there is an appropriate length of time for public displays of that emotion.

18. When natural consequences occur as the result of the student's display of unhappiness, point them out to him/her (e.g., peers prefer not to interact with him/her).

19. Provide the student with as many positive interactions as possible (e.g., recognize the student, call the student by name, compliment his/her attire, etc.).

20. Make certain that positive reinforcement is not inadvertently given for inappropriate behavior.

21. Make certain that consequences for inappropriate behavior are consistent.

22. Encourage and assist the student in joining extracurricular activities, clubs, etc.

23. Remove the student from the peer(s) who is causing his/her unhappiness.

24. Discourage the student from engaging in those activities which cause his/her unhappiness.

25. Encourage the student to use problem-solving skills: (a) identify the problem, (b) identify goals and objectives, (c) develop strategies, (d) develop a plan for action, and (e) carry out the plan.

26. Identify individuals the student may contact concerning his/her unhappiness (e.g., guidance counselor, school nurse, social worker, school psychologist, etc.).

27. Give the student additional responsibilities (e.g., chores, errands, etc.) to give him/her a feeling of success or accomplishment.

28. Structure the environment so that the student does not have time to dwell on real or imagined problems.

29. Teach the student to be satisfied with his/her own best effort rather than perfection.

30. Maintain anecdotal records of the student's behavior to check for patterns or changes in behavior.

31. Teach the student alternative ways to express his/her unhappiness (e.g., talking, writing, creating, etc.).

32. Provide the student with a quiet place to relax when he/she becomes upset. This is not to be used as a form of punishment, but rather an opportunity to function more successfully in his/her environment.

104 Demonstrates inappropriate behavior in a small academic group setting

1. Reinforce the student for demonstrating appropriate behavior in a small academic group setting: (a) give the student a tangible reward (e.g., classroom privileges, line leading, passing out materials, five minutes free time, etc.) or (b) give the student an intangible reward (e.g., praise, handshake, smile, etc.).

2. Speak to the student to explain: (a) what he/she is doing wrong (e.g., failing to take part) and (b) what he/she should be doing (e.g., talking, taking turns, sharing, etc.).

3. Establish classroom rules (e.g., work on-task, work quietly, remain in your seat, finish task, meet task expectations). Reiterate rules often and reinforce students for following rules.

4. Reinforce those students in the classroom who demonstrate appropriate behavior in a small academic group setting.

5. Reinforce the student for demonstrating appropriate behavior in a small academic group setting based on the length of time he/she can be successful. Gradually increase the length of time required for reinforcement as the student demonstrates success.

6. Write a contract with the student specifying what behavior is expected (e.g., working appropriately with peers) and what reinforcement will be made available when the terms of the contract have been met.

7. Communicate with parents (e.g., notes home, phone calls, etc.) in order to share information concerning the student's progress and so that they may reinforce the student at home for demonstrating appropriate behavior in small academic group settings at school.

8. Evaluate the appropriateness of the task to determine: (a) if the task is too easy, (b) if the task is too difficult, and (c) if the length of time scheduled to complete the task is appropriate.

9. Have the student question any directions, explanations, instructions he/she does not understand.

10. DO NOT FORCE the student to participate in a small academic group setting.

11. Assign a peer to sit/work directly with the student (e.g., in different settings such as art, bus, music, P.E.; or different activities such as tutoring, group projects, running errands around the building, recess, etc.).

12. Ask the student questions that cannot be answered "yes" or "no."

13. Call on the student when he/she is most likely to be able to respond successfully (e.g., something in which the student is interested, when you are certain the student knows the answer, etc.).

14. Try various groupings in order to determine the situation in which the student is most comfortable.

15. Have peers invite the student to participate in school or extracurricular activities.

16. Request that the student be the leader of a small group activity if he/she possesses mastery or an interest in the activity.

17. Allow the student to be present during small group activities without requiring active participation. Require more involvement over time as the student demonstrates success.

18. Have the student work with one or two other group members and gradually increase the group size as the student becomes more comfortable.

19. Demonstrate respect for the student's opinions, responses, suggestions, etc.

20. Give the student the opportunity to pick a topic or activity for the group to work on together.

21. Give the student the opportunity to choose a group activity and choose the group members (e.g., along with the teacher decide what the activity will be, what individual group members will do, etc.).

22. Assign the student a role to perform in the group activity that he/she can perform successfully (e.g., secretary, researcher, group behavior monitor, etc.).

23. Make certain the student is productive and accurate in performing individual assignments before placing him/her in small group activities.

24. Go over group rules/expectations at the beginning of each group activity.

25. Make certain that the student can follow classroom rules/expectations independently before placing him/her in small group activities.

26. Reduce the emphasis on competition. Fear of failure may cause the student to refuse to work in small group activities.

27. Help the student to learn to be satisfied with his/her own best effort rather than some arbitrary measure of success. Success is measured individually according to ability level and progress of any kind is a measure of success.

28. Place the student with peers who will be appropriate role models and likely to facilitate his/her academic and behavioral success.

29. Place the student with group members who are least likely to be threatening to him/her (e.g., younger students, students just learning a skill he/she has mastered, etc.).

30. Make certain that the student understands instructions/directions for the group activity (e.g., give instructions in a variety of ways, make certain that the student understands his/her role, go over the rules for group behavior before the activity begins, etc.).

31. Make certain that the student has all needed materials in order to perform his/her role in the group (e.g., paper, pencil, art supplies, reference materials, etc.).

32. Make certain the student has enough room to work successfully (e.g., consider distance from other students, room for all materials, etc.).

33. Make certain the student is actively involved in the group (e.g., call on the student frequently, assign the student a responsibility such as teacher assistant, have him/her be group leader, etc.).

34. Remove the student from the group if he/she behaves inappropriately.

35. Make certain the academic and social demands of the group situation are within the student's ability level.

36. Help the student get to know group members before requiring group participation (e.g., introduce the students to one another, allow the students unstructured free time together, etc.).

37. Reduce distracting stimuli which could interfere with the student's success in a group activity (e.g., provide enough room to move without physical contact, keep noise level to a minimum, keep movement in the environment to a minimum, etc.).

38. Schedule activities in order that your time can be spent uninterrupted with the group.

39. Schedule small group activities as part of the student's daily routine (e.g., small group activities should occur on a regularly scheduled basis so that the student will be prepared and know what to expect).

40. Place the student in group activities he/she prefers and include less desirable activities over time.

41. Provide the student with alternative ways to perform a group assignment and allow him/her to choose the most desirable (e.g., a written paragraph assignment may be accomplished by writing a note to a friend, writing about a recent experience, describing a favorite pastime, etc.).

42. Allow the student to participate in one group activity he/she prefers. Require the student to participate in more small group activities as he/she experiences success.

43. Schedule small group activities when the student is most likely to be successful (e.g., before recess rather than immediately after recess, after the first individual assignment of the day has been completed in order to establish productive behavior, etc.).

44. Program alternative individual activities if the student is unlikely to be successful (e.g., if the schedule has been changed; if holidays or special events have stimulated the student, making successful group interactions unlikely, etc.).

45. Allow the student to join the group after the activity has begun if he/she is unable to participate appropriately at the beginning of the activity.

46. Position the student's desk or work area in such a way that he/she works near other students but is not visually distracted by them (e.g., turn the student's desk away from other students).

47. Allow the student to leave a small group activity and return to independent work when he/she can no longer be successful in the group activity (e.g., as an alternative to disrupting the group, fighting, etc.).

105 Behaves more appropriately alone or in small groups than with the whole class or in large group activities

1. Reinforce the student for working in a group situation: (a) give the student a tangible reward (e.g., classroom privileges, line leading, passing out materials, five minutes free time, etc.) or (b) give the student an intangible reward (e.g., praise, handshake, smile, etc.).

2. Speak with the student to explain: (a) what he/she is doing wrong (e.g., failing to take part) and (b) what he/she should be doing (e.g., talking, taking turns, playing, sharing, etc.).

3. Establish classroom rules (e.g., work on-task, work quietly, remain in your seat, finish task, meet task expectations). Reiterate rules often and reinforce students for following rules.

4. Reinforce other students in the classroom for working appropriately in a group situation.

5. Write a contract with the student specifying what behavior (e.g., working appropriately with peers) and what reinforcement will be made available when the terms of the contract have been met.

6. Communicate with parents (e.g., notes home, phone calls, etc.) in order to share information concerning the student's progress and so that they may reinforce the student at home for participating in group situations at school.

7. DO NOT FORCE the student to participate in group situations.

8. Assign a peer to sit/work directly with the student (e.g., in different settings such as art, bus, music, P.E.; or different activities such as tutoring, group projects, running errands around the building, recess, etc.).

9. Reward or encourage other students for participation in group situations.

10. Give the student the responsibility of helping a peer in group situations.

11. Give the student responsibilities in group situations in order that others might view him/her in a positive light.

12. Call on the student when he/she is most likely to be able to respond successfully (e.g., a topic in which the student is interested, when you are certain the student knows the answer, etc.).

13. Try various groupings in order to determine the situation in which the student is most comfortable.

14. Have peers invite the student to participate in school or extracurricular activities.

15. Have the student lead a small group activity when he/she possesses mastery or an interest in the activity.

16. Allow the student to be present during group activities without requiring active participation. Require more involvement over time as the student becomes more active in group situations.

17. Reduce the emphasis on competition. Fear of failure may cause the student to be reluctant to participate in group situations.

18. Have the student work with one or two other group members. Gradually increase group size as the student becomes more comfortable.

19. Demonstrate respect for the student's opinions, responses, suggestions, etc.

20. Give the student the opportunity to pick a topic or activity for the group to work on together.

21. Give the student the opportunity to choose a group activity and choose the group members (e.g., along with the teacher decide what the activity will be, decide what individual group members will do, etc.).

22. Assign the student a role to perform in the group activity which he/she can perform successfully (e.g., secretary, researcher, group behavior monitor, etc.).

23. Make certain the student is productive and accurate in performing individual assignments before placing him/her in group activities.

24. Go over group rules and expectations at the beginning of each group activity.

25. Make certain that the student can follow classroom rules and expectations independently before placing him/her in a group activity.

26. Help the student learn to be satisfied with his/her own best effort rather than some arbitrary measure of success. Success is measured individually according to ability level and progress of any kind is a measure of success.

27. Group the student with peers who will be appropriate role models and likely to facilitate his/her academic and behavioral success.

28. Group the student with peers who are least likely to be threatening to him/her (e.g., younger students, students just learning a skill he/she has mastered, etc.).

29. Make certain the student understands instructions/directions for the group activity (e.g., give instructions in a variety of ways, make certain that the student understands his/her role, go over the rules for group behavior before the activity begins, etc.).

30. Make certain the student has all needed materials in order to perform his/her role in the group (e.g., paper, pencil, art supplies, reference materials, etc.).

31. Make certain the student has enough room to work successfully (e.g., distance from other students, room for all materials, etc.).

32. Make certain the student is actively involved in the group situation (e.g., call on the student frequently, assign the student a responsibility such as teacher assistant, have him/her be group leader, etc.).

33. Remove the student from the group if his/her behavior is inappropriate.

34. Make certain the academic and social demands of the group situation are within the student's ability level.

35. Evaluate the appropriateness of the task to determine: (a) if the task is too easy, (b) if the task is too difficult, and (c) if the length of time scheduled to complete the task is appropriate.

36. Help the student get to know group members before requiring group participation (e.g., introduce the students to one another, allow the students unstructured free time together, etc.).

37. Reduce distracting stimuli which could interfere with the student's success in a group activity (e.g., provide enough room to move without physical contact, keep noise level to a minimum, keep movement in the environment to a minimum, etc.).

38. Schedule activities in order that your time can be spent uninterrupted with the group.

39. Schedule group activities as part of the student's daily routine. Group activities should occur on a regularly scheduled basis so that the student will be prepared and know what to expect.

40. Place the student in group activities he/she prefers and include less desirable activities over time.

41. Provide the student with alternative ways to perform a group assignment and allow him/her to choose the most desirable (e.g., a written paragraph assignment may be accomplished by writing a note to a friend, writing about a recent experience, describing a favorite pastime, etc.).

42. Allow the student to participate in one group activity he/she prefers. Require the student to participate in more group activities as he/she experiences success.

43. Schedule group activities when the student is most likely to be successful (e.g., before recess rather than immediately after recess, after the first individual assignment of the day has been completed in order to establish productive behavior, etc.).

44. Program alternative individual activities if the student is unlikely to be successful (e.g., if the schedule has been changed, if holidays or special events have stimulated the student and make successful group interaction unlikely, etc.).

45. Allow the student to join the group after the activity has begun if he/she is unable to participate appropriately at the beginning of the group activity.

46. Position the student's desk or work area in such a way that he/she works near other students but is not visually distracted by them (e.g., turn the student's desk away from other students).

47. Allow the student to leave a group activity and return to independent work when he/she can no longer be successful in the group activity (e.g., as an alternative to disrupting the group, fighting, etc.).

106 Demonstrates inappropriate behavior in a large academic group setting

1. Reinforce the student for demonstrating appropriate behavior in a large academic group setting: (a) give the student a tangible reward (e.g., classroom privileges, line leading, passing out materials, five minutes free time, etc.) or (b) give the student an intangible reward (e.g., praise, handshake, smile, etc.).

2. Speak to the student to explain: (a) what he/she is doing wrong (e.g., talking out of turn, failing to take part, etc.) and (b) what he/she should be doing (e.g., talking when appropriate, taking turns, sharing, etc).

3. Establish classroom rules (e.g., work on-task, work quietly, remain in your seat, finish task, meet task expectations). Reiterate rules often and reinforce students for following rules.

4. Reinforce those students in the classroom who demonstrate appropriate behavior in a large academic group setting.

5. Reinforce the student for demonstrating appropriate behavior in a large academic group setting based on the length of time he/she can be successful. Gradually increase the length of time required for reinforcement as the student demonstrates success.

6. Write a contract with the student specifying what behavior is expected (e.g., working appropriately with peers) and what reinforcement will be made available when the terms of the contract have been met.

7. Communicate with parents (e.g., notes home, phone calls, etc.) in order to share information concerning the student's progress and so that they may reinforce the student at home for working appropriately in a large academic group setting at school.

8. Evaluate the appropriateness of the task to determine: (a) if the task is too easy, (b) if the task is too difficult, and (c) if the length of time scheduled to complete the task is appropriate.

9. Have the student question any directions, explanations, instructions he/she does not understand.

10. Assign a peer to sit/work directly with the student in large academic group settings.

11. DO NOT FORCE the student to participate in the group.

12. Reward or encourage others for participation in the group.

13. Give the student the responsibility of helping another student in the group.

14. Give the student responsibilities in the group in order that others might view him/her in a more positive light.

15. Ask the student questions that cannot be answered "yes" or "no."

16. Call on the student when he/she is most likely to be able to respond successfully (e.g., something in which the student is interested, when you are certain the student knows the answer, etc.).

17. Try various groupings in order to determine the situation in which the student is most comfortable.

18. Request the student to be the leader of a large group activity if he/she possesses mastery or an interest in the activity.

19. Allow the student to be present during large group activities without requiring active participation. Require more involvement over time as the student demonstrates success.

20. Reduce the emphasis on competition. Fear of failure may cause the student to avoid participating in large academic group settings.

21. Have the student work with one or two other group members and gradually increase group size as the student becomes more comfortable.

22. Demonstrate respect for the student's opinions, responses, suggestions, etc.

23. Give the student the opportunity to pick a topic or activity for the group to work on together.

24. Give the student the opportunity to choose a group activity and choose the group members who will participate (e.g., along with the teacher decide what the activity will be, what individual group members will do, etc.).

25. Assign the student a role to perform in the group activity that he/she can perform successfully (e.g., secretary, researcher, group behavior monitor, etc.).

26. Make certain the student is productive and accurate in performing individual assignments before placing him/her in large group activities.

27. Go over group rules/expectations at the beginning of each group activity.

28. Make certain the student can follow classroom rules/expectations independently before placing him/her in a large group activity.

29. Help the student learn to be satisfied with his/her own best effort rather than some arbitrary measure of success. Success is measured individually according to ability level and progress of any kind is a measure of success.

30. Place the student with peers who will be appropriate role models and likely to facilitate his/her academic and behavioral success.

31. Place the student with group members who are least likely to be threatening to him/her (e.g., younger students, students just learning a skill he/she has mastered, etc.).

32. Make certain the student understands instructions/directions for the group activity (e.g., give instructions in a variety of ways, make certain that the student understands his/her role, go over the rules for group behavior before the activity begins, etc.).

33. Make certain the student has all needed materials in order to perform his/her role in the group (e.g., paper, pencil, art supplies, reference materials, etc.).

34. Make certain the student has enough room to work successfully (e.g., consider distance from other students, room for all materials, etc.).

35. Make certain the student is actively involved in the group (e.g., call on the student frequently, assign the student a responsibility such as teacher assistant, have him/her be group leader, etc.).

36. Remove the student from the group if he/she behaves inappropriately.

37. Make certain the academic and social demands of the group situation are within the student's ability level.

38. Help the student become acquainted with group members before requiring group participation (e.g., introduce the students to one another, allow the students unstructured free time together, etc.).

39. Reduce distracting stimuli which could interfere with the student's success in a group activity (e.g., provide enough room to move without physical contact, keep noise level to a minimum, keep movement in the environment to a minimum, etc.).

40. Schedule activities in order that your time can be spent uninterrupted with the group.

41. Schedule large group activities as part of the student's daily routine (e.g., large group activities should occur on a regularly scheduled basis so that the student will be prepared and know what to expect).

42. Place the student in group activities he/she prefers and include less desirable activities over time.

43. Provide the student alternative ways to perform a group assignment and allow him/her to choose the most desirable (e.g., a written paragraph assignment may be accomplished by writing a note to a friend, writing about a recent experience, describing a favorite pastime, etc.).

44. Have the student participate in at least one group activity per day. Require the student to participate in more group activities as he/she experiences success.

45. Schedule large group activities when the student is most likely to be successful (e.g., before recess rather than immediately after recess, after the first individual assignment of the day has been completed in order to establish productive behavior, etc.).

46. Program alternative individual activities if the student is unlikely to be successful (e.g., if the schedule has been changed; if a holiday or special event has stimulated the student, making successful group interaction unlikely, etc.).

47. Allow the student to join the group after the activity has begun if he/she is unable to participate appropriately at the beginning of the group activity.

48. Position the student's desk or work area in such a way that he/she works near other students but is not visually distracted by them (e.g., turn the student's desk away from other students, seat the student in the front of a row, etc.).

49. Allow the student to leave a group activity and return to independent work when he/she can no longer be successful in the group activity (e.g., as an alternative to disrupting the group, fighting, etc.).

50. Arrange the student's seating in order that you can interact with him/her frequently (e.g., near the front of the room, on the perimeter of the group, etc.).

51. Assign a peer to sit next to the student to provide assistance.

52. Have the student maintain a list of classroom rules at his/her desk (e.g., attached to the surface of the desk, inside the desk, etc.).

53. Use a "time-out" area to allow the student to gain self-control if problem behaviors occur during a large academic group activity.

54. Provide a carrel or other quiet study area for the student to use if he/she cannot be successful at his/her seat.

55. Use removal from the group as a natural consequence for inappropriate behavior.

56. Present academic tasks in the most attractive and interesting manner possible.

57. Integrate the student into a large academic group activity only after he/she has had success with one other student, a small group, etc.

58. Integrate the student into a large academic group activity gradually (e.g., short periods of time with the group lead to longer periods of time).

59. Provide the student with the opportunity to work with a peer tutor, volunteer, etc., for enrichment or support of content presented in the large academic group activity.

60. Provide structure in order that the large academic group activity does not become overstimulating for the student.

61. Publicly praise the student for appropriate behavior and privately redirect inappropriate behavior.

62. Write group contracts which encourage students to work together for group success.

63. Find related group activities the student can perform successfully (e.g., acting as teacher assistant, giving directions, handing out materials, collecting materials, etc.).

64. Schedule daily activities so that highly desirable activities follow large academic group activities and are contingent upon appropriate behavior in the large academic group activity.

107 Demonstrates inappropriate behavior on the school grounds before and after school

1. Reinforce the student for demonstrating appropriate behavior on the school grounds before and after school: (a) give the student a tangible reward (e.g., classroom privileges, line leading, passing out materials, five minutes free time, etc.) or (b) give the student an intangible reward (e.g., praise, handshake, smile, etc.).

2. Speak to the student to explain: (a) what he/she is doing wrong (e.g., fighting with peers) and (b) what he/she should be doing (e.g., playing appropriately, sharing school equipment with peers, visiting, etc.).

3. Reinforce those students who demonstrate appropriate behavior on the school grounds before and after school.

4. Reinforce the student for demonstrating appropriate behavior on the school grounds before and after school based on the length of time he/she can be successful. Gradually increase the length of time required for reinforcement as the student demonstrates success.

5. Write a contract with the student specifying what behavior is expected (e.g., playing, sharing school equipment, visiting, etc.) and what reinforcement will be made available when the terms of the contract have been met.

6. Communicate with parents (e.g., notes home, phone calls, etc.) in order to share information concerning the student's progress and so that they may reinforce the student at home for demonstrating appropriate behavior on the school grounds before and after school.

7. Identify a peer to act as a model for the student to imitate appropriate behavior on the school grounds before and after school.

8. Establish school ground rules (e.g., remain in assigned areas, share school equipment, use appropriate language, and use school property with care). Reiterate rules often and reinforce students for following rules.

9. Have the student question any school ground rules he/she does not understand.

10. Provide the student with a list of the school ground rules.

11. Separate the student from the peer(s) who stimulates his/her inappropriate behavior on the school grounds before and after school.

12. Have a peer accompany the student when he/she is on the school grounds before and after school.

13. Make certain the behavioral demands are appropriate for the student's ability level (e.g., interacting with peers, entering the building when appropriate, leaving the building when appropriate, using school equipment with care, etc.).

14. Make certain the student is actively involved on the school grounds before and after school (e.g., team activities, responsibilities before and after school, etc.).

15. Have the student carry a point card with him/her at all times so that he/she can be reinforced on the school grounds before and after school.

16. Inform school personnel of any behavior problems the student may have in order that supervision and assistance may be provided on the school grounds before and after school.

17. Be consistent in applying consequences for behavior (e.g., appropriate behavior receives positive consequences while inappropriate behavior receives negative consequences).

18. Reinforce the student for remaining in assigned areas (e.g., play areas, student lounge, recreational areas, etc.).

19. Provide organized activities for the student to participate in on the school grounds before and after school (e.g., kickball, dodge ball, softball, four square, tether ball, jump rope, foot races, etc.).

20. Allow the student to enter the building early or remain in the building after school to work on assignments, special projects, assist teachers, assist the custodian, etc.

21. Reinforce the student for arriving on the school grounds shortly before school begins (e.g., five minutes) and leaving the school grounds shortly after school.

22. Change the student's bus assignment in order that the student does not arrive early and leaves soon after school.

23. Have an older peer meet the student before school begins and remain with the student after school until the student leaves the school grounds.

24. Identify a specified area of the school grounds to be used as a "time-out" area when the student demonstrates inappropriate behavior on the school grounds before and after school.

25. Have the student take responsibility for a younger peer on the school grounds before and after school.

26. Have the student be responsible for organizing and supervising activities and distributing or collecting materials on the school grounds before and after school.

27. Give the student a specific job to perform on the school grounds before and after school (e.g., crosswalk patrol, bus monitor, raising and lowering the flag, picking up litter on the school grounds, etc.).

108 Demonstrates inappropriate behavior going to and from school

1. Reinforce the student for demonstrating appropriate behavior going to and from school: (a) give the student a tangible reward (e.g., classroom privileges, line leading, passing out materials, five minutes free time, etc.) or (b) give the student an intangible reward (e.g., praise, handshake, smile, etc.).

2. Speak to the student to explain: (a) what he/she is doing wrong (e.g., fighting on the bus, taking an indirect route to and from school, etc.) and (b) what he/she should be doing (e.g., sitting quietly on the bus, taking the most direct route to and from school, etc.).

3. Reinforce those students in the classroom who demonstrate appropriate behavior going to and from school.

4. Reinforce the student for demonstrating appropriate behavior going to and from school based on the number of times he/she can be successful. Gradually increase the number of times required for reinforcement as the student demonstrates success.

5. Write a contract with the student specifying what behavior is expected (e.g., sitting quietly on the bus) and what reinforcement will be made available when the terms of the contract have been met.

6. Communicate with parents (e.g., notes home, phone calls, etc.) in order to share information concerning the student's progress and so that they may reinforce the student at home for demonstrating appropriate behavior when going to and from school.

7. Identify a peer to act as a model for the student to imitate appropriate behavior going to and from school.

8. Have the student question any directions, explanations, instructions he/she does not understand.

9. Establish rules for appropriate behavior when going to and from school (e.g., sit quietly on the bus, remain seated on the bus, use a quiet voice while on the bus, take the most direct route when walking to and from school, use sidewalks, follow crossing rules at crosswalks, refrain from fighting on the way to and from school, etc.). Reiterate rules often and reinforce students for following rules.

10. Evaluate the appropriateness of the expectations for the student going to and from school by himself/herself.

11. Assign a peer to accompany the student when going to and from school in order to monitor and encourage appropriate behavior.

12. Accompany the student when going to and from school in order to teach the student appropriate behavior (e.g., using sidewalks, crossing at crosswalks, taking the most direct route, boarding the bus, sitting quietly, remaining seated, leaving the bus, etc.).

13. Assign the student responsibilities to perform when going to and from school (e.g., act as the bus driver's assistant to monitor behavior, accompany a younger peer to and from school, pick up trash on the way to and from school, etc.).

14. Encourage the student to report problems that occur while going to and from school (e.g., being bullied, approached by strangers, teased by other students, etc.).

15. Allow natural consequences to occur if the student fails to demonstrate appropriate behavior when going to and from school (e.g., parents will have to provide transportation and/or supervision).

16. Make certain the student is seated near the bus driver in order to prevent inappropriate behavior when riding on the bus to and from school.

17. Develop a behavioral contract with the bus driver and the student for appropriate behavior on the bus while riding to and from school.

18. Have "block mothers" monitor the student's behavior when going to and from school.

109 Does not finish assignments because of reading difficulties

1. Reinforce the student for finishing assignments: (a) give the student a tangible reward (e.g., classroom privileges, line leading, passing out materials, five minutes free time, etc.) or (b) give the student an intangible reward (e.g., praise, handshake, smile, etc.).

2. Speak to the student to explain: (a) what he/she is doing wrong (e.g., failing to finish assignments) and (b) what he/she should be doing (e.g., finishing assignments).

3. Establish classroom rules (e.g., work on-task, work quietly, remain in your seat, finish task, meet task expectations). Reiterate rules often and reinforce students for following rules.

4. Reinforce those students in the classroom who finish their assignments.

5. Reinforce the student for finishing assignments based on the number of times he/she can be successful. Gradually increase the number of times required for reinforcement as the student demonstrates success.

6. Write a contract with the student specifying what behavior is expected (e.g., finishing assignments) and what reinforcement will be made available when the terms of the contract have been met.

7. Communicate with parents (e.g., notes home, phone calls, etc.) in order to share information concerning the student's progress and so that they may reinforce the student at home for finishing assignments at school.

8. Evaluate the appropriateness of the task to determine: (a) if the task is too easy, (b) if the task is too difficult, and (c) if the length of time scheduled to complete the task is appropriate.

9. Identify a peer to act as a model for the student to imitate completion of assignments.

10. Have the student question any directions, explanations, instructions he/she does not understand.

11. Make certain the student understands that work not done during work time must be completed at other times such as free time, recess, after school, etc.

12. Make certain that the reading demands of the assignment are within the ability level of the student.

13. Tape record directions, explanations, and instructions in order to enhance the student's success.

14. Have a peer read directions, explanations, and instructions to the student in order to enhance his/her success.

15. Require the student to verbally repeat directions, explanations, and instructions.

16. Read directions, explanations, and instructions to the student when necessary.

17. Use a sight word vocabulary approach in order to teach the student key words and phrases when reading directions and instructions (e.g., key words such as circle, underline, match, etc.).

18. Deliver all directions, explanations, and instructions orally.

19. Reduce all directions, explanations, and instructions to a minimum.

20. Shorten the length of assignments that require reading in order that the student can complete his/her assignments in the same length of time as the other students.

21. Provide the student with additional time to complete the assignment.

22. Deliver directions, explanations, and instructions prior to handing out materials.

23. Make certain that the student's knowledge of a particular skill is being assessed rather than the student's ability to read directions, instructions, and content.

24. Maintain mobility in order to provide assistance to the student.

25. Maintain consistency in the manner in which written directions, explanations, and instructions are delivered.

26. Have the student practice timed drills consisting of reading directions, explanations, content, etc., in order to reduce reading time.

27. Plan for the student to have more than enough time to complete an assignment.

28. Assess the quality and clarity of written directions, explanations, instructions, content, etc.

29. Keep written directions as simple and concrete as possible.

30. Reduce distracting stimuli in order to increase the student's ability to follow written directions (e.g., place the student on the front row, provide a carrel or "office" space away from distractions, etc.). This is used as a means of reducing distracting stimuli and not as a form of punishment.

31. Reduce written directions to individual steps and give the student each additional step after completion of the previous step.

32. Make certain the student achieves success when following written directions.

33. Prevent the student from becoming overstimulated by an activity (e.g., frustrated, angry, etc.).

34. Provide the student with a copy of written directions at his/her desk rather than on the chalkboard, posted in the classroom, etc.

35. Seat the student close to the source of the written information (e.g., chalkboard, projector, etc.).

36. Make certain the print is large enough to increase the likelihood of following written directions.

37. Transfer directions from texts and workbooks when pictures or other stimuli make it difficult to attend to or follow written directions.

38. Provide the student a quiet place (e.g., carrel, study booth, etc.) where he/she may go to engage in activities which require following written directions.

39. Work the first problem or problems with the student to make certain that he/she follows written directions.

40. Have the student carry out written directions one step at a time and check with you to make certain that each step is successfully followed before attempting the next.

41. Gradually increase the degree of difficulty or complexity of written directions, explanations, instructions, content, etc., as the student becomes more successful.

42. Modify or adjust the reading level of material presented to the student in order to enhance his/her success.

43. Reduce the emphasis on competition. Competitive activities may make it difficult for the student to finish assignments because of frustration with reading difficulties.

110 Needs oral questions and directions frequently repeated

1. Make certain the student's hearing has been checked recently.

2. Reinforce the student for responding to oral questions and directions without requiring frequent repetition: (a) give the student a tangible reward (e.g., classroom privileges, line leading, passing out materials, five minutes free time, etc.) or (b) give the student an intangible reward (e.g., praise, handshake, smile, etc.).

3. Speak with the student to explain: (a) what he/she is doing wrong (e.g., needing oral questions and directions repeated) and (b) what he/she should be doing (e.g., responding to oral questions and directions without requiring repetition).

4. Establish classroom rules (e.g., work on-task, work quietly, remain in your seat, finish task, meet task expectations). Reiterate rules often and reinforce students for following rules.

5. Reinforce those students in the classroom who respond to oral questions and directions without requiring repetition.

6. Reinforce the student for responding to oral questions and directions without requiring repetition based on the number of times he/she can be successful. Gradually increase the number of times required for reinforcement as the student demonstrates success.

7. Write a contract with the student specifying what behavior is expected (e.g., following directions with one cue) and what reinforcement will be made available when the terms of the contract have been met.

8. Communicate with parents (e.g., notes home, phone calls, etc.) in order to share information concerning the student's progress and so that they may reinforce the student at home for responding to oral questions and directions without requiring repetition at school.

9. Identify a peer to act as a model for the student to imitate responding to oral questions and directions without requiring repetition.

10. Have the student question any directions, explanations, instructions he/she does not understand.

11. Evaluate the appropriateness of requiring the student to respond to oral questions and directions without needing repetition.

12. Present oral questions and directions in a clear and concise manner.

13. Reduce distracting stimuli (e.g., place the student on the front row, provide a carrel or "office" space away from distractions, etc.). This is used as a means of reducing distracting stimuli and not as a form of punishment.

14. Have the student take notes relative to oral questions and directions.

15. Have a peer help the student follow oral questions and directions.

16. Maintain mobility in order to provide assistance to the student.

17. Present oral questions and directions in a variety of ways in order to increase the probability of understanding (e.g., if the student fails to understand verbal directions, present them in written form).

18. Maintain consistency in the manner in which oral questions and directions are delivered.

19. Deliver oral questions and directions that involve only one concept or step. Gradually increase the number of concepts or steps as the student demonstrates success.

20. Stand close to or directly in front of the student when delivering oral questions and directions.

21. Teach the student listening skills (e.g., stop working, look at the person delivering questions and directions, have necessary note-taking materials, etc.).

22. Deliver questions and directions in written form.

23. Identify a peer to deliver and/or repeat oral questions and directions.

24. Tell the student that oral questions and directions will only be given once.

25. Give a signal prior to delivering directions orally to the student.

26. Deliver oral directions prior to handing out materials.

27. Teach the student direction-following skills (e.g., listen carefully, write down important points, etc.).

28. Interact frequently with the student in order to help him/her follow directions for the activity.

29. Have the student repeat or paraphrase the directions orally to the teacher.

30. Establish assignment rules (e.g., listen to directions, wait until all oral directions have been given, ask questions about anything you do not understand, begin the assignment only when you are certain about what you are supposed to do, make certain you have all necessary materials, etc.).

31. Make certain the student is attending while you deliver oral questions and directions (e.g., making eye contact, hands free of writing materials, looking at assignment, etc.).

32. Maintain visibility to and from the student when delivering oral questions and directions. The teacher should be able to see the student and the student should be able to see the teacher, making eye contact possible at all times in order to make certain the student is attending.

33. Call the student by name prior to delivering oral questions and directions.

34. Make certain that eye contact is being made between you and the student when delivering oral questions and directions.

V. Appendix

Preventing Behavior Problems 274
Typical Methods of Modifying Academic Tasks 275
Reinforcer Survey 276
Reinforcer Menu 277
Rules for School Environments 278
Point Record 279
Point Card 280
Sample Contract 281
Contract 282
Group Contract 283
Schedule of Daily Events 284
Schedule of Daily Events Sample 285
Parent Communication Form 286
Student Conference Report 287
A List of Reinforcers Identified By Elementary-Aged Students 288
A List of Reinforcers Identified By Secondary-Aged Students 289

Preventing Behavior Problems

- Determine reinforcer preferences
- Determine academic ability levels
- Determine social interaction skills
- Determine ability to remain on-task
- Determine group behavior
- Monitor and limit contemporary determinants of inappropriate behavior such as having to wait, task length, task difficulty, peer involvement, etc.
- Base seating arrangements on behavior
- Base group involvement on behavior
- Maintain teacher mobility in classroom
- Maintain teacher/student contact: visual, verbal, and physical
- Use criteria for expectations based on observed behavior and performance
- Use shaping, fading, and imitation procedures to gradually change behavior
- Maintain variety in reinforcers
- Use the Premack Principle in arranging schedule (i.e., a more desirable behavior can be used to reinforce the completion of a less desirable behavior)
- Use curriculum as reinforcement
- Use rules, point cards, and schedules of daily events as discriminative stimuli
- Use contracting to individualize, specify expected behavior, and identify reinforcers
- Arrange seating so all students have visibility to and from the teacher and teacher can scan the entire class
- Maintain a full schedule of activities
- Use language that is positive and firm, not demeaning, insulting, or harassing
- Intervene early when any form of conflict occurs
- Do not ignore behavior as an excuse for not intervening
- Use time-out to help the student resolve problem behavior
- Use removal to prevent contagion, destruction of property, and danger to others
- Communicate and coordinate with other teachers
- Communicate with home to prevent students playing one adult against another

Typical Methods of Modifying Academic Tasks

- Reduce the number of problems on a page (e.g., five problems to a page, the student may be required to do four pages of work throughout the day if necessary).

- Use a highlight marker to identify key words, phrases, or sentences for the student to read.

- Remove pages from workbooks or reading material and present these to the student one at a time rather than allowing the student to become anxious with workbooks or texts.

- Outline reading material for the student at his/her reading level, emphasizing main ideas.

- Tape record material for the student to listen to as he/she reads along.

- Read tests/quizzes aloud for the student.

- Tape record tests/quizzes for the student.

- Make a bright construction paper border for the student to place around reading material in order to maintain his/her attention to the task.

- Make a reading window from construction paper which the student places over sentences or paragraphs in order to maintain attention.

- Provide manipulative objects for the student to use in solving math problems.

- Rearrange problems on a page (e.g., if crowded, create more space between the problems).

- Use graph paper for math problems, handwriting, etc.

- Rewrite directions at a more appropriate reading level.

- Tape record directions.

- Have peers deliver directions or explanations.

- Allow more time to take tests or quizzes.

Reinforcer Survey

Name: _____ Age: _____

Date: _____

1. The things I like to do after school are _____
   _____

2. If I had $10 I would _____
   _____

3. My favorite TV programs are _____
   _____

4. My favorite game at school is _____
   _____

5. My best friends are _____
   _____

6. My favorite time of day is _____
   _____

7. My favorite toys are _____
   _____

8. My favorite record is _____
   _____

9. My favorite subject at school is _____
   _____

10. I like to read books about _____
    _____

11. The places I like to go in town are _____
    _____

12. My favorite foods are _____
    _____

13. My favorite inside activities are _____
    _____

14. My favorite outside activities are _____
    _____

15. My hobbies are _____
    _____

16. My favorite animals are _____
    _____

17. The three things I like to do most are _____
    _____

The Reinforcer Survey may be given to one student or a group of students. If the students cannot read, the survey is read to them. If they cannot write their answers, the answers are given verbally.

Reinforcer Menu

REINFORCER MENU

Reinforcer	Points Needed
Working with Clay	30
Peer Tutoring	25
Using Colored Markers	30
Using Colored Chalk	30
Feeding Pets	20
Delivering Messages	15
Carrying Wastebasket	20
Operating Projector	30
Playing a Board Game	35
Leading the Class Line	25
Passing out Materials	20
Using a Typewriter	25

CLASS REINFORCER MENU

Reinforcer	Points Needed
See a Film	30
Class Visitor	25
Write and Mail Letters	30
Field Trip	30
Lunch Outdoors	20
Pop Popcorn	35
Take Class Pictures	30
Tape Songs	15
Put on a Play	25
Have Adults in for Lunch	30

The Reinforcer Menu is compiled from information gathered by having a student or students respond to the Reinforcer Survey.

Rules For School Environments

GENERAL SOCIAL RULES....

- BE QUIET
- REMAIN IN YOUR SEAT
- WORK ON ASSIGNED TASK
- RAISE YOUR HAND

HALLWAY RULES....

- WALK IN THE HALL
- WALK IN A LINE
- WALK ON THE RIGHT
- WALK QUIETLY

CAFETERIA RULES....

- BE QUIET IN THE CAFETERIA LINE
- WALK TO YOUR TABLE
- TALK QUIETLY
- REMAIN SEATED

OUTDOOR RULES....

- TAKE PART IN SOME ACTIVITY
- TAKE TURNS
- BE FRIENDLY
- LINE UP WHEN IT IS TIME

ACADEMIC RULES....

- FINISH ONE TASK
- MEET YOUR CRITERIA TO EARN FIVE POINTS

These rules, except for perhaps the outdoor rules, are applicable to all grade levels and have been used in public schools for general behavioral expectations.

Point Record

ACADEMIC POINTS

Monday | 1 | 2 | 3 | 4 | 5 | 6 | 7 | 8 | 9 | 10 | 11 | 12 | 13 | 14 |

Tuesday | 1 | 2 | 3 | 4 | 5 | 6 | 7 | 8 | 9 | 10 | 11 | 12 | 13 | 14 |

Wednesday | 1 | 2 | 3 | 4 | 5 | 6 | 7 | 8 | 9 | 10 | 11 | 12 | 13 | 14 |

Thursday | 1 | 2 | 3 | 4 | 5 | 6 | 7 | 8 | 9 | 10 | 11 | 12 | 13 | 14 |

Friday | 1 | 2 | 3 | 4 | 5 | 6 | 7 | 8 | 9 | 10 | 11 | 12 | 13 | 14 |

SOCIAL POINTS

Monday

Tuesday

Wednesday

Thursday

Friday

The Point Record form provides for Academic Points, top section, for each task completed with criteria met; and Social Points, bottom section, for demonstrating appropriate behavior in and around the classroom. The Point Record is kept with the student at all times, wherever he/she may be, in order that points may be given for following any school rules.

Point Card

TIME	DAYS OF WEEK				
	M	T	W	T	F
8:00 - 8:50					
9:00 - 9:50					
10:00 - 10:50					
11:00 : 11:30					
11:30 - 12:20					
12:30 - 1:20					
1:30 - 2:20					
1:30 - 2:20					
2:30 - 3:20					

Name: _____

    This is a Point Card for secondary level students and may be used in special education classes or in regular classes. Teachers assign points, give checks, or sign initials for appropriate behavior demonstrated by the student while in the classroom. These points are relative to rules of the classroom, expected behavior, a contract developed with the student, etc. The card is a 3 x 5 inch index card which is easily kept in a shirt pocket and is small enough to reduce embarrassment for some students who would prefer to keep their behavioral support program more confidential.

CONTRACT

I, _Eric Johnson_,

HEREBY DECLARE THAT I WILL _finish my math assignments on time_

THIS JOB WILL BE CONSIDERED SUCCESSFUL _when I finish 3 assignments in a row on time_

NAME _Eric Johnson_

FOR THE SUCCESSFUL COMPLETION OF THE ABOVE JOB YOU MAY _use the computer for 15 minutes_

DATE SIGNED _12/10_

DATE COMPLETED _____

Ms. Cummins
(SIGNED)

The contract is one of the most idividualized and personalized approaches of intervening to improve behavior. This component contributes to the personal aspect of the individual reinforcement system due to the private manner in which teacher, student, and parents may work together for behavior improvement. The contract should specify:

1. Who is working toward the goals
2. What is expected (i.e., social behaviors or academic productivity and quality)
3. The amount of appropriate behavior that is expected
4. The kind of reinforcement that is being earned
5. The amount of the reinforcement
6. When the reinforcement will be made available

CONTRACT

I, _____ ,

HEREBY DECLARE THAT I WILL _____

_____

_____

THIS JOB WILL BE CONSIDERED SUCCESSFUL _____

_____

NAME _____

FOR THE SUCCESSFUL COMPLETION OF THE ABOVE JOB

YOU MAY _____

_____

DATE SIGNED _____

DATE COMPLETED _____

_____
(SIGNED)

GROUP CONTRACT

WE, _____ ,

HEREBY DECLARE THAT WE WILL _____

_____

_____

THIS JOB WILL BE CONSIDERED SUCCESSFUL _____

_____

NAMES _____

FOR THE SUCCESSFUL COMPLETION OF THE ABOVE JOB

WE MAY _____

_____

DATE SIGNED _____

DATE COMPLETED _____

_____
_____
SIGNATURES)

Hawthorne 283

Schedule of Daily Events

SCHEDULE OF DAILY EVENTS

NAME: _____

	#1	#2	#3	#4	#5	#6	#7	#8	#9	#10
Monday										
Tuesday										
Wednesday										
Thursday										
Friday										

SCHEDULE OF DAILY EVENTS

NAME: _____

	#1	#2	#3	#4	#5	#6	#7	#8	#9	#10
Tuesday										

Each individual student's Schedule of Daily Events is developed for him/her and attached to his/her desk for a week at a time or for one day at a time. This schedule identifies each activity/task the student is assigned for the day, and the schedule is filled in by the teacher one day at a time. Students tend to know what they are to do next when the schedule is provided, and teachers can expect fewer interruptions for directions when students refer to their schedules.

Schedule of Daily Events Sample

SCHEDULE OF DAILY EVENTS

NAME: _____

	#1	#2	#3	#4	#5	#6	#7	#8	#9	#10
Monday	Reading	Art (Clay)	Math	Art (Paint)	Science	Creative Writing	Social Studies	Listening	Music	P.E.
Tuesday										
Wednesday										
Thursday										
Friday										

Parent Communication Form

Teacher: _____ Date: _____

Parent(s): _____ Student: _____

Grade or Level: _____ Type of Class: _____

Other School Personnel: _____

—··•··—

TYPE OF COMMUNICATION: Letter _____ Note _____ Telephone _____

Parent Visit to School _____ Teacher Visit to Home _____

Out-of-School Location _____ Other _____

—··•··—

Initiation of Communication: School Scheduled Meeting _____

Teacher Initiation _____ Parent Initiation _____ Other _____

—··•··—

Nature of Communication: Information Sharing _____

Progress Update _____ Problem Identification _____ Other _____

—··•··—

Communication Summary (Copies of Written Communications Should Be Attached): _____
_____
_____
_____
_____

—··•··—

Expectations for Further Communication: _____
_____
_____

—··•··—

Signatures of Participants (If Communication Made in Person): _____
_____
_____

The Parent Communication Form is a record of communication made with parents in person, by telephone, or by notes or letters.

286 Hawthorne

Student Conference Report

Student's Name: _____

School Personnel Involved and Titles: _____

_____

Date: _____ Grade Level of Student: _____

———··•··———

Initiation of Conference: Regularly Scheduled Conference _____

Teacher Initiation _____ Other Personnel Initiation _____

Student Initiation _____ Parent Initiation _____

———··•··———

Nature of Communication: Information Sharing _____

Progress Update _____ Problem Identification _____

Other _____

———··•··———

Conference Summary (Copies of Written Communications Should Be Attached): _____

_____
_____
_____
_____
_____
_____
_____
_____

———··•··———

Expectations Based on Conference: _____

_____
_____

———··•··———

Signatures of Conference Participants: _____

_____
_____
_____

———··•··———

The Student Conference Report is used for recording conferences held with the student to identify problems, concerns, progress, etc.

A List of Reinforcers Identified by Elementary-Aged Students

1. Listen to the radio
2. Free time
3. Watch favorite program on TV
4. Talk to best friend
5. Listen to favorite tapes
6. Read a book
7. Candy, especially chocolate
8. Play sports - baseball, kickball, soccer, hockey
9. Ride a bike
10. Do something fun with best friend
11. Go to the zoo
12. Build a model plane or car
13. Go to the arcade and play video games
14. Camping trip
15. Play with pets
16. Go to a fast-food restaurant
17. Pop popcorn
18. Go to a movie
19. Play in the gym
20. Play outside
21. Help clean up classroom
22. Play with puppets
23. Play with dolls and a doll house
24. Ice cream
25. Cookies
26. Go shopping at a grocery store
27. Tacos
28. Hamburgers and french fries
29. Pizza
30. Money
31. Making buttons
32. Parties
33. Teacher's helper
34. Field trips
35. Eat lunch outside on a nice day
36. Recess
37. Student-of-the-month
38. Honor roll
39. Buy sodas
40. Work on puzzles
41. Write on the chalkboard
42. Gumball machine
43. Race cars
44. Use colored markers
45. Roller skating
46. Puppet show
47. Water slide
48. Stickers
49. Pencils
50. Use the computer
51. Fly model airplanes
52. Visit the principal

A List of Reinforcers Identified by Secondary-Aged Students

1. Free time
    - Doing nothing
    - Reading magazines (from home or library)
    - Reading newspapers
    - Writing a letter (to a rock star, favorite author, politician, probation officer, friend)
    - Peer tutoring (your class or another one)
    - Listen to records (from class, library, home)
    - Visit library
    - Work on a hobby
    - See a film
    - Draw - Paint - Create
2. Acting as teacher assistant (any length of time)
3. Acting as principal assistant (any length of time)
4. Have class outside
5. Field trip
6. Go to a movie
7. Have a soda
8. Have an afternoon for a sport activity (some students play and some watch)
9. Play a game (bingo, cards, board games)
10. Use a camera (take pictures and have them developed)
11. Play trivia games
12. Time off from school
13. Coach's assistant (any length of time)
14. Picnic lunch
15. Run errands
16. Extra time in high-interest areas (shop, art, P.E.)
17. Do clerical work in building (use copy machine, run office errands)
18. Library assistant (any length of time)
19. Custodian's assistant (any length of time)
20. Watch TV
21. Earn a model
22. Typing
23. Attend a sports event
24. Food or treat coupons
25. Iron-on decals

VI. Index

Absenteeism, 122, 138, 215
Abstract concepts, 84
Academic performance, 62, 65, 67, 69, 78, 163, 170, 194
Affect, 95, 110, 132, 136, 142, 184, 190, 196
Agitates, 89, 99, 106, 113, 120, 230
Alcohol, use of, 155, 252
Apathetic, 170, 192, 197
Appearance, 174
Argues, 93, 96, 99, 106, 146, 234, 265
Assignments, 60, 65, 67, 69, 78, 138, 160, 194
Assistance/Attention, waiting for, 140, 220
Avoidance, 78, 138, 250

Blames materials, 128
Blames others, 128
Blames self, 183, 194
Bus behavior, 267

Calls out answers, 118, 120, 140, 217
Careless, 58, 140, 224
Cheats, 160
Communication, 205, 206
Compliance, 72, 75, 140, 146, 163, 168, 217, 248
Comprehension, 86, 271
Constructive criticism, reaction to, 115, 163, 184
Copies, 160
Cries, 96, 196, 234, 254
Critical of self, 183, 194, 197
Curses, 93, 106, 120, 234, 265

Defiance, 72, 75, 146, 163, 168, 217, 248
Denial, 154, 163
Depressed, 170, 190, 194, 196
Derogatory comments, 93, 99, 106, 113, 120, 234, 265
Destroys property, 201, 234, 236, 265
Disorganized, 55, 67, 152
Distracted, 50, 55, 67, 152, 199
Disturbs others, 113, 236, 256, 262
Drugs, use of, 155, 252

Embarrassed, 95
Environmental cues, 246
Exaggerates, 154

Fails quizzes, 62, 65, 69
Fails tests, 62, 65, 69
Falsetto voice, 205
Family problems, 183, 199
Fights, 89, 96, 140, 152, 234, 265

Following directions, 55, 72, 75, 81, 140, 146, 163, 168, 217, 236, 244, 248, 256, 262, 271
Free time, use of, 113, 116, 157, 236

Gestures, inappropriate, 99, 120, 150, 212, 234, 265

Hand raising, 230
Hits, 89, 96, 140, 201, 234, 265
Homework, 53, 65, 160
Hugs, 126
Hurts self, 186, 201
Hygiene, 174

Illegal materials, 155, 252
Illegible, 58
Illness, 138, 214
Impatient, 96, 118, 140, 203, 248
Impulsive, 58, 67, 96, 113, 118, 126, 140, 144, 152, 203, 219, 248
Independent functioning, 60, 244
Instigates, 89, 99, 106, 113, 120, 234, 265
Interactions, peer and teacher, 101, 104, 108, 110, 111, 113, 115, 116, 118
Interest, 58, 101, 104, 170, 192
Interrupts, 113, 120, 140, 152
Involuntary movement, 203, 212

Jealous of others, 132

Large group behavior, 259, 262
Learns slowly, 81, 88
Leaves seat without permission, 152, 203, 217, 248
Lies, 154
Line behavior, 162
Loses assignments and materials, 53, 55

Makes fun of others, 99, 106, 113, 120, 234, 265
Makes noises, 99, 113, 120, 134
Masturbates, 150, 176
Materials, use of, 224, 240
Mechanical voice, 205
Memory, short-term/long-term, 81, 88, 244, 246, 271
Mood, 140, 170, 190, 215
Motivation, 64, 67, 69, 78, 138, 170, 180, 192

Name calling, 106, 110, 234, 265
Nervous behavior, 208
Note taking, 232
Notes, writing and passing, 242

Obscenities, 93, 96, 106, 150, 234, 265
Off-task, 50, 60, 67, 78, 113, 138, 152, 203

Participation, 67, 78, 101, 104, 116, 118, 138, 152, 170, 180, 192
Peer relations, 104, 106, 110, 111, 113, 115, 188, 199, 234, 265
Personal problems, 183, 199, 254
Personal relationships, 199
Pessimistic, 183, 190, 194, 197
Physical aggression toward teacher and students, 89, 96, 162, 234, 265
Physical contact, 108, 126, 162
Praise, response to, 95, 115, 132, 136
Prepared, assignments, activities and tests, 53, 65
Property, care of, 224, 227, 240

Reading comprehension, 72, 86, 269
Reads slowly, 269
Recall, 81, 246
Recognition, response to, 95, 115, 194
Reinforcement/Reward, 64, 172
Responsibility, 65, 128, 138, 224, 232, 250
Routine, following of, 165, 246
Rude comments, 93, 106
Rules, following of, 168, 217, 230, 256, 262
Runs away, 234, 250
Rushes through tasks, 58

Sarcastic remarks, 110, 113, 234, 265
Schedule, following of, 165, 246
Seat behavior, 113, 134, 203
Self-control, 60, 67, 72, 75, 89, 91, 93, 95, 113, 118, 120, 126, 132, 134, 140, 144, 152, 168, 178, 203, 212, 219, 224, 227, 236, 248, 256, 259, 262, 267

Self-destructive behavior, 186, 201
Sexual comments, 93, 106, 150, 176
Sexually-related behavior, 93, 106, 150, 176
Sharing, 115, 116, 236, 240
Skips classes, 122, 138
Small group behavior, 256
Sportsmanship, 96, 115, 116, 118, 132, 144, 152, 194
Steals, 130
Studying, 65
Substitute teacher, 165, 221
Suicide, 186

Talks without permission, 113, 120, 140, 152, 217
Taking turns, 118, 140, 152
Tardy, 124, 138
Task completion, 50, 53, 60, 65, 67, 78, 138
Tattles, 243
Teases/Teasing, 89, 99, 110, 113, 120, 265
Temper tantrums, 210
Threatens, 93, 96, 234, 265
Touches, 113, 126, 134
Tutoring, behavior during, 238

Unhappiness, 170, 190, 192, 194, 196

Vandalism, 157, 265

Walking to and from school, 267
Whines, 254
Withdrawn, 96, 101, 104, 111, 190, 192
Work habits, 60, 65, 67, 78, 113, 138, 170, 172, 192, 203

BEHAVIOR DISORDERS IDENTIFICATION SCALE - SECOND EDITION (BDIS-2)
SCHOOL VERSION

*by Stephen B. McCarney, Ed.D. &
Tamara J. Arthaud, Ph.D.*

Copyright © 2000

The *Behavior Disorders Identification Scale-Second Edition School Version* **(BDIS-2 SV)** is based on the federal definition of emotional disturbance and was designed to meet all state and federal guidelines for the identification of emotionally disturbed/ behaviorally disordered students from 5 through 18 years of age. The **BDIS-2 SV** subscales are *Learning Problems, Interpersonal Relations, Inappropriate Behavior, Unhappiness/ Depression,* and *Physical Symptoms/Fears*.

The **BDIS-2 SV** was standardized on a total of 3,986 students and provides separate norms for male and female students 5 through 18 years of age. It can be completed in approximately 20 minutes and includes 83 items easily observed and documented by educational personnel. As a comprehensive evaluation instrument, the **BDIS-2 SV** leads from assessment to program development to intervention, thus maximizing the likelihood of student success in the educational environment.

H A W T H O R N E
Phone: (800) 542-1673 FAX: (800) 442-9509